MUSLIM DIASPORA IN THE WEST

Research in Migration and Ethnic Relations Series

Series Editor:
Maykel Verkuyten, ERCOMER
Utrecht University

The Research in Migration and Ethnic Relations series has been at the forefront of research in the field for ten years. The series has built an international reputation for cutting edge theoretical work, for comparative research especially on Europe and for nationally-based studies with broader relevance to international issues. Published in association with the European Research Centre on Migration and Ethnic Relations (ERCOMER), Utrecht University, it draws contributions from the best international scholars in the field, offering an interdisciplinary perspective on some of the key issues of the contemporary world.

Forthcoming

Managing Ethnic Diversity
Meanings and Practices from an International Perspective
Edited by Reza Hasmath
ISBN 978 1 4094 1121 5

Full series list at back of book

**EUROPEAN RESEARCH CENTRE
ON MIGRATION & ETHNIC RELATIONS**

Muslim Diaspora in the West

Negotiating Gender, Home and Belonging

Edited by

HAIDEH MOGHISSI
York University, Toronto, Canada

and

HALLEH GHORASHI
VU University Amsterdam, The Netherlands

ASHGATE

Published by
Ashgate Publishing Limited
Wey Court East
Union Road
Farnham
Surrey, GU9 7PT
England

Ashgate Publishing Company
Suite 420
101 Cherry Street
Burlington
VT 05401-4405
USA

www.ashgate.com

British Library Cataloguing in Publication Data
 Muslim diaspora in the West : negotiating gender, home and
  belonging. -- (Research in migration and ethnic relations
  series)
  1. Muslim diaspora. 2. Muslims--Non-Muslim countries--
  Social conditions.
  I. Series II. Moghissi, Haideh, 1944- III. Ghorashi,
  Halleh.
  305.6'97'091713-dc22

Library of Congress Cataloging-in-Publication Data
Muslim diaspora in the West : negotiating gender, home and belonging / by Haideh Moghissi and Halleh Ghorashi.
    p. cm. -- (Research in migration and ethnic relations series)
  Includes index.
  ISBN 978-1-4094-0287-9 (hardback) -- ISBN 978-1-4094-0288-6 (ebook) 1. Muslim women--Western countries. 2. Muslim families--Western countries. 3. Muslim diaspora. 4. Islam--Customs and practices. 5. Multiculturalism. I. Moghissi, Haideh, 1944- II. Ghorashi, Halleh.
  HQ1170.M8466 2010
  305.6'97091821--dc22

                                                                    2010026830

ISBN 9781409402879 (hbk)
ISBN 9781409402886 (ebk)

Mixed Sources
Product group from well-managed forests and other controlled sources
www.fsc.org Cert no. SA-COC-1565
© 1996 Forest Stewardship Council
FSC

Printed and bound in Great Britain by
MPG Books Group, UK

Contents

PART III   REFLECTIONS ON ISLAMIC POSITIONINGS OF YOUTH IN DIASPORA

PART IV   DIASPORIC SPACE AND LOCATING SPACE

Notes on Contributors

Fauzia Erfan Ahmed has worked in gender and development projects with the United Nations and grassroots organizations in the global South as well as with African American communities in the US. Her current research focuses on Islam and theories of masculinity and feminist. She is writing a book entitled, *Redefining Manhood: Gender Empowerment, Poverty Alleviation and Masculinity*, based on her ethnographic research with Grameen Bank sharecropper families in Bangladesh. Her writings have appeared in the *National Women's Studies Association Journal*, the *International Feminist Journal of Politics,* and the *Encyclopedia for Women in Muslim Cultures*. She is currently Assistant Professor of Sociology and Women's Studies at Miami University in Ohio.

Cassandra Balchin is an independent researcher, writer and human rights advocacy trainer, specializing in the interconnections between gender, law and culture. She is a founder of the Muslim Women's Network-UK, is on the Planning Committee for Musawah: A Global Movement for Equality & Justice in the Muslim Family, and has been part of the international network, Women Living Under Muslim Laws for over 15 years. She has published on Muslim family laws, and international development policy regarding gender and religion.

Marjo Buitelaar is associate professor Anthropology of Muslim societies at the Faculty of Theology & Religious Studies, University of Groningen, the Netherlands. Her present research focuses on the narrative construction of identity by descendants of Moroccan migrants in the Netherlands and on the practice of Islam in everyday life in Morocco

Halleh Ghorashi is Professor of Management of Diversity and Integration in the Department of Culture, Organization, and Management at the VU University Amsterdam. Professor Ghorashi received her PhD in Anthropology and Women's studies from the University of Nijmegen (2001). She is the author of *Ways to Survive, Battles to Win: Iranian Women Exiles in the Netherlands and the US* (2003, Nova Science Publishers, New York) and several articles on questions of identity, diaspora, diversity in organizations and (Iranian) women's movement. Her most recent publication is the edited volume, *Paradoxes of Cultural Recognition: Perspectives from Northern Europe* (together with S. Alghasi and T.H. Eriksen, eds, Ashgate 2009). As an active participant in the Dutch public debates on diversity and integration issues, she has received several awards. Most recently, the 2008 De Triomf award for her work on and with migrant women. She is conducting research, questioning why is it important to be culturally sensitive in this culturalist world and how can this cultural sensitivity be created while at the same time avoiding culturalism?

Fataneh Farahani is an ethnologist and works at the Centre for Research in International Migration and Ethnic Relations at Stockholm University. Trained in Ethnology at Stockholm University and Gender Studies at Department of Women Studies at York University, Toronto, she wrote her doctoral thesis under the title, *Diasporic Narratives of Sexuality: Identity Formation among Iranian-Swedish Woman* (2007) which is an ethnographical account of sexuality among Iranian women living in Sweden. Fataneh's thesis was awarded the best dissertation in the faculty of humanity at Stockholm University. The topic of Fataneh's research and teaching are primarily on sexuality, Islam, postcolonial theories, diaspora, feminist and queer theories, and masculinities and whiteness studies. She has published in different anthologies and journals on her subjects of interest. Building upon her doctoral thesis, Fataneh's current research, Cultural and Racial Politics of Representation: A Study of Diasporic Masculinities among Iranian Men *s*eeks to examine the under-researched area of (re)presentation of masculinity and sexuality of Iranian men in three heterogeneous cities; Stockholm, Sydney and London.

Sepideh Farkhondeh is a researcher and a journalist. She began her sociological research in 2000 as a student in Sciences-Po Paris where she completed her PhD in 2006. After years of fieldwork, she published several articles and two books in French, most recently *Civil Society in Iran, Myths and Realities*, about the obstacles and aspirations of Iran's civil society. Since 2007, she has been working as a journalist on a number of nation-wide French radio channels and programs with a focus on human rights in Iran.

Jaqueline S. Ismael is Professor of Social Work at the University of Calgary and is co-editor of the *International Journal of Contemporary Iraqi Studies*. She has published extensively on Canadian social policy and international social welfare, including *The Canadian Welfare State: Evolution and Transition* (1989) and *International Social Welfare in a Changing World* (1996). She has also written articles and monographs on social change in the Middle East and co-authored a number of works with Tareq Y. Ismael, including *The Communist Movement in Syria and Lebanon* (1998) and *The Iraqi Predicament* (2004). Her latest work, with William Haddad, are entitled *Barriers to Reconciliation: Case Studies on Iraq and the Palestine-Israel Conflict* (2006); and *Government and Politics of the Contemporary Middle East: Continuity and Change* (2010).

Shereen T. Ismael is Associate Professor of Social Work in the School of Social Work, Carleton University, Ottawa. In addition to her book *Child Poverty and the Canadian Welfare State: From Entitlement to Charity* (2006), she is the editor of *Cultural Cleansing in Iraq: Why Museums Were Looted; Libraries Burned* *and Academics Murdered*, with Raymond Baker and Tareq Y. Ismael (2010); and *Globalization: Policies, Challenges and Responses* (1999). She has published numerous articles on Canadian and international social welfare issues. Her latest journal articles have appeared in the *Journal of Comparative Family Studies*, *Arab Studies Quarterly* and *The International Journal of Contemporary Iraqi Studies*.

Martijn de Koning is an anthropologist working at Radboud University Nijmegen, the Netherlands. In 2008 he defended his PhD 'Searching for a 'pure' Islam. Identity construction and religious beliefs among Moroccan-Dutch Muslim youth.' Currently he is part of the research program Salafism as a Transnational Movement focusing the production and distribution of Salafism and the development of Salafi networks in Europe. He maintains his own weblog at http://religionresearch.org/martijn.

Haideh Moghissi, is Professor of Sociology and Political Science and Associate Dean, Faculty of Liberal and Professional Studies at York University, Toronto. She was a founder of the Iranian National Union of Women and member of its first executive and editorial boards, before leaving Iran in 1984. Her publications (in English) include articles in refereed journals and chapters in edited volumes and following books: *Diaspora by Design: Muslims in Canada and Beyond* (co-authored, University of Toronto Press 2009) *Muslim Diaspora: Gender, Culture and Identity* (ed.) (Routledge 2006); Three volume reference, *Women and Islam: Critical Concepts in Sociology* (ed.) (Routledge 2005); *Feminism and Islamic Fundamentalism: The Limits of Postmodern Analysis,* (Zed Press, 1999, winner of Choice Outstanding Academic Book Award) and *Populism and Feminism in Iran: Women's Struggle in a Male-Defined Revolutionary Movement* (Macmillan Press and St. Martin's Press 1994).

Vida Nassehi-Behnam graduated from Sorbonne University in Paris in 1975 and was an Assistant Professor at Tehran University, Faculty of Social Sciences. She was coordinator of the Social Psychology Program at the Institute of Social Sciences and Research where she directed research projects on Family and Women studies. After leaving Iran in 1980 she worked as a lecturer and working group animator at Nanterre University (IEP, 1982–86) and later as freelance researcher in various international projects, including the one conducted at York University in Toronto. Her publications include articles on sociology of family, woman and old age, domestic violence and migration. She now lives in Paris.

Anne Sofie Roald is professor of Religious Studies and senior researcher at Chr. Michelsen Institute, Bergen, Norway. Among her research interest are Islamist movements, Islam in Europe, Islam and gender, and Multiculturalism. She has published books and articles in Swedish, Norwegian, and English. Her publications include *Women in Islam. The Western Experience* (Routledge 2001); *New Muslims in the European Context. Scandinavian Converts to Islam* (Brill 2005), and

Muslimer i Nya Samhällen. Individuella och kollektiva rättigheter (Muslims in New Societies. Individual andcollective rights) (Daidalos 2009).

Femke Stock graduated in Religious Studies at the University of Groningen in 2007, specialising in Islam and Muslims in Western Europe. Her current PhD project *Making a Home: Identity and Belonging for Second-generation Turkish and Moroccan Migrants* was made possible by a research grant from the NWO Top Talent programme.

Thijl Sunier is an anthropologist and holds the VISOR chair of 'Islam in European Societies' at the VU University Amsterdam. He conducted research on inter-ethnic relations, Turkish youth and Turkish Islamic organizations in the Netherlands, comparative research among Turkish youth in France, Germany, Great Britain and the Netherlands, and international comparative research on nation-building and multiculturalism in France and The Netherlands. Presently he is preparing research on styles of popular religiosity among young Muslims in Europe, religious leadership, and nation-building and Islam in Europe. He is a member of the Amsterdam School for Social Science Research (ASSR), chairman of the board of the Inter-academic School for Islam Studies in the Netherlands (NISIS). He is the editor of the anthropological journal *Etnofoor*, and chairman of the board of the Dutch Anthropological Association (ABV).

David Thurfjell is Associate Professor and Research Fellow in Religious Studies at Södertörn University, Stockholm, Sweden. He has published mainly within the fields of Islamic and Romani studies but his academic interest also includes Muslim minorities in Europe, interreligious relations and postcolonial theory.

Acknowledgements

We would like to express our gratitude to colleagues and friends who provided us with support and assistance in the process of preparing this volume. At VU University in Amsterdam the support of graduate students and colleagues in particular in the Department of Culture, Organization, and Management, and the Faculty of Social Sciences made the forum a pleasant and fruitful one. We acknowledge gratefully the support of the 'Education, Sexuality, Religion Unit', Ford Foundation, particularly Dr Constance Buchanan who provided for a forum through conferences in Toronto and Amsterdam for the exchange of ideas and knowledge among scholars in the field. At York University, Toronto, we benefited from the enthusiastic assistance of graduate students and colleagues and the support of the then Office of the Dean, Faculty of Arts, Office of the Dean, Atkinson Faculty and the Office of Vice President Research and Innovation. We are thankful to contributors for their collective efforts in turning some of those ideas into the present volume. Our thanks are also due to the editorial staff at Ashgate Publishing and to the anonymous readers of the manuscript for their valuable comments. Needless to emphasize that no one but us is responsible for the shortcomings that remain.

Chapter 1

Introduction

Haideh Moghissi

It seems that each historical period has its own heroes and villains, its own revolutionary and counter-revolutionary archetypes. And in each period one specific group and what it represents, or is imagined to represent, becomes the target of fascination, obsession and fear. The early 20th century had the Bolshevik revolution and the hopes and fears that it generated; then there was the rise of fascism and the resistance movements against that; the post-war anti-communism that followed also gripped the attention of protagonists and victims alike. We now have Islam. Islam represents, to some people, a merciless, backward and oppressive faith that sets off shock waves of terror around the world and to others represents the most or, indeed, the only egalitarian, compassionate faith. The fact is that Islam can be both, depending on who represents it and for what purpose uses it.

The rise of politicized Islam to prominence has in fact obscured the fact that even in terms of religion, the world's one and a half billion Muslims are more divided than united. For, in addition to Sunni and Shi'i divisions, we have many different schools and sub-sects within the faith. Besides, Muslims, like other people, include in their ranks orthodox believers, practising individuals, non-practising skeptics, secular and laic members. For this reason many scholars of Islam use the plural term 'Islams' rather than the singular Islam. Indeed, internal clashes and uncompromising, irrational hostility amongst the followers of the faith, be they between Sunnis and Shi'is or between absolutist and moderate Muslims, are much more profound than between Muslims and non-Muslims. The horrifying number of Muslims in Iraq, Pakistan, Afghanistan and elsewhere who fall victim to blind, brutal terror at the hands of other Muslims, in the name of defending Islamic prescriptions and values testifies to this reality.

Muslim populations in the Middle East and South Asia bear the brunt of these clashes in addition to the consequences of devastating wars imposed from outside. But life is certainly not free of trying experiences for the small sections of these populations who have managed to settle in Europe and North America, saving themselves from the devastating impacts of war, ethnic and religious persecution, and political and economic chaos. These realities, however, are lost to the overwhelming majority of people, even if they interact with Muslim migrants on a daily basis in one way or another. Indeed, the essentialist view in the West of Muslims, which overlooks the remarkable diversity of people inside and outside Muslim-majority countries in particular the existence of a large number of secular and laic persons has 'invented' a 'Muslim community' that is held collectively responsible for the senseless violence committed by small groups. Moreover, not only do the socio-historical forces that have aided the actions of the violence not prompt interrogation, but the negative psychosocial and political consequences of stereotyping, particularly on the younger generations of Muslim diaspora, are not seriously investigated and addressed. Instead, we see ongoing barrages of commentaries, practices and policies for the control and containment of Muslim populations in Western countries where the socio-religious landscape is changing as a result of the growth of Muslim populations, either because of migration or birth rate. Hence, in place of well-thought-out plans and integration policies aimed at removing barriers to the full involvement of Muslims in the economic, social and political lives of their adopted countries, overt and covert racist statements warning the public of threats to European cultural identity and social values poison the minds of the public on a daily basis. Muslims are supposedly conquering the West step by step, destroying it from within.

The media, and terrorism 'experts,' call on the public to watch out for Muslim populations. In the words of a Canadian journalist, 'Most of the ones who are likely to attack the West are already here.' This same pundit went on to state that '80 to 90 per cent of known *jihadis* come from the great Muslim diaspora,'[1] hence implicating all migrants and citizens of Muslim cultural background in extremist activity. Security-driven immigration and settlement policies from country to country focus on how to watch, contain and control Muslims and thus protect their societies from cultural contamination. The Swiss electorate vote to change the country's constitution to include a blanket ban on the building of minarets; French leaders push for legal restrictions on Muslim women's full-face veils; and in Britain concerns over Muslims transforming the country into 'Eurobia' are reflected, among other ways, in anti-terrorist raids on Muslim-populated neighbourhoods, often based on purely speculative evidence.[2] On the Muslim side, mistrust, suspicion and alienation feed the notions of hard-core Islamists and the actions of disgruntled individuals, be they segregationist and missionary insistence on Muslim women's dress code or harsh punishment of the young generation, again mostly women, for defying rigid moralistic rules of conduct, which only intensifies the difficult relations between Muslim communities and their new countries. Ironically, the moral panic does not prevent Western governments from continuing their misguided policy of talking only or mainly to the most conservative elements within the Muslim community whenever they need to address an issue related to the population, ignoring the existence of a rainbow of Muslims of differing national origin, rural–urban roots, class, gender, language, lifestyle and degree of religiosity, as well as political and moral conviction. In a sense it seems

---

1   *The Globe and Mail*, January 9, 2010, p. 17.

2   For example, in April 2009 a group of students of Pakistani origin were arrested and sent to Pakistan after an anti-terrorist raid. No evidence of terrorist activities, such as bomb-making equipment or a specific plot, have emerged. *The Guardian Weekly*, November 12, 2009, p. 13.

that conservative Muslims, rather than being influenced by the secular cultural and political values and practices of their new countries, are influencing them to make religion the guiding principle in dealing with their ethnic minorities. All this makes one wonder about the prospects of integration, issues of human rights and democratic values.

The chapters in this collection are the outcome of two conferences on the subject held in Toronto and Amsterdam in 2006 and 2008. They have one overarching goal in common, that is, to show how wrong it is to homogenize and weld together individual citizens from Muslim-majority countries and single out culture and/or religion as defining every aspect of their lives. Different experiences reflected and retold in these contributions clearly speak to the fallacy of a singular, crude and naive reductionist emphasis on the notion of 'culture' that obscures the many different factors shaping the experiences of individuals of Muslim cultural background. Reducing everything to 'culture' causes confusion for the public in their encounters and interactions with their fellow citizens; it also confuses those individuals from Muslim-majority societies who never thought of themselves as religious in their home countries and are now compelled to identify themselves as Muslims or let such identity be imposed on them. Obsessive preoccupation with culture also prevents Western governments from standing up firmly and clearly against the aggressive demands of conservative factions within Muslim communities who seek 'special' or 'exceptional rights' for the imagined Muslim community – rights that could trample the individual rights of other community members, particularly women, and should have no place in an open and democratic society.

Taken together, the chapters in this volume point to incredible links and similarities among the chapters, or rather among important aspects of diasporic life related to the larger society, despite different geographical locations and specific differences in other aspects. Gender, home and belonging are central themes in the majority of chapters in this collection. Surely, in no area is misconception about Islam and Muslims more profound and overpowering than in relation to Muslim women. The global context of the 'War on Terror,' which has given Muslim women's rights centre stage, is thus reflected in the choice of contributors to the two conferences and in the experiences and voices they reflect. The problem with wrapping populations of Muslim cultural origin in a single religious cloth, leading to the racialization of Muslims through faith, is also a linking thread throughout the collection.

The culturalist approach to integration, as Halleh Ghorashi in Chapter 2 argues, is ironically the very reason why Dutch society has become harsher and more disrespectful towards the immigrant women it seeks to emancipate. The reluctance to acknowledge the ability of these women to identify the problems hindering full-integration into their adopted homes, and the refusal to include them in decision-making processes that have direct effects on their lives, are demonstrated in Ghorashi's discussion of various empowerment courses launched by various immigration agencies in the Netherlands for such women, and clearly demonstrates that when the focus is on the shortcomings of migrant women, viewing them as 'walking deficits,' they and their voices are not taken seriously. An instrumentalist approach to potentially useful integration practices, Ghorashi argues, would limit the type of reflection and evaluation that is necessary to grasp the complexity of the real problems.

The problem of negative stereotypes of Islam and Muslim women, and how they may negatively affect women's attempts to challenge patriarchal gender roles is also discussed by Fauzia Erfan Ahmed in the United States, in Chapter 3. Through a historical review of Muslims' presence in the US, Ahmed shows the binaries faced by women within and without Muslim communities. The binaries result from the conservative Muslim communities and the patriarchal nostalgia they harbour, with the expectation that the Muslim woman act as the citadel of an endangered culture, and white feminists' well-intentioned wish to assist women's emancipation on their own terms, without attention to the differences inherent to women of colour, including Muslim women. Ahmed is concerned that post-9/11 legal changes that have reduced citizenship rights for Muslims in the US, and their greater marginalization, have intensified patriarchal expectations. This imposes silence on women who have historically played leadership roles within their communities and pulled them together since the dawn of slavery in the US. Cassandra Balchin's discussion of the rise of transnational Muslim feminist consciousness in Chapter 4, however, demonstrates that Muslim women refuse to allow either governments or religious leaders within their communities to dominate the discourse regarding women's legal rights. Critical of the British policy of multiculturalism, which induces homogenization of Muslim communities, and the government's frequent failure to 'talk to' entire communities through a larger number of representatives, Balchin tell us that the women are now beginning to question the doublespeak of both the government and the supposedly moderate Muslims within their communities.

Chapters in Part II of the collection turn attention to two major areas of women's lives: family and sexuality. Through qualitative research among women of Muslim cultural background in countries with sizable Muslim populations, women's experiences and self-perception about the impact of migration and relocation on two central cores of their lives are examined. Two of the contributors, Anne Sofie Roald (Chapter 5) and Fataneh Farahani (Chapter 8) focus on Sweden. Vida Nassehi-Behnam's study (Chapter 6) is about the experiences of Iranian migrants in Britain, while Haideh Moghissi's contribution, Chapter 7, discusses the results of an expansive study conducted among migrants from four communities of Muslim cultural background in Canada.

Roald's chapter explores Islamic family legislation in view of Sweden's multicultural policies. She points to a contradiction in marriage and divorce laws in that country, where marriage ritual, based on the Christian tradition, is a sacrament ordained by God; hence, religious associations have the legal right to perform marriage ceremonies. Issuing divorce documents, however, is a civic act and the sole responsibility of the government. Roald argues that this practice derives from a conception of matters related to marriage as part of the collective right of religious minorities, whereas divorce is an individual right recognized and administered by the state. However, this dualistic legal approach causes confusion and conflict, not least because of Islamic practices such as, among others, dowry, the unilateral right of a man to divorce, and the women-instigated right to ask for divorce. Roald argues that Muslim women coming to Sweden enjoy some legal protection and, particularly, the economic possibility of living without a man, and this new dynamic provides the opportunity for them to challenge the prerogatives of men more than they could in their countries of origin. The question still remains as to how much the recognition of the collective rights of a Muslim minority serves the interests of women in the community.

Vida Nassehi-Behnam's observations of Iranian women in exile has led her to the conclusion that generally they have proven to become their own agents. The lives they lead in Britain show that not only have they escaped the general stereotype of the helpless, subordinate, Middle Eastern woman who follows her husband into immigration, but in fact many Iranian women in her sample have been the instigators of their family's displacement. Feeling responsible for the consequences of displacement, they subsequently try to effectively protect and manage their families' interests. Nassehi-Behnam argues that in fact Iranian women in Britain have turned the harsh reality of exile into opportunity, and this has improved their status within the family and within the Iranian community. A relatively high percentage of Iranian women are now financially independent, either because they work (47 per cent in France and about 50 per cent in Britain) or because they are covered by the social security systems in those countries. All these factors have totally changed the marital relations of Iranian immigrants and forced couples to accept more egalitarian attitudes. My study of changing family relations among four populations of Muslim cultural background in Canada – Afghans Iranians, Pakistanis and Palestinians – explores how the changes in life circumstances resulting from migration are processed and absorbed or made the subject of a continuing contestation by married couples within these communities. Two major themes emerge in this study. First is the remarkable difference in perspective, lifestyle and religious identification among the four groups. Secondly, the interviewees' responses show that marital contestation depends to a large extent on social and economic conditions that negatively or positively influence the process of adjustment, and hence relations within the family.

Fataneh Farahani analyses the narratives of a group of Iranian-born women in Sweden regarding their experiences in intimate relationships within or outside conjugal bonds and the impacts of 'home' and 'host' cultures on these women's self-perceptions about their sexuality as well as the more general conception of identity, subjectivity, sameness, difference, otherness, agency, and marginality. The interviewees' navigations between past and present and socio-cultural comparisons, as well as the dominant cultural stereotypes they encounter as 'Iranians,' 'Muslims,' 'immigrants' and 'Middle Easterners', Farahani suggests, shape the way these women experience intimacy within or outside marriage and whether or not their moral values regarding appropriate sexual behaviour have been transformed.

The three chapters in Part III explore the experiences, expectations and reactions of Muslim youth in Europe. Thijl Sunier in Chapter 9 draws attention, once more, to the sharp, post-9/11 politicization of religious issues and the polarization of debate in Europe in general with examples from the Netherlands. He posits that this reality forces even young people of Muslim background who no longer practise Islam to relate to it one way or the other. The interplay between Islam, mass media, popular culture and the commoditization of religious experience, Sunier argues, shows the increasing diversity of the forms in which Islam is imagined, mediated and performed. He takes issue with the tendency of looking at young European Muslims as victims of a cultural clash or as being trapped in an identity crisis. Analysing some of the creative ways the youths use in expressing their religious identity, he offers, Muslim youths in Europe are agents of their own cultural environment, and they sometimes break away from the 'Islamic culture' of their parents in search of a pure Islam. In his view, the religious practices of young Muslims in Europe invite us to more thoroughly interrogate the 'religious' and 'secular' categories.

David Thurfjell's analysis (Chapter 10) also focuses on youth in Europe, and poignantly points to the enormous challenges faced by the Muslim diaspora's second generations. Culturally distant from their parents' origins and with no longing for a remote motherland, they are pressured nevertheless by social forces that draw them away from the religious middle ground straddling radicalization and religious abandonment. Thurfjell argues that the meaning of a particular Islamic practice, such as the veil or daily prayers, like all other elements of culture, is not only dependent on the choices or preferences of the individual believer, but also on the meaning-making forces and societal discourses external to them. The tension between the desired meaning of a particular attribute and the ascribed meanings of it, along with the difficulty of full participation in society, forces Muslim youths to choose between two extremes: either to abandon Islam altogether or to accept a radical interpretation of it.

Sepideh Farkhondeh (Chapter 11) focuses on young Frenchwomen of Muslim descent. She identifies social and economic discrimination, mass unemployment and racism as the main causes of frustration amongst French Muslim youth. These problems in some cases force the youths to turn to the underground economy and, sometimes, illegal criminal activities, violence and ghettoization, which in turn give rise to the influence of underground Islam or 'les imams des caves.' Radicalized, disgruntled youths turn on young women of Muslim descent to exert some control over their own lives. The young women in Farkhoneh's study are caught between the racialized representation of Arabs in political debate and in the media, and the requirements of family customs. However, they yearn to be accepted as full-fledged Frenchwomen without being forced to deny their ethnic identities, which the dominant culture denies.

Two of the chapters in the last section focus on the post-9/11 experience of Muslim communities in the Netherlands, a country marked by the fear of fundamentalist Islam. Through an analysis of individual stories of home-making and belonging, Marjo Buitelaar and Femke Stock (Chapter 12) show how highly embedded these notions are in individuals' minds and in the larger society. The ambivalence about belonging to either the present home or the distant home, as expressed by their interviewees, speaks perhaps to the lasting experience of 'foreignness' and out-of-place existence of an uprooted person. This tortured existence, they observe, is more profound in individuals who are constantly under scrutiny and hostility for their use of Islamic symbols such as the head-cover. Buitelaar and Stock point to the preoccupation with Islam and the pressure to privatize religion in the Netherlands. This alienates Muslims who choose to be identified as Dutch Muslim citizens and yet are made to feel that they cannot fully belong in Dutch society as a Muslim.

Martijn de Koning's contribution (Chapter 13) also draws attention to the transformation of the Dutch liberal approach to its non-Dutch citizens and migrants post-9/11, and particularly in the aftermath of the murder of filmmaker Theo van Gogh. He points to a shift in public attitude along with the focus in the media and in politics on the notion of 'integration,' and, hence, the emergence of a rude and harsh discourse on multiculturalism, Islam and migrants. To de Koning, some of the ideas of the Salafi imams about, say, homosexuality and the rights of women have no place in a secular and democratic society, but they are not any different from those of orthodox Protestants and members of Pentecostal churches. However, it is only the positions of orthodox Muslims that are considered radical and against 'typical Dutch values.'

Chapter 14 focuses on the experiences of Iraqi émigrés in Canada, the United States, Britain, France and Jordan. These are individuals who left their country prior to its invasion in 2003 by the US and its allies. Providing a politico-historical context for the mass population movement from Iraq, Jacqueline Ismael and Shereen Ismael show that Iraqi displacement is the culmination of a long process of political shocks, from colonial intervention and political turmoil to Ba'th Party terror under Saddam Hussein's regime. Ismael and Ismael point to the strong sentiments of home felt by Iraqi migrants, and their connections to the home country through folk culture and artifacts and to each other through memories of the homeland.

The size of Muslim populations in the West is rapidly increasing. The fusion of religion with indigenous cultures means that we have among us Muslims from a variety of cultures, national origin, rural–urban roots, class, gender, age, and language. Presumably, depending on political and/or socio-economic circumstances, some of these factors may play a more significant role in the sense of selfhood felt by these populations. We hope to bring to the attention of our reader through these chapters the fact that the rigid, conservative and punishing interpretations of religious texts that have found discursive prominence in the West for political reasons are not to be considered as the voice of Muslims in general.

We also hope to draw attention away from an understanding of Islamic 'culture' that is radically disconnected from the social and economic conditions and self-perceptions of people from Muslim cultural backgrounds. The prepackaged identity assigned to Muslims, which is translated into overt and covert forms of social and economic discrimination, not only affects their quality of life in practical terms, but instills in them a sense of insecurity, uncertainty and outsiderness. These are not qualities that promote feelings of belonging and loyalty to an adopted country. They may compel those in the older generation to withdraw and create their own self-sufficient, isolated communities and networks, but for the new generation born or raised in the West, withdrawal is no option. They have every right to expect from the larger society openness, tolerance, mutual respect, acceptance, and the abandonment of its sense of moral and ethical superiority. They have a legitimate right to ask that their governments take responsibility for eliminating socio-economic and political barriers to the dignified integration of its new citizens.

Finally, the chapters taken together have one message, that given the diversity of Muslim populations in the West, conservative cultural practices and traditions do not have the power to compromise Western liberal lifestyle and cherished values. The real threat comes when, frustrated by marginalization, migrants turn to religious practices and traditions to compensate for their exclusion from the larger society, following old norms self-consciously and resentfully. Only then can the circumstances be successfully manipulated by ideologically driven, self-appointed religious leaders against the interests of Muslim communities and the larger society.

PART I
Women's Agency Within
Intersection of Discourses

Chapter 2

Culturalist Approach to Women's Emancipation in the Netherlands

Halleh Ghorashi

Introduction

In the June 2009 elections for the European Parliament, the anti-immigrant party in the Netherlands, PVV (Party for Freedom), was the major winner. Unfortunately, this was not a great surprise in a country that until recently had enjoyed an international image of openness and tolerance. Since the beginning of this century, 'multiculturalism' has been discussed on an almost daily basis in the Dutch media, even more after the November 2004 murder of the filmmaker and columnist Theo van Gogh, the creator of a controversial film about Muslim culture. Because the person charged with the murder was a young Moroccan man with Islamic convictions, a side effect of the case has been that Islam itself has become the core issue in the political debate on migration and integration in the Netherlands. In addition to the political murders of Van Gogh and, two years earlier, Pim Fortuyn, leader of the Livable Netherlands party, was the dispute over the nationality of politician and activist Ayaan Hirsi Ali, which resulted in the fall of the Dutch Cabinet in June 2006, and the controversy over *Fitna*, a film criticizing the Qur'an by populist, anti-immigrant politician Geert Wilders (PVV leader).

The dominant discourse on migration and integration in the Netherlands is not simply about Islam or cultural and/or ethnic difference: at its core it also has a gender component. Much of the discourse focuses on the emancipation of migrant women, particularly Muslim women. Issues such as 'honour killing', 'forced marriages' and 'female circumcision' are commonly discussed in the public arena. The most prominent aspect of the debates in the public sphere is the image of migrant men as aggressors and migrant women as passive victims. In addition, violence is often described exclusively through culture. I believe that this exclusive focus on culture, along with the dominant images of migrant men and women, has enormous implications both for policymaking and for the space allowed for cultural diversity within the country.

My focus in this piece is on the core elements and the implications of the present attention on the emancipation[1] of migrant women in the Netherlands.

---

1   Although *emanicapation* is not often used in recent international academic literature, it is a dominant word within Dutch public and academic works.

Policymaking sensitive to diversity and gender is welcome and needed in all new multicultural societies such as the Netherlands. But the Dutch focus on the emancipation of migrant women has peculiar aspects that may hamper real understanding and the desired results. A combination of three approaches: the culturalist perceptions, a touch of 'new realism', and deficit assessments of women's lives, deepens the already existing divide between the native Dutch and the non-native Dutch.

Culturalist Dominance

It is remarkable that current emancipation policies focus extensively and explicitly on the emancipation of non-Dutch women and, in particular, Muslim women.[2] The assumption is that Dutch women are emancipated and do not need the explicit attention of policymakers, and that it is only migrant women who need help in order to gain emancipation. At the end of 2005, a study of women's emancipation in several European countries (http://www.maqeeq.net) concluded that the Netherlands is the only country in which emancipation is culturalized. In other words, in the Netherlands, emancipation matters are often related to cultural/ ethnic groups.

To understand this culturalization of emancipation in the Netherlands, we need to go back a few years and identify the ways that culture has been defined and discussed within the country's public sphere. It was one of the previous leaders of the Liberal Party (VVD), Frits Bolkestein, who for the first time in the 1990s introduced the Dutch version of the 'clash of civilizations', stating openly that Western and Islamic cultures are incompatible. This essentialist notion of culture takes for granted that cultures are static, homogeneous, and, most importantly, closed entities. It further assumes that what is true of a culture is also true for all individual members of that culture, thus reducing individuals to their culture's perceived attributes and leaving little space for personal agency. Taking this view means that there is not much room for individuals – in this case, migrants – to re-evaluate, change and construct their identities in a variety of ways.

The essentialist view of culture, especially with regard to migrants, is neither new to the Netherlands nor unique to the Dutch situation. Jan Rath (1991) shows that ethnic minorities in the Netherlands have always been considered culturally deviant. This demonstrates the deep historical roots of culturalist thinking in the Netherlands. However, Verena Stolcke believes that cultural exclusion is the new exclusionary rhetoric in Europe as a whole, and is based on a homogeneous, static, coherent, and rooted notion of culture. She calls this new rhetoric 'cultural fundamentalism' (1995: 4). Stolcke argues that it is not the race that needs to be protected but a historically rooted, homogenous national culture: 'racism without

---

2   For an example of this approach see the campaign 'Emancipatie & Integratie: "Thuis in Nederland? Doe mee!"' [At home in the Netherlands? Participate!].

race' (idem). Thus, the essentialist discourse on culture not only has historical roots in the Netherlands, but is also embedded within broader European tendencies.

New Realist and Deficit Discourse

Yet, what makes the current-day Netherlands unique compared to other European countries and to its own past practices is a new shift in the debates towards what Baukje Prins (2002) calls the 'new realistic' discourse. One of the important features of this new genre of thinking is that having the 'guts' to solve problems of integration leaves no room either for 'compromise' or for 'taboos'. This new element in the Dutch public debate began in the mid-1990s and gained vitality with Pim Fortuyn in the beginning of this century. Prins analyzes this new genre as follows: 'Fortuyn […] managed to turn new realism into its opposite, into a kind of hyperrealism. Frankness was no longer practised for the sake of truth, but for its own sake' (2002: 376). The events of September 11, 2001 accorded him more credibility. In the minds of many, the potential enemy – read Islamic migrants – that Bolkestein had discussed in the 1990s became actualized. This made it easier for Fortuyn to say things that had been implied before, but had never been said explicitly. In an interview in *de Volkskrant* in February 2002, Fortuyn made statements such as 'Islam is a backward culture' and 'The real refugees do not reach Holland'.[3] These comments shook the foundation of politics in the Netherlands. Even with his death, in 2002, Fortuyn's influence has remained significant.

The Dutch context is thus unique in the way that the culturalist approach to integration and emancipation is combined with this 'new realistic' discourse. Not only is there a strong essentialist conviction in the ways that migrant cultures are defined as being completely different from that of the Dutch, but it is now also permitted to state that their culture is 'backward' compared to Dutch culture. It is the combination of essentialism, a sense of superiority, and bluntness that underlies the public debates on integration in the Netherlands. In addition, there is another component present within the emancipation debates and policies, and that is the emphasis on migrant women from Islamic countries as people with deficits and shortcomings. It is often argued that migrant women do not have the required skills – knowledge of the language and education – to become active participants in Dutch society. Dominant discourses hold that migrant women, considered 'prisoners' within their culture, or at least within their homes, are socially isolated and need to be freed from isolation and released from their marginalized position. Such attention to deprived and marginalized groups is not new in the Netherlands. According to Rath (1991), the Dutch welfare state has always engaged in decreasing the deprivation of once-called 'unsociables'. The experiences of the Dutch welfare state served as a background for the formation

---

3   See the interview of Fortuyn in *de Volkskrant* on February 9, 2002 with the title: 'De islam is een achterlijke cultuur' [Islam is a backward culture].

of policies for and images of migrants in the Netherlands. The causes of isolation have historically been explained both through socio-cultural and socio-economic factors. This is also the case with migrants in general and with migrant women specifically, since they are assumed to be ultimate victims, both of their gender and of their culture.

In recent years, the deficit and culturalist approaches have been interwoven in explaining the isolation of migrant women. As a result of these developments within the new realist framework, we see that Dutch society is becoming harsh: it has become quite common to disrespect the culture and religion of migrants in public, to call them backward and inherently undemocratic. An example of these developments – a tightening of the rules, regulations and attitudes towards migrants – even affected Somalia-born Hirsi Ali when it came to the dispute over her Dutch citizenship – years after she had received political asylum in the country. Both the national and international media covered this issue extensively. The case of Hirsi Ali shows that the 'rightist', 'new realist' turn within the discourse over integration and migration could not safeguard the position of one of the most integrated, if not assimilated, non-native Dutch people in the country, not to mention one of the key contributors to the 'culturalist' discourse on migrants. These examples show that the 'culturalist' discourse has gone so far that it has become absurd, and has mainly served to fuel public fears and insecurities instead of working towards new insights on diversity and migration. This combination of deprivation and victimization by means of culture or religion, with its clear link to gender, has specific consequences for migrant women in the societal field.

Consequences in the Field

The first consequence of the dominant discourse as described above is that migrants in general, and migrant women in particular, are often not included in decision-making processes that have direct effects on their lives. These groups are not deemed capable of designing solutions for their own problems, and consequently, there is not much room for the many initiatives they do develop to expand their own space. Decisions are frequently based on the frames of reference of 'the emancipated people', which are often poorly connected to the social environment of migrant women. A good example of this is an anecdote concerning a conversation with one of my research assistants:

> Some time ago one of my assistants had become involved in an empowerment project[4] that provided several courses and activities for migrant women. Various plans were developed, and it seemed that all was going well. After the first session of one of the courses, my assistant came to me and said, 'We have a

---

4   Empowerment projects in the Netherlands refer to the projects that help to increase the political, social and economic strength of individuals and communities.

huge problem. We have developed so many interesting things for the women, but they have all kinds of limitations that keep them from participating in the courses and activities.' 'What kinds of limitations and problems?' I asked. The answer was almost too obvious. 'They have children and cannot leave their home; their command of Dutch is not good enough; their husbands limit them in their freedom to come to the meetings.' My response was, 'Okay, but have you asked the women themselves how they see the solutions to their problems, and how they expect the organization to facilitate them in that regard?' The answer of my assistant was a simple, 'No, the organization did not think of that.' When the migrant women participants of the project were asked about this, they came up with a number of simple solutions to their problems. Some did not even need to be facilitated by the organization at all. This is one of many examples of how migrant women are often seen as carriers of problems but not as people who can also devise possible solutions to those problems.

The negative image of these women is often so strong that they are not even taken seriously during the training and courses that are offered to them and in which they participate.

The second consequence is that the political and societal urgency to help migrant women with their emancipation brings with it an associated pressure to get a lot done within a short period of time. All organizations compete for available means. Groups design one rushed project after another. Most of these projects start by assuming that when the shortcomings of the targeted migrant women are solved and they have become 'emancipated', they will have no problem fully participating in society. This approach ignores various causes of isolation, such as societal exclusion. For example, there are many highly educated women who cannot find access to the job market, or have no opportunities to grow in their jobs. This is often brushed aside as a luxury problem. A common reaction is: 'Look at all those women who cannot even leave their homes! *They* are the ones who need help.'

The Case Study[5]

I would like to illustrate these two points through a case study. In the second half of the 1990s a large-scale urban renewal project began in Amsterdam (KEI kenniscentrum stedelijke vernieuwing: website). This project, which is still in progress, focuses on the far western part of Amsterdam, which consists of four adjoining districts. These districts were mostly built during the first few years

---

5   The summary and translation of this case study was done by Ismintha Waldring. A shorter version of this case study and some of the arguments in this piece are already published in another article by Ismintha Waldring (see also Walderling and Ghorashi 2007).

after the Second World War (1939–1945), when there was a great shortage in housing. Nowadays the houses do not meet modern standards: they are small and relatively poor in quality. In addition, the area has other problems, such as high levels of long-term unemployment among its inhabitants, along with the departure of middle and higher incomes inhabitants, growing feelings of insecurity, and a bad public image (ibid.). These socio-economic factors have led the City of Amsterdam to focus not only on the physical renewal of the areas in question, but also on possible social investments in their inhabitants. Given the fact that many Moroccan and Turkish migrants live in these western areas of Amsterdam (Onderzoek & Statistiek: website), and that, as mentioned earlier, Turkish and Moroccan women receive abundant attention in the Netherlands when it comes to emancipation and participation in Dutch society, social investments in the project have also been focused on them.

The initial idea of one of the projects that targeted Turkish and Moroccan women in the Western areas of the city was to train and empower them so that they would be able to participate in decision-making boards related to their neighbourhoods. The whole process of this project, including many of the empowerment and diversity training courses, was coupled with academic research that I supervised. The choice of using academic research in order to monitor and evaluate all the phases of this project from the start was a daring one. Including this learning component in the project not only created moments of reflection throughout the process, but also allowed for vulnerability by including possible criticism.

The research was done in three phases, by three junior researchers, among different groups of women, and lasted a total of two years (2005–2007). All three researchers used the same method of participant observation, each one building on the results of the other. In this chapter, only the first two phases of the project will be presented. The research started by dividing the work into three phases; each phase was followed intensively by one of the researchers. At the end of each phase, the research findings were used to reflect upon the initial aims of the project. The findings helped to rethink the initial planning of the phase to follow. In addition to taking account of participant observation throughout the project, individual in-depth interviews were conducted. In the first study a total of 16 interviews were conducted (ten with participants of the course 'Living in the West', four with coordinators of the self-organizations where the courses were held, and two with project coordinators). In the second study a total of twelve interviews were conducted (ten with participants of the course, and two with the course trainers).

Migrant women were approached to participate in various empowerment courses through different migrant organizations located in the four districts. One noticeable observation of the study was that the project coordinator had not consulted the migrant organizations about the contents of the course; the organizations were only asked to help out with finding the required number of women to participate in the project (Choi 2006). This resulted in little awareness of what the course was about and little interest in investing time to recruit participants. A further consequence was that the women who were approached did not receive thorough and motivating information concerning the course they were asked to follow, resulting in low attendance (ibid.). It is remarkable that this project, with its initial ambition of making women's voices heard in the public sphere, considered the local women's organizations mere instruments to reach the targeted women. Hence, both the contribution of migrant women and self-organizations remained negligible in the first phase of the project. This is only one example of the ways in which migrant women become visible when it comes to serving as background figures and invisible when it comes to serving as experts and specialists in various societal fields. Various formal and informal interviews, both inside and outside this project, show that this overload of attention, coupled with ignorance of the qualities and voices of the stakeholders, can trigger emancipation/integration exhaustion.

The same blind spots that marked the first phase of this project started to resurface during the second phase. The main concern of the participants in the project was to be trained so that they could obtain better access to the job market. They did not show any interest in participation in the urban renewal program that was the initial goal of the project. Also, there seemed to be a disparity between the migrant women who were approached (mainly lowly educated and with low social participation) and the requirements for participation in the decision-making board setting (i.e. people active and experienced in the field). The interviews with migrant women involved in the project made it possible to realize this mismatch quite early in the process and so reflect upon the initial goals of the project. This realization and reflection helped to change those goals so that they could meet the preferences of migrant women who participated in the project. This meant also a shift in activities towards training migrant women for the job market by offering short internships that would provide work experience. Seven of the ten women interviewed did not have a paid job. They did express the wish to find employment, but were aware of the hindrances, e.g. insufficient education, lack of recent work experience, responsibilities for families (especially towards their young children) and, to some extent, command of the Dutch language (Balker 2006). Organizations such as social housing offices, local government offices, political parties, primary schools, foundations and other social organizations were approached. However, getting in touch with these organizations and obtaining access proved to be difficult (ibid.). The unwillingness of organizations to take in migrant women, even just temporarily and on an intern basis, manifestly explains the multi-layered causes of isolation and lack of participation of these women. Within public debates and societal practices, the main cause of assumed non-participation and isolation of migrant women is often explained as the fault of the women themselves: their own possible shortcomings or lack of motivation are blamed. This suggests that the power of the dominant discourses and other societal factors are not examined well enough in order to understand the processes of exclusion of different groups within Dutch society. The unexpected unwillingness of organizations to provide internships did not diminish the enthusiasm of the trainers or the feeling of empowerment gained by these women in their efforts to find jobs. The insistence and enthusiasm of all parties involved in the project resulted in some success by the time of its conclusion.

In addition to its sensitivity to the women's ideas, the partial success of the project was due to the flexibility of the two female trainers involved, who were responsive to the wishes of the migrant women enrolled in the course. This became especially obvious when comparing it to the first-track training – enhancing administrative participation for migrant women – which was conducted by a trainer who, in sticking to her fixed program and schedule, ignored the specific wishes of the women whom she was training (Balker 2006). The trainer in question was intent on following the schedule from A to Z, even if this meant that it would not entirely meet the needs of the women involved and would neglect critical voices. This led to a course that failed to attract and involve participants. In addition to the significant role of the trainers, this comparison showed that success was only possible when the project was evaluated and space was created for the insights and contributions of the participants in the process. In this way, the research component of this project proved to be of essential importance in creating enough reflective room to be able to include the voices of the participants in the project.

Even though the project was at the end unsuccessful in meeting its initial goals of preparing and enabling migrant women to participate in decision-making boards within housing organizations, it was successful in responding to the women's voices and needs, such as providing internships of up to six months for most participants despite the initial unwillingness of the organizations. Some of them found paying jobs during this trajectory, thanks to the networks they had established during the training and coaching sessions; four participants completed the course with internships and six found jobs. These successes were made possible by the non-patronizing approach of the trainers, who did not see the women as passive and 'unemancipated', but rather as active and enterprising, thus facilitating the process for the women to make their own choices based on their own needs and interests.

What this case study clearly shows is that the first consequence of the dominant discourse – focusing on the shortcomings of migrant women as culturally deviant – was at work from the beginning. Even an undertaking that planned to go beyond the basic assumptions of the dominant discourse by presenting an innovative project seemed unable to seriously listen to the women's voices. This is partly due to the generally time-consuming process of obtaining funds in a rather competitive field. But it is also due to the instrumental and results-oriented approach required by the funders. This often results in a lack of time to actually consult the women in question about their needs and wishes, which was the case at the start of this project. A common point made by the different groups of migrant women was: 'After all the courses we took, we have become truly empowered. Now, we need a job but we can't get one.' Yet what made this project different was the coupling of research and reflection, through which those involved in overseeing the project became sensitive to voices from the field. These voices served as necessary feedback to allow a reformulation of initial goals and plans as needed. It is usually the case, however, that the basic assumptions of the dominant discourse, combined with a sense of urgency and growing instrumental tendencies in projects of this sort, do not allow for the type of reflection and evaluation that is necessary to grasp the complexity of the real problems involved. Consequently, these projects fail to achieve promised goals, and the target groups are mostly blamed for the failure. Focusing on the shortcomings of migrant women and viewing them as 'walking deficits' means that they are not taken seriously. Also, the haste and pressures of competition in obtaining funds result in a lack of time to actually consult the women in question about their needs and wishes. What's more, the present attention focused on migrant women from Islamic countries excludes other groups of women, such as the black and refugee women who also constitute a large group within the Dutch society that barely receive any attention, let alone native Dutch women, whose emancipation is assumed to have been completed already. This excessive attention on migrant women with Islamic backgrounds is unpleasant for other groups of women who feel that their problems are misunderstood or overlooked, and increases tension among women. The increasing poverty of single mothers and the difficulties in finding decent childcare or proper jobs for women returning to the job market are nationwide problems that also deserve attention.

Is There a Way Out?

With so much attention focused on the emancipation of migrant women, we have to make sure that this does not just embody a cultural emancipation with essentialist features. Care should be taken not to draw a picture of women from Muslim-majority countries as merely suppressed or isolated. It is crucial to keep an eye open for the real causes of isolation without prematurely categorizing these causes as cultural, which would inevitably cloud other possible causes. For example, the main cause of possible isolation for many of the women involved in this project was not so much their culture or religion, but their level of education and their financial and legal dependency on men. If we look further, we could in fact learn much about the causes of social isolation of women from the history of the women's movement in the Netherlands, where, as well as in much of the rest of the world, women's struggle has been to create a balance between a career and the care of children. The lack of balance can result in a situation in which women cannot claim the position they aim for or deserve. This factor is still true for many native and non-native Dutch women. Financial dependency on men is often one of the major limitations for women to pursue their goals optimally. In the case of migrant women, an additional factor is in play, which is a possible dependency on their husband for gaining a residence permit. In addition, the role of social exclusion, even in the case of highly educated, non-native Dutch women, should not be overlooked as one of the main causes of isolation. Despite relatively remarkable efforts and their own competencies, non-native Dutch women are often denied chances for social mobility. The causes of social isolation are manifold, but the fact that they are often viewed mainly as 'problem cases', and therefore 'risk groups' for companies, is an important factor.

This calls for a broad approach, beginning with a policy that is based on seeing the diversity of Muslims and Muslim women in the causes of social isolation, and not reducing everything to culture. This would enable emancipation policies to focus on the practical needs of all women in need of assistance. Such a diversity-sensitive policy would build upon the positive forces that are already present in the field, thus stimulating different forms of alliances in support of the inclusion-seeking policy, which at present makes it difficult to even form such alliances.

Beyond the Policies

The greatest challenge for Dutch society in the coming years, apart from policy, however, will be countering the dominant gap between natives and non-natives. This will require making room for diversity instead of dichotomizing non-native Dutch populations as cultural others with negative connotations based on their culture and religion. As is stated in the UNDP report of 2004,[6] the real challenge of new multicultural states such as the Netherlands is to avoid cultural determinism – read cultural fundamentalism, to use Stolcke's term – since this can have 'dangerous policy implications'. 'They can fuel support for nationalistic policies that would denigrate or oppress 'inferior' cultures which are assumed to stand in the way of national unity, democracy and development. Such attacks on cultural values would then fuel violent reactions that could feed tensions both within and between nations' (UNDP 2004: 5). As I have argued, the Dutch case is a perfect example of this cultural determinism because of the present configuration of culturalism, a deficit approach and 'new realism' within the dominant discourse on integration. The deficit approach invites the public to focus on the culture-based deprivation of these women, and even though it aims to help women overcome their isolation, it contributes paradoxically and unintentionally to their marginalization. This is the tendency against which the UNDP report warns us and is completely ignored within the Dutch context, even though the increasing tensions between native and non-native Dutch, with potentially dangerous consequences, are becoming more and more visible. Studies on diversity management show that short-term inclusion attempts based on the goodwill of organizations and institutions backfire in the long run. This has to do with the fact that this kind of inclusion is not based on trust in the qualities of the people they take in, but on the moral obligation of the organization. This means that even when target groups are included temporarily, the organizational structure and culture send signals of exclusion, and therefore keeps them out of the system. The only way that social inclusion can have long-term effects is when the participation of the new members is needed and appreciated. At

---

6   http://www.undp.org.in/hdr2004/Report_hdr2004/hdr04_overview.pdf (visited on 24 January 2005).

present, as argued, existing integration policies in the Netherlands do not trigger the inclusion of migrant women based on appreciation and need.

The inclusion of black, migrant and refugee women can have lasting effects only when the women are seen and assessed based on their qualities and talent. To create space for this kind of inclusion, the dominant discourse in the Netherlands and its pursuant policy-making must be countered by a non-essentialist, non-culturalist approach to integration. In this new approach the situational logic of practices and possible conflicts and various factors – including cultural differences and perception – are used to help define and thus solve societal problems. At present, however, a combination of growing populism and 'rightist' sentiments in the Netherlands, combined with a strong belief in instrumental solutions, do not leave much space for evaluation of the policies in this manner. Most importantly, it does not leave much room for reflection upon the paradoxical characters of the present debates and policies.

Having said this, there is room for optimism, as a growing number of young migrant women have gone to university despite the low socio-economic and educational backgrounds of their parents and, increasingly, a relatively large number of passionate and ambitious black, migrant and refugee women are becoming quite visible in various fields in Dutch society. Many of these women have been successful in changing their lives from being filled with limitations to being filled with opportunities. They are sharing their experiences with other women who need their examples. It is to be hoped that their successes will gradually change the prevailing image of migrant women as 'helpless victims'.

References

Balker, B. (2006), *Tot op het bod gemotiveerd! Een onderzoek naar de weg van migrantenvrouwen tot de arbeidsmarkt* (Masters thesis, VU University Amsterdam).

Choi, T. (2006), *Gender- en Etniciteitsubtekst vs. Emancipatie: Over de belemmerende werking van de gender- en etniciteitsubtekst op de emancipatie van migrantenvrouwen* (Masters thesis, VU University Amsterdam).

Ghorashi, H. (2010), 'From absolute invisibility to extreme visibility: Emancipation trajectory of migrant women in the Netherlands', *Feminist Review* 94, 75–92.

Prins, B. (2002), 'The Nerve to Break Taboos: New Realism in the Dutch Discourse on Multiculturalism', *Journal of International Migration and Integration* 3(3 and 4): 363–79.

Rath, J. (1991), *Minorisering: de sociale constructie van 'etnische minderheden'*, (Amsterdam: SUA).

Stolcke, V. (1995), 'Talking Culture: New Boundaries, New Rhetorics of Exclusion in Europe', *Current Anthropology* 36(1): 1–24.

UNDP Report (2004), *Human Development Report 2004: Cultural Liberty in Today's Diverse World* (New York: The United Nations Development Programme).

Waldring, I. and Ghorashi, H. (2007), *Bureau Parkstad 'Vrouwenstemmen kleuren de vernieuwing'.* (Rapportage, VU University Amsterdam).

Internet-based References

KEI kenniscentrum stedelijke vernieuwing (2008), http://www.kei-centrum. nl/view.cfm?page_id=1897&item_type=project&item_id=96 (visited on 24 January 2008).

Onderzoek & Statistiek (2008), http://www.os.amsterdam.nl/pdf/2001_factsheets_ 4.pdf (visited on 24 January 2008).

Chapter 3
Globalization and Women's Leadership in the Muslim Diaspora: An Intersectional Analysis

Fauzia Erfan Ahmed

Introduction

Popular images of Muslim women leaders in the US media that focus on their personal traits, however well meaning, convey a misleading impression of the diverse settings of Muslim women's leadership in the North American diaspora. Leadership is also contextual, an aspect now acknowledged by different disciplines (Graen 2007; Kellerman 2008; Molm 1986). However, the neo-Orientalist image of a Muslim woman throwing off the veil to courageously assume leadership (or assuming leadership despite it) has shown remarkable tenacity. Vivid and dramatic as it is, I argue that this scenario is only part of the story.

While I challenge prevailing media representations of Muslim women leaders as unidimensional paper cutouts, I certainly do not disagree that personal qualities, such as courage, distinguish individual leaders. Based on my fieldwork with rural, low-income Bangladeshi women (Ahmed 2008), I argue that a Gramscian perspective or one that is derived from the women themselves, of these qualities is essential. Muslim women, whom I interviewed, felt that a leader is a woman who has *boodhi*, which they described as wisdom.[1] A combination of intelligence and compassion, *boodhi* is seen as a tangible asset. It creates vision and the fearlessness that is imperative to imagine and develop new horizons. *Boodhi* also creates bridges of solidarity between women by sharing this courage. But this definition of a leader did not develop in a vacuum. Clearly, the distinction between individual leaders and their personal qualities and contextual leadership and its followership needs to be made. In this chapter, I focus on various leadership models of Muslim women in the diaspora which, as we shall see, are replete with the cross currents of many contextual intersectionalities.

Globalization has been the context of Muslim women's leadership in the North American diaspora ever since the first Muslims arrived in slave ships in the sixteenth century. Studies of globalization, leadership, and Islam (Roy 2004) focus on Muslim men and how male leadership has influenced women followers. Little

---

1   *Boodhi* has multiple meanings in Bengali which depend on the context.

is known about the impact of globalization on women's leadership in Muslim communities in the United States. Intimately linked to history, geography, political economy, and society, this leadership has been determined by the changing structure of globalization. Multiple meanings of nation, imagined geographies of home, contradictory notions of citizenship, and dramatic shifts in state policy have intersected in different ways throughout history to form the contours of Muslim women's leadership in the US.

These intersections have also shaped the followership, which is as central as leadership in my exploration of this globalized landscape. As a sociologist, I contend that not only do leaders arise from followers, but that the shape of leadership depends on the shape of followership in any given historic period. In their path-breaking work, Kellerman (2008) and Kelley (2008) analyse the power of followers and their ability to change leaders. But I argue, as does Mills (1992), that a broader perspective is imperative for the exercise of the sociological imagination, perhaps even more so in the exploration of the globalized panorama of Muslim women's leadership.

The nexus of nation, home, citizenship, and state provides this necessary perspective. In this chapter, I provide an intersectional analysis of the ways in which this nexus impacted upon the forms of leadership among Muslim women in the United States in different historic periods. I investigate the following specific questions: How did intersections of nation, home, citizenship, and state impact upon the followership and, consequently, its expectations of Muslim women's leadership? What was the leadership model of each period, and what were its strategies?

Clearly, a textured analysis of the changing interconnections of nation, home, and citizenship, the essential backdrop for these questions, cannot be limited to changing cultural meanings. These contextual components are as concrete as they are abstract: they are the axes of globalized social structures. For example, an investigation of what the notions of the state mean to women of the Muslim diaspora cannot avoid the impact of state policy on its leadership, which, as this chapter illustrates, becomes increasingly globalized over time. Therefore, I also explore how these concepts, as configurations of a globalized structure, impacted upon Muslim women's leadership – its emergence, shape and strategies. I combine Appadurai's superb (1990) definition of the global cultural economy and its 'scapes' with Kim-Puri's (2005) intersectional theories of gender, state, and nation in my analytical framework of inquiry. After a description of the theoretical framework I use for my analysis, I investigate leadership in the early enslaved community of the sixteenth century and in the immigrant community of the early 1970s. I conclude with an analysis of the post-9/11 era, introducing the intersectional model of leadership as the kind of women's leadership that is needed by the Muslim community in the United States today.

Intersectionality and the Globalized Landscapes of Muslim Women's Leadership

Fluid, perspectival, and structural, Appadurai's (1990) use of 'scapes' to describe different dimensions of the global cultural economy reflect the physical and imagined situatedness of various actors. These scapes constitute imagined worlds. They demonstrate how the global cultural economy is a series of disjunctures amongst economy, culture, and politics. The global cultural economy has five such scapes: ethnoscapes; mediascapes; technoscapes; financescapes; and ideoscapes. Ethnoscapes consist of moving persons – tourists, immigrants, refugees, exiles, and guest workers. Fast-moving and unbounded, the global frameworks of technology are technoscapes. As the recent global financial crisis, which originated in faulty mortgage lending in the United States indicates, movements of global capital comprise financescapes. Unpredictable and uneven, the relationships of ethnoscapes, technoscapes, and financescapes now constitute the global cultural economy. The mediascapes and ideoscapes are interrelated landscapes of images that arise from the global political economy. Mediascapes, such as newspapers and television stations, produce information that also provides narratives about the ethnoscapes, thus blurring the distinction between reality and fiction. Ideoscapes are images that are related to power over competing ideologies. Building on Appadurai (1990), I define ideoscapes as the narratives of the dominant ideology, which serve to provide the rationale for the structures of power. All together, these scapes form the global cultural economy.

This theoretical perspective is useful in any investigation of the Muslim diaspora, because the concept of a global *ummah* (community) has been contained in Islam since, perhaps, its very inception. Indeed, in less than a hundred years after the Prophet's death, the Muslim empire had expanded from Spain to India. From this perspective, all Muslims are diasporic, their true home being Mecca, in the direction of which they are all are supposed to pray five times a day. This concept of a diasporic identity is further complicated by geographic migration, which opens possibilities of simultaneously existing in different worlds, with various cultural and social ways of being and thinking. Not surprisingly, when examined through a gendered lens, the ideoscapes and mediascapes of the Muslim diaspora contain imagined and mythic masculinities and femininities that impact upon the leadership and followership therein. Clearly, an examination of Muslim women's leadership also needs a transnational feminist approach.

The intellectual canon of intersectionality theory (Collins 2009; Crenshaw 1991), which combines three indicators of race, class, and gender, needs to be expanded in order to explore this globalized landscape. The origins of this model, based on the experiences of Black women in the United States, are not explicitly transnational. Intersectionality is useful in locating inquiry of the centre in the periphery; it also provides structural and historical perspectives on the micro-contexts in marginalized populations. But in the case of the globalized Muslim diaspora, which is simultaneously distant yet close, real yet imagined, I argue that it is insufficient to limit this context to the three social markers.

I therefore use Kim-Puri's (2005) conceptual intersection of gender, sexuality, state, and nation to create a transnational sociological framework for the analysis of women's leadership in the Muslim diaspora against the backdrop of these globalized scapes. (For the purposes of this chapter, I do not examine sexuality, but this should of course not be taken to mean that I consider this marker unimportant.) In an attempt to avoid replicating mainstream discourse, Kim-Puri (2005) challenges transnational feminist cultural studies on the grounds that it ignores structure. Similarly, they critique feminist sociology because it ghettoizes scholars working in international and American contexts in separate theoretical arenas. In fact, they argue, as does Appadurai (1990), that there is a disjuncture between the state and the nation and that relations of the state, nation, gender, sexuality, and gender are mutually constituted. As Haddad (2001) writes, the question of what it means to be a good Muslim woman in the United States is central to the Muslim diaspora. It is a contested theme, central to Muslim women's leadership. I argue that in a globalized world, this leadership cannot be examined through culture and formal religion alone, because neither culture nor religion can escape structure. Women's leadership therefore must be analysed in a framework that theorizes how these scapes are mutually constituted with gender, state, and nation. For the best illustration of the application of this theoretical approach, I now turn to the sixteenth century, when the first Muslims arrived in the United States.

Leadership as Resilience in the Enslaved Community: Islam as Spiritual Nation

The first Muslims to arrive in North America were African. In fact, more than half the slaves brought to the continent came from predominantly Muslim West Africa; a number of them were educated and of high status in their community (Austin 1997). This group also contained clerics and teachers of the Quran who travelled within Africa to spread Islam. Forced to cross the ocean to the New World in the filthy holds of slave ships, a journey in which large numbers perished, the first Muslims arrived in North America in chains. This involuntary migration, a result of the globalized slave trade, frames the scapes of Muslim women's leadership in this period.

The ethnoscape and ideoscape of enslavement began with capture and the journey across what Africans termed the Bitter Passage to the New World. They were, by definition, private property, and the legal apparatus of state policy reflected this. Slaves could neither own property nor achieve an education. Women were raped; runaways were punished; families were separated. But execution was reserved for those suspected of any kind of organizing ability and activity. The ideoscape or the socio-cultural ideology of the slave-owning classes focused its searchlight on the male slave as capable of organizing insurrection and raping white women. Slave owners not only wanted to buy the bodies of their slaves; they also wanted to own their souls. Forced to eat pork, to change their names, and to marry outside their faith, Muslim slaves were forced to convert to Christianity. Impoverishment and imprisonment, buttressed by state law, created an environment for the enslaved community of unremittingly dehumanization. The construction of a slave identity was imposed by brute force.

Despite this, as Davis (1972) points out in her pioneering article, women were pivotal in what was essentially a 'community of resistance' (Davis 1992: 87). But the fond eye of the liberal historian who studies leadership in the enslaved population falls, inevitably, on male slaves and the insurrections that they led. However, if little is known about African Muslim men who were enslaved, even less is known about African American Muslim women of the antebellum period.

In this chapter, I write of a different kind of leadership, the everyday leadership of women, which is, perhaps, a leadership that is more enduring. In this context, clearly, the emergence and very survival of this leadership was dependent on its invisibility to the legal, social, and cultural apparatus of enslavement. Though beyond the scope of this chapter, I believe that other indigenous African religions and traditions have also contributed to this ideology of female resistance and sabotage. Clearly, I do *not* consider Muslim women and their faith to be the only sources of women's leadership in the early enslaved communities. However, I contend that this leadership, subterranean yet strong, quiet yet insistent, was imperative to the very survival of the enslaved community. But who were these leaders?

The Spiritual Guide Model of Leadership

I argue that in keeping with West African tradition, older Muslim women of the early enslaved communities did in fact assume the task of leadership. Austin (2007) writes about male slaves who continued to write Arabic even after forty years of enslavement. Though he focuses on men, it would be a serious mistake to assume that the women who accompanied them were illiterate. It is the religious duty (*farz*) of every Muslim, regardless of ethnic background and gender, to learn how to read the Quran, which is written in Arabic. Wives of *qadis* (Muslim judges), *imams* (Muslim clerics), and *muezzins* (Muslims who issue the call to prayer), these women leaders were also teachers of the Quran in *madrassahs* (Islamic schools). Clearly, the qualities of these women leaders were important. Teachers of the Quran, wives of travelling clerics, these enslaved women possessed an enormous reservoir of spiritual strength. Their adherence to their faith was remarkable. When the rigours of the daily slave routine prevented them from completing their prayers, they practised *dhikr*, a form of Muslim mediation the goal of which is to praise Allah by expressing thankfulness for the gift of life. This spiritual exercise can also consist of praising God by reciting the hundred names of Allah that reflect different aspects of the Divine. *Dhikr* can be recited under one's breath, a practice eminently well suited to the everyday life of a slave. Such Muslim women were amongst the most vibrant of their community. Cosmopolitan, well-educated, and multilingual, they knew how to be resourceful even under the harshest of circumstances. They were determined not only to learn, even from the most dehumanizing of environments, but also to share their courage with their community. As Diouf asserts, they were 'unafraid of the unknown' (1998: 39). Not surprisingly, they knew that leadership was needed and seized the opportunity.

Leadership as Spiritual Resilience

The social structure of slavery created a followership that needed resilience, and indeed the women leaders rose to meet the expectations of their followers. The primary task of leadership was to create an affirming ideoscape as a counterpoint to the dehumanizing ideology of the slave-owners, which was an accompaniment to the social structure of slavery. In the abstract as well as the everyday, Islam became synonymous with home, nation, and citizenship. It represented, therefore, not just an imagined community but also an imagined world. As Appadurai (1990) states, living in an imagined world can subvert the imagined world of the official mind. The task of leadership was subversion through spiritual resilience, and it was accomplished in two ways: first, through the continued daily practice of Islam even though it was dangerous; and second, through the conscious syncretization of Islam.

How did enslaved women practice Islam in an environment of forced conversion? Accounts reveal that they made honey rice cakes (*saraka*) during Ramadan and shared them with the entire community, which also included non-Muslims (Diouf 1998). The cakes symbolized alms-giving (*sadakha*) in the name of Allah, a common practice in Muslim communities. In addition to their efforts to maintain the daily prayers, they maintained *zakat* (a tax that amounts to one-fortieth of total personal income), one of the five tenets of Islam. As can be imagined, these were no mean feats in an enslaved existence. The preparation of this food and the breaking of the fast were important to the cohesion of an identity that was under daily assault. These rituals were not simply the tasks of a leadership that envisioned its work as located in its physical environment. Muslim women used these rituals to connect the enslaved community with the imagined world of the global Muslim community (*ummah*). This leadership strategy made it clear to Muslim slaves that despite differences in region of origin in Africa and language, they shared common values as Muslims.

In addition to the daily practice of their faith, Muslim women leaders also consciously syncretized Islam as part of their vision of an imagined world and a free national identity. Syncretic Islam, in essence, is the spiritual fusion of Islam with other local religious and folk traditions (Roy 1993). In the context of slavery, in the face of enforced conversion, women leaders also fused Islam with Christianity by reciting the Sura Fatiha (opening verse of the Quran) in place of the Lord's Prayer. Muhammad (Sm) was linked to Jesus. Dancing in a circle around the church simulated circumambulation around the Kaaba during *hajj* (the pilgrimage to Mecca), yet another pillar of Islam but impossible in an enslaved existence. I disagree with scholars (Diouf 1998; McCloud 2001) who argue that Islam in enslaved populations could not survive the rigours of slavery and eventually died out. Instead, I argue that it was this conscious syncretization of Islam by enslaved women leaders that kept its spiritual essence, indeed the very backbone of Islam (Kassam 2006), alive. Syncretization, which has taken place throughout Muslim history in various parts of the world, has largely been an unconscious process. The leadership work of enslaved Muslim women leaders is one of the few instances of conscious syncretization that I have found.

These leadership strategies helped the followership recognize the power of self-definition as everyday resistance to slavery. In *Black Feminist Thought*, Collins (2009) analyses the ways in which self-definition and spiritual resistance enabled Black women to resist negative stereotypes. They used Islam as a concept that united a past heritage with a future vision of a free identity. As such, the leadership of enslaved Muslim women represented a backbone of resistance because of its simple yet profound message: physical enslavement does not have to mean spiritual bondage. In this way, it created the resilience necessary to overcome the unbearable realities of the present.

Leadership as Defying Binarism: Islam as Private Patriarchy and Public Stereotype

A change in state policy in 1965, embodied in the revocation of the *Asia Exclusion Act*, changed the ethnoscape of Muslims in the United States. It brought not only larger numbers of Muslim immigrants, but also more women from diverse ethnic, religious, and national backgrounds. Many of these Muslim women were highly educated; a number were physicians, lawyers, and professors. This generation came from countries that were young. In general, migration to the US represented an opportunity for this generation to live a life of equality.

But when they arrived in America, these Muslim women found themselves at the heart of controversy, a disjuncture that was created between state policy, which putatively welcomed them, and the negative mediascapes and ideoscapes that confronted them in the country they had chosen to call home. The mediascapes were not favourable: Islam was not understood, much less appreciated in all its dimensions, in the US, and the new immigrants had to confront hurtful stereotypes about their communities, especially if they were of Arab origin.

Muslim women simultaneously faced two ideoscapes that represented different axes of power, but were rooted in a binary social construction of the Muslim woman. The first ideoscape represented upper-middle-class white women who dominated the feminist movement in the US. Well-connected, outspoken and wealthy, these women promoted a liberal feminism that ignored the differences between women and assumed a homogenous stereotype of women of colour. Though many were well-intentioned, they were quite ignorant about the various cultures and histories of immigrant Muslim women. This ideoscape of Western feminism was binary, and their unidimensional model of the 'liberated woman' imposed a dualistic construction on Muslim women. Binarism consists of absolutes: Oppressed Muslim (Third World) women vs Liberated Western women; Passive Muslim women vs Independent Western women. Muslim women immigrants found that Western women pitied them and wanted to save them from the dictates of their oppressive religion (Abu Lughod 2007). In this schema, modern, progressive Muslim women looked and thought like them, whereas backward Muslim women remained imprisoned in their cultural traditions. In essence, this duality meant that Muslim women had to be like the white, middle-class woman in the United States.

In the post-colonial world, this ideoscape of Western feminism was also connected to global structures of power. This second-wave white feminists wanted to change the world and to improve things for women overseas but, again, on their own terms. Created in 1970s by women (Connell 1987) who belonged to the Society for International Development, an American non-governmental organization (NGO) based in Washington DC, WID), otherwise known as 'add women and mix,' quickly gained credibility with the United States Agency for International Development (USAID), which established a WID office in 1973. Self-contained though not comprehensive, WID is best understood as a 'regime of representation' (Escobar 1995: 10) that determines what is seen and what remains unseen. WID has been critiqued by feminist scholars as depicting Third World women as passive and uniformly lacking in agency (Mohanty 1991) and by gender and development experts as imposing a Western modernization on non-Western women. However, it remains popular among policy-makers throughout the world, who find its non-controversial binary message easy to implement.

But immigrant Muslim women leaders, among others from the Third World, were unable to affect WID because globality did not translate into globalized leadership. A transnational existence did not translate into transnational power. Despite their efforts, these women lost ground in the international arena, in the very international socialist women's movement in which they had participated as freedom fighters for their countries of origin. Up rootedness and diminished financial resources, a double burden combined with negative ideoscapes and mediascapes in the United States, consumed their attention and energy. The ethnoscape of immigration of this generation of Muslim women leaders reduced the reach of their influence. This is, in my opinion, the central tragedy of this generation; the socialist movement was deprived of the vision and vitality of these Muslim women leaders, and at a time when it was most needed.

They also had to confront the second ideoscape: patriarchy within their own immigrant Muslim communities. The philosophy of the patriarchal Muslim imam, yet another leadership model in the immigrant community, posed a counterpoint. Imams wrote texts on Muslim women in the US that emphasized traditional gender roles. In this ideoscape, good Muslim women were submissive, and bad Muslim women were outspoken; good Muslim women conformed, and bad Muslim women deviated. These binaries focused on the depiction of an imagined world, imbued with patriarchal nostalgia, in which everybody (especially women) 'knew their place.' In stark contrast to the white feminist model, this binarism focused on the depiction of the good Muslim immigrant woman as remaining 'true' to the culture of her origin instead of falling 'prey' to the evils of the West. This ideoscape constructed the Muslim woman as the citadel of an endangered culture, a common theme in minority Muslim cultures (Ahmed 2006). Contradictory ideoscapes made the Muslim woman a 'political football' (Haddad 2001) in America. Clearly, these scapes of followership had an impact on who the leaders were and, more importantly, on the leadership model.

The Scholar–Activist Model of Leadership

Though age is respected in many of the cultures of origin, Muslim women immigrants who comprised the followership did not follow tradition. They did not look towards older women for guidance in how to navigate these contradictory territories. Instead, they conferred leadership on educated professional women who were fluent in English and who had high-status jobs in the US. The highly educated nature of the followership, the racialized context of US feminism, and patriarchy within Muslim communities created a new scholar–activist model of leadership in the Muslim diaspora. Dr Azizah al Hibri is one such example. As a law professor, she researches women's issues in Islam based on a critique of patriarchal medieval jurists. Her writings frequently appear in major newspapers. She also created Karama, an organization of Muslim lawyers that provides legal aid to Muslim women in the United States.

The Muslim women leaders of this period had fought Western imperialism; they had rejected traditional gender stereotypes; they had participated in the public sphere. For these women, 'globality was more than a state of mind,' as Scholte (2000) defines it. As founders of women's organizations in their countries of origin, they did not relinquish their roots. They went back as often as possible, and those women who could not do so maintained ties in other ways. At the same time, they quickly became a focal point of their own immigrant community, a leadership node around which other women coalesced. Clearly, they lived a transnational existence in body and spirit: meanings of home lay in the in-between.

This simultaneity was heightened by the fact that many of these women leaders did not come to the United States voluntarily. Though they had fought for freedom in their countries of origin after independence, these women had met heartbreak when patriarchy reasserted itself in the newly independent countries, enforcing the oppression of women. But in the United States they encountered the compound, simultaneous oppression of negative scapes of race, gender, class and nation.

Leadership as Defiance of Stereotypes

These scholar–activists were neither quiet nor invisible; their response was public and immediate. Unwilling to conform to expected stereotypes, Muslim women leaders challenged liberal feminism through scholarly writings and public advocacy. They also wrote op-eds in major newspapers questioning such stereotypes. They took issue with the leadership of the National Organization of Women (NOW) when it failed to condemn Israel's bombing of civilians in Lebanon in 1982. They created their own organizations.

As scholars, they focused on feminist interpretations of the Islamic texts, the Quran and the Hadith. They also revived *ijtihad* (Ahmed 2008) or moral reasoning, an aspect of Islamic jurisprudence that had been neglected by Muslim jurists (Webb 2000). Based on a Hadith that says that the outpost of God is one's conscience, *ijtihad* presents the philosophy of Islamic jurisprudence as an interpretative process that is simultaneously contextual and contemporary. In essence, *ijtihad* implies that the meaning of justice and how it was implemented in seventh-century Arabia, when Islam began, cannot mean precisely the same thing today. Not surprisingly, patriarchal Islamicists found this objectionable. Riffat Hasan, one of the early pioneers of feminist leadership of this generation, explored an interpretation of the Quran as a basis for gender equality, and subsequently challenged Muhammad Abdul Rauf, imam of the Islamic Center in Washington DC. In the public confrontation that followed, he publicly chastised her for assuming the authority to analyse the Quran in such a manner. African American Muslim scholars, such as Amina Wadud, who led a group in prayer at a mosque, and Amina McCloud, have been equally outspoken and courageous. It is as a result of their courage that, unlike other minority-Muslim cultures in the world, the patriarchal imam leadership model does not remain undisputed in the United States. Today, the feminist scholar–activist model is also recognized as valid.

Leadership after 9/11: Islam and the De-Americanization of Muslims

In what must be one of the superlative ironies of history, Islam, which was forcibly brought to America in the holds of slave ships in the sixteenth century and then suppressed, is now one of the fastest growing religions in the United States. The Muslim diaspora is rapidly increasing: in mid-2000, there were over 4 million Muslims, out of whom 1.6 million were African American. Approximately 17,500 African Americans converted to Islam each year between 1990 and 1995. The community is very diverse, Muslims having migrated from all of the five continents. Most are immigrants (77.6 per cent), but an increasing number are

US-born (22.4 per cent).[2] Yet despite this increase in followership, the context of leadership in post-9/11 America is dire.

Scapes of vulnerability frame the Muslim diaspora in the United States today. The ideoscapes and mediascapes now assume fearful proportions, and gender, nation, and Islam are at the heart of these images and discourses. Like two sides of a coin, different dualities have been simultaneously created: Muslim men as terrorist-against-nation and oppressor-of-women (Abu Lughod 2007; Cainkar 2009). The mediascape has created a hegemonic Muslim masculinity and its counterpart, an emphasized and subordinate veiled femininity. In her study of Arab Muslims in Chicago, Cainkar (2009) noted that Muslim males, when accompanied by women wearing *hijab*, were more frequently attacked than those who were not. Muslim men are constructed as outcasts in American culture because they devalue Muslim women. As terrorists, they are constructed as non-citizens, disloyal to the red, white and blue. Islam as the 'morally deviant' religion (Cainkar 2009) that sanctions terrorism is the axis on which this coin spins. Imaged as a barbaric colossus, the Muslim world is juxtaposed with the United States, a civilized modern nation in which freedom for women is valued.

These media images, in fact, serve as the ideoscapes of state policy. Within six weeks of the September 11 attack, Congress passed the *USA Patriot Act* of 2001 (Uniting and Strengthening America by Providing Appropriate Tools Required to Intercept and Obstruct Terrorism Act),[3] which gave the US government sweeping powers of surveillance and investigation. For the first time, Muslims became a social category marked by law. In order to justify constitutional violations of due process and free speech, the *Patriot Act* needs a vivid narrative. This is conveniently provided by the mediascapes that portray Muslims as 'terrorists' who not only threaten the safety of 'peace-loving peoples' but also have the potential to harm the very foundations of Western civilization itself. Thus, any measure must be taken to stop these terrorists, no matter what the costs.[4]

State policy is condoned by popular opinion. Not surprisingly, hate crimes increased immediately after 9/11 (Maira 2004). As time went on such incidents decreased, but civil rights complaints in airports and workplaces have increased. Maira's (2004) study revealed that prior to 9/11, about 80 per cent of the American

---

2   This information was provided by Zogby International in August 2000 in a survey commissioned by the American Muslim Council. Obtained from the website of the official US State Department fact sheet http://www.islamfortoday.com/historyusa.4.htm accessed October 28, 2009.

3   For an excellent detailed description and analysis of the *Patriot Act* see Hines, Barbara (2006).

4   The fact that US authorities failed to catch Nigerian hijacker Omar Farouk Abdulmuttalab despite a warning from his own father only serves to highlight my thesis that the scapes of terror have their own logic and that homeland safety may not be the real issue.

population considered racial profiling wrong; since 9/11, 60 per cent favour it as long as it is directed towards Muslims and Arabs. At first glance, it seems that 9/11 represented a dramatic reversal. Indeed, well-meaning liberal commentators have referred to the blatant xenophobia in the weeks following 9/11 as a deviation from traditional American values of tolerance. Others, such as Cainkar (2009) and Schumann (2007), also point out that the social construction of Muslims, particularly Arabs, as a monolithic people innately prone to violence is not a new ideology. It can legitimately be argued that 9/11 only consolidated a hitherto latent cultural antipathy towards Muslims.

What is new is that legal changes after 9/11 essentially reduced citizenship rights for Muslims. The *Patriot Act* and the convergence of negative scapes have created a climate in which it is permissible to heighten surveillance and summarily deport Muslim immigrants as state policy. There were large-scale deportations of Pakistani nationals on chartered planes from New York State in the middle of the night (Ryan 2003). Constructed as 'moral aliens' (Yuval-Davis 1997) not citizens, as perpetual outsiders not Americans, for American Muslims today 'nation' does not mean safety.

It is only too easy to lose sight of Muslim women's concerns in the midst of the confusion and the fear. Maira (2009) analyses how the ideoscape has divided the Muslim community into 'good' or 'bad' Muslims. But the ways in which the scapes affect gender relations at the micro and meso levels cannot be ignored. What is happening to women in the Muslim community and how the scapes have impacted upon relationships between men and women therein have not been systematically studied. Indeed, silence has become a watchword for survival. But survival for men doesn't always mean the same thing as survival for women, especially in marginalized communities. As Lateef's (1990) work on Muslim women in India indicates, they are a 'minority within a minority.' I argue that the greater the marginalization of the community without, the greater the rise of patriarchy within, because external oppression imposes internal silence on women. It is likely that the vulnerabilities of immigrant women to domestic violence (Menjivar and Salcido 2006) have increased for Muslim women. Perhaps, as never before, it is the beacon of leadership that is needed. But a woman's leadership model that meets the expectations of the followership of the post-9/11 Muslim women's diaspora has yet to emerge.

The Intersectional Leadership Model

The scholar–activist model that served Muslim female followership in the past may not be sufficient in the post-9/11 era. I present an intersectional leadership model that combines the philosophical vision of Aristotelian citizenship as participating in governance as well as being governed with what I call intersectional agency. I define this agency as the ability to not only simultaneously lead different coalitions, but to effectively enable their intersections on a number of political projects relevant to the followership. It is no longer enough to confine oneself to the Muslim community. The capacity to navigate the sensitive terrain of Muslim women's oppression within the Muslim community at a time when Muslim men are being stereotyped as brutish and violent is crucial. This ability to connect and intervene at the meeting points of different scapes is a key feature of this leadership model, which Collins (2009) implies in her discussion of transversal politics. An intersectional leader has to engage in the globalized praxis of intersectionality. This means that such a leader would have, for example, the vision to philosophically intersect the mediascape with the ethnoscape of the immigrant Muslim woman on the intersectional meeting point of a political project, such as domestic violence.

Leadership as Globalized Transversal Dialogue

The scapes of post-9/11 America are not only dire; they are stark; they are globalized. The strategies of leadership, therefore, though not simple, are unambiguous. Building on the work of Italian feminists Yuval-Davis (1997) and Collins (2009), I argue that the key strategy of Muslim women's leadership is to engage in globalized transversal dialogue. For the purposes of this chapter I shall highlight three specific tasks: self-definition; coalition-building; and youth-leadership development. I focus on the latter since little has been written about intersectionality and Muslim girls.

First, the demonization of Islam and the de-Americanization of Muslims make self-definition paramount for Muslim women; it is a strategy that draws from the spiritual legacy of the resistance of Muslim women in the early enslaved communities. Second, transversal coalitions need to be built across diverse religious and ethnic group lines. To this end, the grassroots interfaith dialogues started after 9/11 need to be expanded. This alliance-building must also be virtual, in order to counter not only the mediascapes of the Western media but the also the ideoscapes of Islamicist groups that oppress Muslim women. The fact that despite the binary scapes, provisions for immigrant women who face domestic violence have been expanded (Hines 2006) is an example of the effectiveness of such transversal coalitions. Third, leadership development for Muslim girls in the diaspora reflects the expectations of a followership whose demographics have changed and increasingly comprises Muslims born in the United States. This group is young, multi-class, and vociferous. An ethnographic study (Maira 2004) revealed that working-class Muslim youth are speaking out; often they will publicly voice opinions that the middle-class leaders are unwilling to express. The scapes of repression force these Muslim students to engage in a citizenship of dissent. Muslim immigrant youth link domestic and foreign policies in a philosophy that views globalization and nationalism as part of the ideoscape of US imperialism. Targets of the 'War-on-Terror' and the 'War-on-Immigrants,' and lacking the money and connections to get expert legal advice, these Muslim youth use sophisticated political analyses to define themselves in the scapes of outsiderness. I also think that they speak out because they feel that they have nothing to lose, a clear indication that leadership development is needed.

Conclusion

Muslim women's leadership always emerged from a globalized context, even as structures of nation, citizenship, and state changed over time. Each historic period created its own leadership model and strategies. Spiritual resilience, the leadership strategy of the women in the early enslaved communities, survives today as an eternal gift to the Muslim diaspora. The scholar–activist model is a testimony to the struggle of women in the 1970s who openly confronted the compound oppressions of Western liberal feminists and patriarchal Islamicists. I have no doubt that an intersectional leadership model will emerge, because the gleams of a constant river of courage, sinuous and flowing, illuminate the history of women's leadership in the American diaspora.

References

Abu Lughod, Lila (2007), 'Do Muslim Women Really Need Saving? Anthropological Reflections on Cultural Relativism and its Others', in Taylor, V. and Whittier, N. (eds) *Feminist Frontiers* 7th ed. (New York: McGraw Hill), 484–93.

Ahmed, Fauzia Erfan (2008), 'Hidden Opportunities: Grassroots Muslim Feminism, Masculinity, and the Grameen Bank', *International Journal of Feminist Politics*, 10(4): 542–62.

—— (2006), 'Women, Gender, and Reproductive Health: South Asia', *Encyclopedia of Women and Islamic Cultures*, Vol. 2 3.041i (Netherlands: Brill Academic Publishers).

Appadurai, Arjun (1990), 'Disjuncture and Difference in the Global Cultural Economy', *Theory, Culture and Society*, 76, 295–310.

Austin, Allan D. (1997), *African Muslims in Antebellum America: Transatlantic Stories and Spiritual Struggles* (New York and London: Routledge).

Cainkar, Louise A. (2009), *Homeland Insecurity: The Arab American and Muslim Experience After 9/11* (New York: Russell Sage Foundation).

Collins, Patricia Hill (2009), *Black Feminist Thought.* 2nd ed. (London: Routledge).

Connell, Robert W. (1987), *Gender and Power: Society, the Person and Sexual Politics* (Stanford, CA: Stanford University Press).

Crenshaw, Kimberlé Williams (1991), 'Mapping the Margins: Intersectionality, Identity, Politics, and the Violence Against Women of Color', *Stanford Law Review* 43(6): 1241–99.

Davis, Angela (1972), 'Reflections on the Black Woman's Role in the Community of Slaves', *Massachusetts Review*, 88–100.

Diouf, Sylviane A. (1998), *Servants of Allah: African Muslims Enslaved in the Americas* (New York and London: New York University Press).

Escobar, Arturo (1995), *Encountering Development: The Making and Unmaking of the Third World* (Princeton: Princeton University Press).

Graen, George B. (2007), 'Asking the Wrong Questions about Leadership', *American Psychologist* 62, 604–18.

Haddad, Yvonne Yazbeck (2006), 'Islam, Women, and the Struggle for Identity in North America', in Rosemary Skinner Keller and Rosemary Radford Ruether (eds) *Encyclopedia of Women and Religion in North America*, Vol. 2, Part VIII (Bloomington: Indiana University Press).

Hines, Barbara (2006), 'An Overview of U.S. Immigration Law and Policy Since 9/11', *Texas Hispanic Journal of Law & Policy* 12, 9–28

Kassam, Tazeen. R. (2006), 'Response', *Journal of Feminist Studies in Religion* 22(1): 59–66.

Kellerman, Barbara (2008), *Followership: How Followers are Creating Change and Changing Leadership* (Cambridge: Harvard Business Press).

Kelley, Robert E. (2008), *The Power of Followership*, quoted in Kellerman, Barbara (2008), *Followership: How Followers are Creating Change and Changing Leadership* (Cambridge: Harvard Business Press).

Kim-Puri, H.J. (2005), 'Conceptualizing Gender-Sexuality-State-Nation: an Introduction', *Gender & Society* 19(2): 137–59.

Lateef, Shahida (1990), *Muslim Women in India: Political and Private Affairs* (New Jersey: Zed Books).

Maira, Sunaina (2004), 'Youth Culture, Citizenship and Globalization: South Asian Muslim Youth in the United States after September 11th', *Comparative Studies of South Asia, Africa, and the Middle East* 24(1): 219–31.

—— (2009), '"Good" and "Bad" Muslim Citizens: Feminists, Terrorists, and US Orientalisms', *Feminist Studies* Fall 35(3): 631–56.

McCloud, Aminah Beverly (2001), 'African American Muslim Women', in Rosemary Skinner Keller and Rosemary Radford Ruether (eds) *Encyclopedia of Women and Religion in North America*, Vol. 2, Part VIII (Bloomington: Indiana University Press).

Menjivar, Cecilia and Olivia Salcido (2006), 'Immigrant Women and Domestic Violence', *Gender & Society* 16(6): 898–929.

Mills, C. Wright (1992), 'The Promise of Sociology' in *Seeing Ourselves: Classic, Contemporary, and Cross Cultural Readings in Sociology* (New Jersey: Prentice Hall), 1–5.

Mohanty, Chandra (1991), 'Under Western Eyes: Feminist Scholarship and Colonial Discourse', in Chandra Mohanty, Ann Russo, and Lourdes Torres (eds) *Third World Women and the Politics of Feminism* (Bloomingdale: Indiana University Press).

Roy, Asim (1993), *The Islamic Syncretic Tradition in Bengal* (New Jersey: Princeton University Press).

Roy, Olivier (2004), *Globalized Islam: The Search for a New Ummah* (New York: Columbia University Press).

Ryan, Oliver (2003), 'Empty Shops, Empty Promises for Coney Island Pakistanis', *ColorLines* 6(2): 14–16.

Scholte, Jan. A. (2000), *Globalization: A Critical Introduction* (New York: St. Martin's Press).

Schumann, Christoph (2007), 'A Muslim Diaspora in the United States', *The Muslim World* 97, 11–32.

Wallerstein, Immanuel (1974), *The Modern World System: Capitalist Agriculture and the Origins of the European World Economy in the Sixteenth Century* (New York: Academic Press).

Webb, Gisela (2000), *Windows of Faith Muslim Women Scholar Activists in North America* Syracuse (New York: University Press).

Yuval-Davis, Nira (1997), 'Women, Citizenship and Difference', *Feminist Review* 57, 4–27.

Chapter 4

Emergence of a Transnational Muslim Feminist Consciousness among Women in the WENAAZ (Western Europe, North America, Australia and New Zealand) Context

Cassandra Balchin

Introduction

Since, according to the feminist mantra, 'sisterhood is global,' and since the *ummah* by definition traverses borders and boundaries, it stands to reason that feminist consciousness among Muslim women should also be transnational. Yet this transnational feminist consciousness has emerged in quite distinct forms and at diverse paces in different contexts. This brief chapter cannot possibly do justice to the whole area of transnationalism within women's rights activism in Muslim contexts, which has a long history (Hélie-Lucas, 1990; Shaheed, 1994; Sunder, 2003). It will, however, attempt to briefly outline a few examples of transnational activism for women's human rights, as well as discuss their main features and subject focus. It will then discuss the British context, wherein a transnational feminist consciousness appears now to be emerging.

This chapter is based on more than 20 years of women's rights activism in Muslim contexts, including several years as a journalist in Pakistan and nine years with Shirkat Gah Women's Resource Centre (SG), one of the country's most active women's organizations. SG is also the Asia Regional coordination office for the international solidarity network, Women Living Under Muslim Laws, and much of my work at SG related to WLUML. In 2000, I moved to Britain to help relocate WLUML's International Coordination Office from France to London; I worked there until 2007, when I left the network to focus on my voluntary work with women in Britain's Muslim communities. Since 2002 I have been involved with the Muslim Women's Network UK (MWN-UK), which was formally established as an autonomous women's organization in 2007. What struck me most in moving from South Asia's vibrant feminist scene and my involvement in global women's activism in Muslim contexts was the apparent lack in Britain of a collective feminist consciousness among women from the dominant Muslim migrant communities of Bangladeshi, Indian and Pakistani origin. There are women's groups, such as Imece, serving the Turkish-speaking community with a feminist outlook, and many long-standing support groups, such as Southall Black Sisters and Newham Asian Women's Project, working in areas dominated by South Asian migrant communities; there are also feminist groups linking Iraqi, Iranian and Afghan exile communities.[1] All of these groups have a long history of transnational feminist networking, but always within a secular framework. Women who sought to combine feminist perspectives with progressive interpretations of Islam seemed either non-existent or invisible as a collective. Moreover, there was no evidence of any linkage with international feminist networking – general or Muslim-specific. That situation now appears to be rapidly changing.

Feminist Transnational Networking in Muslim Contexts

Consciously feminist, collective and transnational organizing for women's legal rights has been visible for more than two decades in Muslim majority and minority contexts outside the main 'diasporic' centres in Western Europe, North America, Australia and New Zealand (which I shall abbreviate to WENAAZ). This chapter avoids the term 'The West' and 'diaspora' while discussing Muslims in these contexts because these dichotomous terms imply that Muslims are not 'of' these regions but are rather in the apparently lesser position of being merely 'in' these contexts. Yet research has found that 99.2 per cent of British-born Muslims identify themselves as British (Manning and Roy, 2007: 9). Moreover, the significant differences between the experiences of Muslim women organizing in Britain and organizing in their families' countries of origin (aside from English, Welsh, Scottish and Irish converts to Islam) also indicate that there is a specifically British form of Muslim feminist collective action. Generally, it is more accurate to refer to 'women in Muslim communities' rather than 'Muslim women,' given that those born into a Muslim community may not wish to identify as such or, in the case of women married to Muslims, may indeed not be Muslim themselves. This is the long-standing position of WLUML, and elsewhere I have discussed the serious problems arising from the label 'Muslim women' (Balchin, 2007; Balchin, 2003). However, as this chapter deals specifically with women in Britain who identify themselves as feminist and Muslim, in that context I shall occasionally use the term 'Muslim women.'

Collective organizing outside WENAAZ has taken various forms. One example is the aforementioned Women Living Under Muslim Laws, formed in 1984, which now links women in over 70 countries, ranging from Senegal to Indonesia, and Uzbekistan to South Africa. WLUML's trilingual website receives well over one million hits per month. Its largest initiative to date, the Women and Law in the Muslim World Programme, ran for over 10 years and involved thousands of researchers, activists, sociologists, scholars and lawyers in some two dozen countries, all sharing a common methodological and analytical approach. The

---

1   www.imece.org.uk/; www.southallblacksisters.org.uk/; www.nawp.org/; Organization of Women's Freedom in Iraq.

project produced numerous publications, including *Knowing Our Rights: Women, family, laws and customs in the Muslim world* (WLUML, 2006), which was the international synthesis of this project. The knowledge and experiences shared as a result of this project strengthened women's activism for positive reform of family laws and practices across the network and beyond.

Using the 1995 Beijing World Conference on Women as its anchor, the Collectif 95 Maghreb Egalité launched a major regional initiative to push for family law reform in North Africa. This was a key contributing factor in the new Moroccan Family Code, or Moudawana, of 2004 (which moves towards envisaging marriage as a partnership of equals) and significant reforms to the Algerian Family Code in 2005. Although the initiative remained regional, broader transnational links played important roles at various points in the process: there was a sharing of information and experiences with Turkish feminists undertaking a similarly sweeping reform effort in the early 2000s, and when women leading the reform campaign in Morocco were personally threatened, international solidarity helped ensure their safety.

Noticeably, in the region of the Middle East and North Africa (MENA), it is only within about the last ten years that transnational feminist activism, and specifically activism around legal matters, has shifted to include regular networking with women in Muslim contexts in South and Southeast Asia and sub-Saharan Africa. The reluctance to network *as Muslims* stemmed from the dominant pan-Arab nationalist project and the determination of local feminists to resist the fracturing they felt would arise from apparently acceding to religious rather than ethnic definitions of identity. To date, of course, the pan-Arab project has failed and the privileging of religious identity – courtesy of the visibility of groups such as the Muslim Brotherhood – has triumphed. Nevertheless, in the past, women activists in the Maghreb region networked regularly with migrant Maghrebi women in France, often regarding legal rights issues. This networking was far more visible than that between, for example, Pakistani or Bangladeshi women activists and migrant women in Britain's, Canada's or Norway's Muslim communities. The reasons for this, which can be largely understood through an analysis of class and ethnicity, are too complex to discuss here.

In contrast to the more formal structures of the WLUML network and Collectif 95, in Malaysia, for example, Sisters in Islam (SIS) has used shared language linkages to network informally with progressive Indonesian scholars and thus strengthen their analyses of and challenges to conservative interpretations of Muslim family laws in the country. The African-American Muslim scholar, Amina Wadud, lived in Malaysia for several years and became a founding member of SIS; to this day she contributes to the organization's legal-reform advocacy efforts with her scholarship. Through these initiatives, transnational feminist legal activism in Muslim contexts has ranged in form from large international formal networks to more individualized connections.

Since 2007, a movement has been quietly developing that brings together women and some men from diverse Muslim contexts who are working to reform family law and a total reimagining of the Muslim family based on the changed realities shared in so many Muslim contexts. A global movement for equality and justice in the Muslim family, Musawah was launched in February 2009.[2] In structure, it is emerging as a far looser entity than either WLUML or the Collectif 95 initiative. However, it is cohesive in seeing transnational knowledge-sharing as a vital contribution to successful strategies to promote legal reform and to protect women's existing rights in diverse Muslim contexts.

It is not surprising that transnational feminist activism in Muslim contexts has focused on family laws and practices. To paraphrase the work of sociologist Nira Yuval-Davis (1997), women are the physical and symbolic bearers of the collective's identity, and thus family law, which regulates the community's control of women's bodies in both the private and public spheres, is central both to the preservation of dominant constructions of that identity and to challenges to that construction. This applies to the perspectives of both state and non-state actors such as religious fundamentalist groups. In an era where identity politics in general, and religious fundamentalism in particular, have become so visible and powerful, the tussle between the ideologically opposing forces of feminism and fundamentalism have naturally sharpened this focus on women and the family.

This is not to ignore transnational feminist activism around penal laws, especially, those relating to sexuality and violence against women (VAW). WLUML is currently coordinating The Global Campaign to Stop Killing and Stoning Women!, which is designed to address the misuse of religion and culture to justify killing women as punishment for violating the 'norms' of sexual behaviour. When several northern Nigerian states announced the 'sharianization' of penal provisions a decade ago, WLUML networkers from Pakistan shared with Nigerian activists their analysis of the discriminatory aspects of laws supposedly based on Muslim penal provisions, or Hudood, as well as case law from positive judgements in zina (sex outside a valid marriage) cases before Pakistan's Federal Shariat Court. This networking strengthened the arguments used to secure the dismissal of cases against women charged with zina in Nigeria. There was similar feminist transnational networking when a Malaysian state, which had elected a fundamentalist political party to power, sought to introduce zina laws. Any claim by apologist and fundamentalist male analysts, such as Tariq Ramadan, that 'serious debate is virtually non-existent' regarding the death penalty in Muslim contexts, and that there have been 'silences' and 'timid responses'[3] clearly overlooks the vibrant and transnational women's activism in Muslim contexts that has been going on for years regarding this issue.

Also addressing an area in which women have faced discriminatory legislation, the 2003 Machreq/Maghreb Gender Linking and Information Project's, 'Gender, Citizenship and Nationality' survey sought to mobilize and share information across women's groups in the region and has inspired nationality and citizenship law-reform efforts in other parts of the Middle East.

---

2   www.musawah.org.

3   http://www.tariqramadan.com/spip.php?article264m accessed 30.12.2009.

Less visible but equally important have been the legal advice and support provided to individual women seeking asylum and those whose children have been kidnapped by fathers across international borders. With globalization's increasing human movement across jurisdictions, transnational legal activism is best placed to address the growing number of conflicts of laws, or private international law, issues and cases. For example, understanding the validity of Muslim marriage and divorce in English law also requires reference to Pakistani law, and certainly in Britain research has found that legal professionals and state officials lack the kind of transnational knowledge that Pakistani women's organizations have been obliged to acquire in order to address the problems facing many migrant women (Warraich and Balchin, 2006).

The Added Value of Transnational Legal Activism

Almost all transnational legal initiatives have been characterized by a multidisciplinary approach, a determination to cross dominant religious and social boundaries, and an increasing tendency to draw upon jurisprudential and theological arguments. While the success of their efforts is hard to measure, the emergence of increasingly vocal and visible initiatives indicates that women in Muslim contexts see a value in transnational legal activism. This value apparently lies in the sense of solidarity, the sharing of strategies and information, and the visibility that collectivity brings.

In many Muslim contexts today, conservative and fundamentalist forces seek to preserve or impose a regressive vision of gender roles; they use religion and claims that they are protecting the right of Muslims to their identity to justify these efforts (BAOBAB, 2003; Othman, 2005). Wherever activists have succeeded in advancing women's legal rights, this has invariably occurred despite resistance from such forces, as has been the case in, for example, Egypt, Morocco, Pakistan and Turkey, all of which have seen recent positive law reform (CEWLA, 2003; Collectif 95 Maghreb Egalité n.d.; ACHR, 2006; WWHR, 2005). Thus activists in Muslim contexts who challenge 'Islamization' and identity politics frequently face the accusation that their demands for gender justice are somehow not in consonance with 'tradition' and the accepted norms of what constitutes a 'good Muslim woman.' This is by no means unique to Muslim contexts; research has found a shared pattern across all religious fundamentalisms in all regions (AWID, 2008a, 2008b, 2008c).

International networking brings four important advantages to women's rights activists in Muslim contexts. First, those struggling to resist regressive forces become aware that their struggle is mirrored across the world; this brings relief from knowing that they are not alone and helps build confidence. Secondly, networking across boundaries involves a sharing of information about how women experience their lives – laws, policies and legal practice – in other Muslim contexts; this enables them to deconstruct and analyse more effectively the power structures and political objectives behind the forces that oppose women's rights in Muslim contexts. Thirdly, networking allows a sharing of strategies; while these may not transfer effectively from one particular context to another, the sharing of ideas can undoubtedly inspire new initiatives. And fourthly, and perhaps most importantly, transnational interaction across Muslim contexts enables women to understand both the similarities and the diversities encountered in their struggles for their rights. Put simply, the realization of the immense diversity – of customs, of laws, of political structures, of women's status – found in Muslim contexts explodes the myth that there is one homogenous 'Muslim world,' that there is, as right-wing political–religious forces would have us believe, only one way of being a 'good Muslim woman.' And the realization that women across such a variety of contexts share a struggle against remarkably similar efforts to discriminate against the marginalized and to use religion to gain social and political control strengthens their collective activism. An added reason for feminist transnationalism in Muslim contexts is that religious fundamentalism is also undoubtedly transnational (AWID, 2008b).

Transnational Feminist Activism in WENAAZ

The state of women's collective activism for their human rights in Muslim communities in WENAAZ – Western Europe, North America, Australia and New Zealand – presents quite a startling contrast to the vibrant transnational activism described above. This chapter focuses on the British context, but comments about the organizing of Muslim women in Britain may apply more broadly across WENAAZ.

First, a few clarifications. Muslim women in Britain have not engaged in transnational feminist legal activism *as Muslims* until now largely because there has not been a collective feminist consciousness in the local Muslim community. When WLUML's Women and Law in the Muslim World Programme launched in 1992, and even as it expanded throughout the next ten years and was joined by emerging women's groups in, for example, Uzbekistan and Mali, despite the significant number of Muslims in WENAAZ, no group from the various areas asked to be included in the project – or even to receive the materials it generated. The sole exception was women from North African communities living in France. Most had a history of engagement with leftist political parties, promoted French-style laïcité, and identified as 'Muslim' at most in a cultural rather than a religious sense. At all the international conferences throughout the 1980s and 1990s where women from across Muslim contexts coincidentally met and formed linkages, there were few women from WENAAZ; again, the rare exceptions were usually immigrants from North Africa or exile communities from Iran, Afghanistan and Turkey. Certainly, there was no routinely visible representation from WENAAZ of women who wished to claim simultaneous feminist and Muslim identities. One could conclude, then, that the migrant and convert Muslim communities did not have an organized Muslim feminist consciousness.

This is not to say that there have been no feminists of a Muslim background in Britain; there have been some, such as Deniz Kandiyoti, Hannanah Siddiqui, Samia Bano, Aisha Gill, and Maryam Namazie, who have a history of women's rights analysis and collective activism. They have often focused on legal activism, particularly in the area of violence against women in mainstream and, especially, 'Asian' women's organizations. However, they have usually not identified themselves as 'Muslim women.' There have equally been many feminists in Britain who do indeed identify as Muslim but who have not engaged in collective feminist organizing – at least not until recently.

Before discussing these recent developments, there is a need for some background to the British context. Multiculturalism induces an unnatural homogenization within a community, as the government needs to 'talk to' entire communities through a more manageable number of 'representatives.' In Muslim communities, these 'representatives' have invariably been male, South Asian and of a conservative, if not fundamentalist, political orientation.[4] In the absence of a visible Muslim feminist collective, the result was that conservative forces were able almost completely to dominate the local discourse regarding the legal rights of women in Britain's Muslim communities, as well as actual bodies such as informal 'Sharia councils' and formal expert opinion in court cases. Women were told that in Islam only men have the right of divorce – in stark contrast to codified laws operating in Muslim contexts; women, even highly educated and apparently autonomous women, believed the lie that the 'proper Muslim way' to get married was through an unwritten *nikah* (marriage contract) in front of an unrecognized imam and not to have a civil registry marriage (all of which leaves them with few rights both under the law and in informal religious forums such as 'Sharia councils'). They had no idea that in 1961 women in Pakistan had gained a marriage contract that facilitated *talaq-e-tafweez* – the unconditional delegation of the right of divorce to the wife; they had no idea that Muslims have been concluding written marriage contracts with detailed terms and conditions favouring women since the beginning of Islam. They had no idea that there was all this dynamic, transnational feminist networking happening in Muslim contexts. The overwhelming majority appeared to have accepted the lie that feminism and Islam were simply incompatible.

The Emergence of a Feminist Collective Consciousness in Britain

I do not wish to overstate the impact of 9/11. Many of the forces, not least globalization and transformations in information and communication technologies that have contributed to the emergence of a collective feminist Muslim consciousness in WENAAZ and that now offer the possibility of transnational

---

4   Excellent critiques of British multiculturalism can be found in Bhatt (2006), and Sahgal and Yuval-Davis (2000).

legal activism, including women from these contexts, were already in process long before 9/11. Nevertheless, that deplorable event was undoubtedly a catalyst for social change amongst Muslim women. Many of the currently most visible women's organizations in Britain that specifically focus on Muslim women were – coincidentally or otherwise – formed in late 2001 and 2002: FATIMA Women's Network in Leicester; the Safra Project for lesbian, bisexual and transgender Muslim women; the MWN-UK. In France, the migrant women's group from the *banlieux*, Ni Putes Ni Soumises, was also formed in 2002. Two of the few examples of organizations predating this period are the Canadian Council of Muslim Women, founded in 1982, and the Islamic Women's Welfare Council of Victoria (Australia), founded in 1991 – and notably no similar activity in Britain at the time.[5] To put it another way, across WENAAZ the contrast between the number of women's groups claiming a Muslim identity before 2000 and after is remarkable.

With the US-led coalition supposedly going to war over Afghan women's rights, and veiled women experiencing increased racist attacks in Britain, it was clear that the new, global context of 'war on terror' placed Muslim women centre stage. Suddenly, the British government declared an interest in Muslim women, primarily lumping them in with the responsibility for 'Preventing Violent Extremism' – as the major British government initiative is called (for a detailed discussion, see Balchin, 2007). Whatever the government's intentions, by holding several meetings with a large number of women who had been engaging in social work within the Muslim community, it above all enabled these women from across the country to meet each other. There is an entire herstory to be written about the development of events in Britain, which for reasons of space cannot be dealt with here, but by 2005 those who were engaging in collective Muslim women's organizing had become disillusioned both with the male-dominated 'community leadership' and with the British government's policies, particularly in the wake of the London bombings of 2005, when terrorists claiming Muslim identity killed over 50 on London's transport network. These policies included attempts to prevent the publication of the recommendations and demands made by Muslim women in a series of *government-funded* focus-group discussions. The demands (which relate to discrimination both at the hands of the non-Muslim majority and patriarchal forces within the Muslim community) were eventually published, but minus the numerous and concrete recommendations that women in Muslim communities had made for positive government interventions (MWN-UK-WNC, 2006). In contrast, Muslim men were granted immediate and concrete concessions, such as the establishment of the Mosques and Imams National Advisory Board (MINAB). MINAB remains dominated by groups representing highly conservative visions of Islam; women, sexual minorities, and minority groups such as the Ahmedis

---

5   http://www.ccmw.com/about_ccmw.html and http://www.islamicwomenswelfare. org.au/ Although the CCMW and IWWCV do not use the 'F' word (feminism), their perspectives are largely feminist.

and Zikris are either grossly underrepresented or absent. As a government-funded body, it thus runs the risk of violating national equalities legislation.

By 2005, the Muslim women's groups had clearly had enough of the men dominating their communities and enough of the government, and began talking in terms of a movement, of 'autonomy' and of an 'independent voice.' The organized, feminist, Muslim collective consciousness had finally arrived in Britain. Given the many hundreds of tiny, voluntary, welfare-oriented, voiceless and isolated Muslim women's groups scattered across the country, it was about time, too.

This development has yet to be comprehensively analyzed, and the observations in the present chapter are admittedly based entirely on anecdotal evidence and my work as a board member of the MWN-UK. Undoubtedly, this is an area begging for academic enquiry.

There are numerous examples illustrating the emergence of a Muslim feminist consciousness in Britain, especially among younger women. Even in the more deprived Bangladeshi and Pakistani communities, young Muslim women are excelling in education and entering well-paid professions in the public and private sectors. Their confidence in themselves and in their multiple identities is clearly growing. While the word 'feminist' may not feature directly in their interactions, the content of their discussions increasingly highlights women's autonomy. Women are now beginning to question the doublespeak of supposedly more 'moderate' Muslim groups in Britain influenced by Tariq Ramadan and Yusuf al-Qaradawi.[6] During interactions with Muslim women, I come across increasing numbers who question whether apparently moderate statements that women should be encouraged to become educated and go out to work hide a fundamental belief that women's priority must remain the heterosexual, male-headed household, where any commitment to equality is in practice greatly watered down by continued insistence that rigidly defined gender roles are 'natural' and ultimately divinely ordained. Many Muslim women in Britain are now hungry for information about women's rights in Islam (MWN-UK-WNC, 2006), and are no longer as afraid to question the apparent dichotomy between their gut feelings that Islam does not mandate gender inequality and their daily lived experiences of discrimination.[7] This hunger and anger means that many are actively seeking out transnational

---

6   For an in-depth analysis of Ramadan's positions see Fourest, 2004. In 2005 a controversy arose over the positions of al-Qaradawi with groups both attacking and defending his various positions as extremist and as moderate (see http://www.london.gov.uk/news/docs/qaradawi_dossier.pdf). As regards women, al-Qaradawi is on record as supporting female genital mutilation ('I personally support this under the current circumstances in the modern world') even while acknowledging it is not obligatory in Islam, (http://www.islamonline.net/servlet/Satellite?pagename=Islamonline-English-Ask_Scholar/FatwaE/FatwaE&cid=1119503543886, accessed 30.12.09), and has not taken steps to reverse this opinion since 2002.

7   Events such as the Muslim Women's Network-UK's five-day Gender, Islam and Advocacy training in 2008 illustrate these developments.

sources of information – and finding them. Feminists from other Muslim contexts, such as South Asia and North Africa, who have bitter experiences arising from religious fundamentalism, may be horrified by the websites routinely visited by Britain's young Muslim women; these are invariably dominated by fundamentalist perspectives, simply because the greater resources of such groups ensure their command of online information. But research recently completed at the University of York (UK) indicates that it is important to recognize that women visiting Muslim online discussions are perfectly capable of interacting with them with discernment and with the determination to raise difficult questions.

Moreover, the long-standing isolation of Britain's Muslim women from international feminist gatherings and from transnational activism is increasingly being broken down. As Britain's Muslim women become more visible locally, they find themselves in greater demand at the international level, allowing them to build their transnational linkages: contacts mushroom once the ball starts rolling. A sizeable number of participants from WENAAZ contexts attended the Musawah launch in Malaysia in February 2009. The MWN-UK took part in the Second Global Conference of WISE (Women's Islamic Initiative in Spirituality and Equity), itself initiated by Muslim women from North America. Meanwhile, Women Living Under Muslim Laws has published its first analysis of the experiences of women in Britain's Muslim community,[8] although it has yet to develop a regional networking focal point for women in migrant contexts.

As regards the relationship between longer-standing feminist groups in Muslim contexts and feminists who do not claim a religious identity on the one hand, and the very nascent Muslim feminist groups in the WENAAZ context on the other, it is still far too early to identify the possible points of collaboration and tension, if any. Moreover, any attempt at analysis at this early stage would likely unhelpfully homogenize all of the groups involved. The relationship between faith and feminism has preoccupied many of us for some years now (Gokal, 2006), and it is probable that the challenges in bridging the dichotomization of faith and feminism will be repeated in this instance.

Even in their daily lives, acting out the feminist slogan that 'the personal is political,' young Muslim women in Britain find themselves pushing the boundaries of acceptability, discrimination and autonomy. With so many of them being more educated, better salaried, and more comfortable than their male peers with their intersecting identities as British and Muslim, there is an increasing question as to whom they can marry; the pool of eligible male peers is extremely limited and informally numerous young Muslim women are asking themselves the question: what's so wrong about marrying a non-Muslim? Indeed, this is a question that surfaces in many European-dominated online discussion pages.

Although collective feminist activism and transnational linkages are certainly newer in WENAAZ Muslim communities than in, for example, Egypt, Pakistan,

---

8   Kariapper, Ayesha Salma (2009), *Walking the Tightrope: Women and Veiling in the United Kingdom* (London: WLUML).

Sudan, or Nigeria, it is conceivable that Muslim women's activism in WENAAZ may become a leading force in the coming years. Certainly a number of important female scholars of Muslim jurisprudence (*fiqh*) and Quranic exegesis (*tafsir*), such as Amina Wadud, Asma Barlas, Keica Ali, and Ziba Mir-Hosseini, are based in the United States and other WENAAZ countries. Besides, other factors, such as the growing numbers of Muslim women post-graduate scholars in WENAAZ, the increasing financial independence of Muslim women, and the relatively stable political and infrastructural environment, will likely facilitate the generation of feminist analysis in WENAAZ in ways that feminists from Muslim contexts in the south can only dream of. Finally, converts to Islam in the WENAAZ context may also play a role: it appears that some women from societies with a more clearly articulated belief in gender equality, especially in the Scandinavian countries, are particularly likely to push the boundaries of what modern Muslim women can demand and achieve as women (van Nieuwkerk, 2006). The board of the MWN-UK has a sizeable representation of converts.[9]

These comments are admittedly entirely speculative at this stage, and rigorous research is required to examine whether they hold water. But could it be that transnational legal activism among feminists in Muslim communities will not only flow across the WENAAZ region in the same vibrant way that it has for decades across other regions, but that the region will become a source for some of the most frontline thinking in this sphere in the coming years?

References

ACHR (Asian Centre for Human Rights) (2006), *Appeasing the Mullahs: Protection of Women (Criminal Laws Amendment) Bill 2006 of Pakistan.* http://www.achrweb.org/Review/2006/132-06.htm, accessed 30.12.2009.

AWID (Association of Women's Rights in Development) (2008a), *Religious Fundamentalisms on the Rise: A Case for Action.* (Toronto: Association for Women's Rights in Development (AWID)).

AWID (Association of Women's Rights in Development) (2008b), *Religious Fundamentalisms Exposed: Ten Myths Revealed about Religious Fundamentalisms.* (Toronto: Association for Women's Rights in Development (AWID)).

AWID (Association of Women's Rights in Development) (2008c), *Shared Insights: Women's Rights Activists Define Religious Fundamentalisms.* (Toronto: Association for Women's Rights in Development (AWID)).

Balchin, C. (2003), 'With Her Feet on the Ground: Women, religion and development in Muslim communities', *Development* 46(4): 40–47, Society for International Development.

---

9   http://www.mwnuk.co.uk/grid2.php?id=85, accessed 30.12.09.

—— (2007), '"Muslim Women" and "Moderate Muslims": British Policy and the Strengthening of Religious Absolutist Control over Gender Development', in Rosalind Eyben and Joy Moncrieffe (eds), *The Power of Labelling: How and Why People's Categories Matter* (London: Earthscan).

BAOBAB (BAOBAB for Women's Human Rights) (2003), *Sharia Implementation in Nigeria: The Journey so Far* (Lagos: BAOBAB). http://www.baobabwomen.org/Sharia%20&%20BAOBAB%20publication.pdf

Bhatt, C. (2006), 'The Fetish of the Margins: Religious Absolutism, Anti-Racism and Postcolonial Silence', *New Formations* 59, 98–115.

CEWLA (Center for Egyptian Women Legal Assistance) (2003), *The Harvest Two Years After Khol: An Analytical Study*. CEWLA and Women Living Under Muslim Laws.

Collectif 95 Maghreb Egalité. n.d. *Women in the Maghreb Change and Resistance,* Friedrich Ebert Stiftung.

Fourest, C. (2004), *Frère Tariq: Discours, stratégie et méthode de Tariq Ramadan* (Paris: Grasset & Fasquelle).

Gokal, S. (2006), 'Faith, Feminism and the Power of Love', *Development* 49, 81–83.

Hélie-Lucas, M. (1990), 'Strategies of Women and Women's Movements in the Muslim World *vis-à-vis* Fundamentalisms: From entryism to internationalism'. *Occasional Paper No. 2* (Grabels: Women Living Under Muslim Laws).

Manning, A. and Roy, S. (2007), 'Culture clash or culture club? The identity and attitudes of immigrants in Britain', Centre for Economic Performance, London School of Economics, CentrePiece Summer 2007. http://cep.lse.ac.uk/centrepiece/v12i1/manning_roy.pdf, accessed 25.01.09.

Muslim Women's Network UK and Women's National Commission (2006), *She Who Disputes: Muslim Women Shape the Debate*, (London: Women's National Commission), http://www.thewnc.org.uk/publications/doc_view/355-she-who-disputes-.raw?tmpl=component, accessed 25.01.09.

Van Nieuwkerk, K. (2006), (ed.) *Women Embracing Islam: Gender and Conversion in the West* (Austin: University of Texas Press).

Othman, N. (2005), (ed.) *Muslim Women and the Challenge of Islamic Extremism* (Kuala Lumpur: Sisters in Islam).

Sahgal, G. and Yuval-Davis, N. (2000), *Refusing Holy Orders: Women and Fundamentalism in Britain*, (London: Women Living Under Muslim Laws), www.wluml.org/english/pubs/pdf/misc/refusing-holy-orders-eng.pdf, accessed 25.01.09.

Shaheed, F. (1994), 'Controlled or Autonomous: Identity and the experience of the Network Women Living Under Muslim Laws', *Occasional Paper No. 5* (Grabels: Women Living Under Muslim Laws).

Sunder, M. (2003), 'Piercing the Veil', *Yale Law Journal* 112, 1399.

Warraich, Sohail Akbar and Balchin, C. (2006), *Recognising the Unrecognised: Inter country Cases and Muslim Marriage and Divorce in Britain* (London:

Women Living Under Muslim Laws). http://www.wluml.org/english/publistheme.shtml?cmd%5B23%5D=c-1-Law%20reform, accessed 25.01.09.

WLUML (Women Living Under Muslim Laws). 2006, *Knowing Our Rights: Women, family, laws and customs in the Muslim world.* (London: Women Living Under Muslim Laws). http://www.wluml.org/english/pubs/pdf/knowing%20our%20rights/kor_2006_en.pdf, accessed 25.01.09.

WWHR (Women for Women's Human Rights-NEW WAYS) (2005), *Turkish Civil and Penal Code Reforms from a Gender Perspective: The Success of Two Nationwide Campaigns* (Istanbul: WWHR-NEW WAYS).

Yuval-Davis, N. (1997), *Gender and Nation* (London: Sage).

PART II
Shifting Notions of Sexuality and Family in Diaspora

Chapter 5
Multiculturalism and Religious Legislation in Sweden

Anne Sofie Roald

Introduction

In Sweden, certificated religious associations have the legal right (*vigselsrätt*) to perform marriage ceremonies. Thus, couples married by a religious association are automatically considered married according to the state's legal system. This legal right to marry might be regarded as a (collective) right for religious minorities, whereas divorce is based on the pattern of individual rights, with the state legal system being the sole provider of official divorce documents. If a marriage between two Muslims is conducted by an Islamic organization in Sweden, a document issued by the national court is legally sufficient to complete a divorce, although many Muslims request additional religious divorces due to social and psychological factors. A couple married in a country with a Muslim majority population, on the other hand, would need an Islamic divorce document in addition to the legal divorce obtainable in Sweden.

The present study deals with Islamic family legislation in Sweden in view of multicultural policies. How does the Swedish state deal with religious minorities in matters of marriage and divorce? And what implications does this policy have for majority/minority dynamics?[1]

Multiculturalism

The notion of multiculturalism, which is probably the outcome of Article 27[2] of the United Nations' 1966 International Covenant on Civil and Political Rights

---

1   This study builds on participating observation in Muslim communities in Sweden and interviews with Muslim actors; five Muslim leaders of various national and ethnic backgrounds, key persons in various national and ethnic communities, and 12 women living in 'limping' marriages.

2   Article 27 says: In those states in which ethnic, religious or linguistic minorities exist, persons belonging to such minorities shall not be denied the right, in community with the other members of their group, to enjoy their own culture, to profess and practice their own religion, or to use their own language.

(ICCPR), has since the 1970s been a strong underlying societal force, particularly in northern Europe, the US, Canada, New Zealand and Australia. Multiculturalism is mainly concerned with *communal diversity[3] and the various identity formations found in minority communities in a nation-state. Communal diversity* relates to organized communities living and acting according to a particular belief system, or *nomos* (a community's normative universe, in which legislation and cultural structures are intertwined).[4]

There is a tendency of arbitrary use of the term 'multiculturalism' leading to a conceptual confusion in the discourse of multiculturalism. The term has often been applied without a clear definition, in public debate as well as in some scholarly works. The necessary distinction between 'multicultural' and 'multiculturalist' society is rarely found in scholarly or political work on multiculturalism (Parekh 2000). Whereas most nation-states today exist of more than one cultural community, and can thus be said to be 'multicultural societies,' very few societies are 'multiculturalist societies,' in the sense of cherishing and encouraging more than one cultural approach. Such a multiculturalist approach implies the incorporation of various cultural patterns into the majority system of belief and practice, and it furthermore requires respect for the cultural demands of the nation-state's minority communities. Despite the fact that few nation-states have a policy of multiculturalism in this ultimate sense of the word, the discourse on multiculturalism tends to be of a hegemonic nature in many countries in the Western world today.[5]

In the late 1960s there was a slight shift away from the strict emphasis on individual rights manifested in the Universal Declaration of Human Rights of 1948 towards an awareness of minority groups being deprived of their rights as a collective. This was mainly due to the rise of the Civil Rights Movement in the United States, as well as to American anthropologists' perception of Western political and economical exploitation of underprivileged countries and communities (Merry 2001: 33, Baumann 1999: 2). This new awareness caused a particular (re)focus[6] on 'culture' in the public discourse,[7] leading to the formation of 'multiculturalism' as an ideal. Thomas Hylland Eriksen claims that the concept of 'multiculturalism' includes 'a positive evaluation of cultural traditions and,

---

3   See Parekh (2000: 3–4).

4   See Shachar (2001: 2).

5   See for instance Carlbom (2003), for a critic against multiculturalism as a hegemonic discourse in Sweden.

6   The protection of minorities has a history going back to the nineteenth century. The interwar policy of international protection of minorities was put into force by the League of Nations at the Paris Peace Conference in 1919 (Fink 1995). The Nazis' utilization of minority protection in order to invade Poland and Czechoslovakia, together with their pogroms of the Jews, made an emphasis on individual rights precarious in the early years after World War II (Eriksen 1997: 50).

7   See Cowan, Dembour and Wilson (2001: 2).

particularly, the cultural or ethnic identities of minorities' (Eriksen 1997: 49). The pertinent question that some researchers ask, however, is whether or not the ideology of 'multiculturalism' is at odds with individual human rights.[8] In contrast, Eriksen believes that 'multiculturalism' reflects both the Enlightenment ideal of individual rights, and the Romantic concept of 'people' and the right of groups to survive (Eriksen 1997: 3–4). There seems thus to be a tension within the notion of multiculturalism itself between the individual's right to freely choose to join a cultural group and the group's right to survive. The contemporary integration debate in many Western countries reflects this tension between individual and collective rights. One prominent example of this are the recurring pro and cons in the Islamic headscarf debate: whether the main issue is protecting a woman's individual right to choose what to wear or sustaining a (religious/cultural) custom that is part of an identity policy staged by patriarchal forces in Muslim communities.

The ideology of *multiculturalism* has been under scrutiny since it came into being as a response to post-war Western Europe's ethnically homogenous societies (Becket and Macey 2001). Some anthropologists have, for instance, discussed how the concept of 'multiculturalism' presupposes an essentialist view of culture, in which it is regarded as fixed and unalterable.[9] It was the political scientist Susan Moller Okin, however, who in 1997 highlighted the notion of 'multiculturalism' as bad for women. Previously, liberal scholars such as Will Kymlicka, Charles Taylor and Iris Marion Young had promoted a 'weak' form of multiculturalism, accepting minority claims within the liberal framework of every individual's right to live the 'good' life on the condition that freedom and autonomy for all other individuals were respected (Kymlicka 1995: 78–9). Okin, herself belonging to the liberal tradition, went one step further than her colleagues by introducing the private sphere into the multicultural discourse. Her view of multiculturalism as implying fixed and unalterable cultures, on the one hand, and elitist understandings within communities of which elements minority 'cultures' consist of, on the other, brought a new dimension into the public debate (Okin 1999). Okin's criticism of multiculturalism was disapproved of by scholars such as, for instance, the post-colonial theorist Homi K. Bhabha, who claimed that Okin tended to highlight the extreme cases, such as female genital cutting, forced marriages, etc.[10] Liberal scholars such as Kymlicka, on the other hand, accepted much of Okin's criticism of his and other liberalists' work, although he claims that the success of feminism is much due to such affirmative actions as he sees necessary for improving the status of members of minority groups. Kymlicka believes that his distinction between internal and external restrictions, refusing the 'internal restrictions,' i.e.,

---

8　See Eriksen (1997) and Okin (1999).

9　See Merry (2001); Carlbom (2003); Baumann (1999) for discussion on reification of culture, identity and religion.

10　It is interesting to note how Bhabha (1999) himself tends to emphasize the extreme cases of immigrants who are deprived and discriminated against and who are alienated 'from the comforts of citizenship.'

a community's 'right to restrict individual choice in the name of cultural 'tradition' or cultural 'integrity' while accepting 'external restrictions,' i.e., 'rights which are claimed by a minority group against the larger society in order to reduce its vulnerability to the economic or political power of the larger society,' is sufficient to protect minorities within minorities (Kymlicka 1999). Okin, however, points out that Kymlicka's account of 'internal restriction' does not address the fact that women's abilities to question traditional gender roles are limited, as 'a "closed" or discriminatory culture cannot provide the context for individual development that liberalism requires' and because collective rights might otherwise result in subcultures of oppression within and aided by liberal societies (Okin 1999). Although Kymlicka agrees with Okin to a great extent, he rejects the absolute emphasis on individual rights promoted by her, and continues to promote a 'weak' form of multiculturalism.

Multiculturalism in Sweden

Most Western countries have committed themselves to following international conventions such as the Declaration of Human Rights, and CEDAW (Convention on the Elimination of All Forms of Discriminations Against Women), as well as the ICCPR (The International Convention of Civil and Political Rights). In Sweden, 'multiculturalism' was introduced in 1974, in the aftermath of the approval of the ICCPR in the United Nations. However, at the same time the legislation of the European Convention guaranteed every individual the right to be treated as an individual and not as part of a collective group. In principle, the state makes it easy for individuals to belong to a community and conform to its cultural and religious traditions, but at the same time ensures the individual the right to *not* belong to an ethnic or a religious community. Sweden thus, to a certain extent, promotes a 'weak' form of multiculturalism in tune with the liberal ideas of, among others, Kymlicka.

The term 'multiculturalism' was not explicitly stated in the beginning; rather, the Swedish state's official report spoke in terms of freedom of choice for members of 'linguistic' minorities between 'retaining and developing their original cultural identity and assuming a Swedish cultural identity.'[11] Up to the late 1990s the Swedish state cherished the notion of freedom of choice, and the discrepancy between the state and the immigrant leadership in their understanding of this official policy of multiculturalism was rarely highlighted. However, in the mid-1990s the concept of 'diversity' (*mångfald*) was introduced as a key concept in official reports as well as in the public debate, indicating the emphasis on getting immigrants into the labour market. However, this change of concept has also to be regarded in terms of the authorities' rethinking of the consequences of multiculturalism, particularly in family issues, as the Swedish policy of gender equality (*jämställdhet*) is one of the main social values in the public sphere. It seems, however, that when it comes to religious associations' legal right to marry couples (*vigselrätt*), Swedish policy

---

11   See SOU (State's Official Reports) 1974. See also Sander (1997: 288).

turns towards a 'strong' form of multiculturalism, in which internal restrictions within minorities, with the possibility of group pressures forcing women into oppressive situations, are not taken into consideration. *Vigselrätt* is regarded within the framework of freedom of religion, and it seems that with regards to the principle of religious rights, the state is careful to not take a 'wrong step'.

Vigselrätt might be regarded as an affirmative action; by granting the communities this right, the minorities' attitude towards the state could be felt, potentially, in positive terms. However, the consequence of this affirmative action has been that for immigrant women, who, as Okin points at, do not have the same possibilities as women in the majority society for the individual development required by liberalism, approval of such cultural action could 'result in subcultures of oppression' within the liberal state of Sweden, with its strong emphasis on gender equality and gender-equal opportunities on all levels of society. In view of Okin's reflections, it is pertinent to ask what possibilities there are for individuals within such 'closed' communities to choose the system they want to follow. And, more importantly, is there a possibility for individuals within communities to adhere to more than one system? There are gray spots on the borderline between belonging and not belonging, and the present paper attempts to discuss what happens between these states of being. Is it possible that the image Swedish religious minorities have of their collective rights within the pattern of the state's professed policy of 'multiculturalism' causes restrictions on women within religious communities?

Islamic Legislation

Many religious and ethnic minority communities adhere to a set of customs and codes that tend to either limit or strengthen their members. Although divorce used to be and in many cases still is problematic in many of these communities, it is particularly so in Judaism, Catholicism, and Islam, wherein actual legislation, with matters of marriage and divorce being circumvented by rituals and conventions, links the issue of divorce directly to religious dogma. In Catholicism, divorce is restricted both for men and for women. In Islam, divorce in general is accepted, but the divorce instigated by a man is much easier to procure than a divorce instigated by a woman. In Judaism, divorce is also accepted, and similarly to the Islamic case, it is easier for men than women to obtain. However, in the Orthodox and Conservative sects of Judaism, divorce papers have to be signed by both the husband and the wife in order to be valid. Although this appears to be divorce on equal terms, a man without proper divorce papers can live together with a new woman, due to the acceptance of polygyny in classical Jewish law.[12] A woman, on the other hand, does not have the same option, as she might be regarded as an

---

12   Adin Steinsalz, *The Essential Talmud,* (New York: Basic Books) (1976), 133. See also Bente Groth, 'Mann og Kvinne skapte Han dem. Ekteskapets betydelse i jødisk tradisjon', I.B. Thorbjörnsrud, (ed.) *Evig Din? Ekteskaps- og samlivstradisjoner I det flerreligiöse Norge,* (Oslo: Abstrakt Forlag) (2005), 146.

outcast socially, and this procedure of requiring both signatures often impedes the divorce process, leaving Jewish women in a state of suspension between being married and being divorced. Below I will use the Islamic case; although the Jewish legislation on marriage and divorce has many parallels to the Islamic law, this matter will not be discussed.

It is not uncommon to discuss sharia in terms of a modern understanding of what law is. This is true if we consider personal status law, which in most Muslim countries is a set of laws and regulations built on sharia legislation. However, historically speaking, sharia was not a homogenous law. Sharia consists of sources of legislation – the Koran and the *hadiths* (stories about the Prophet's sayings and doings) – and interpretations of these sources. The division of sharia into schools of law (*madhhabs*) indicates the variety of understandings of how these sources should be interpreted, as the schools apply different principles in the process of interpretation.[13] The notion of Islamic legislation, or sharia, as an unchangeable unit has recently been contested by Muslim feminists and liberals in general, claiming alternative interpretations of the Islamic sources (see Wadud 1999 and Roald 2001).

The aspect of time is important in considering Islamic law. Sharia legislation became more or less institutionalized in the period around 900–1000 CE, and its rules and regulations are thus influenced by the particular cultural traits common in most of the Muslim world at that time. The question is then whether or not personal status law, which builds on traditional Islamic law-school legislation, is suitable to societies with different socio-economic circumstances than 11th century Muslim society. Ziba Mir-Hosseini, a prominent writer within Islamic legislation issues, claims that the reason personal status law is still dominated by sharia legislation is because of the way modern Muslim leaders dealt with the modernization process started by Western colonial powers. Following the ideals of liberalism, these political leaders did not touch upon the domestic sphere, leaving this domain to religious scholars. By doing this, the religious scholars were kept content and the secular leaders could secure the religious establishment's support for their policies in other fields (Mir-Hosseini 2000: 10). Moreover, as modern Muslim leaders codified the personal status law after independence from Western colonial powers, they tended to select those parts of sharia legislation suitable to their purposes of nation-building. According to researchers, sharia was previously more flexible, with a much wider range of legal judgments to refer to compared to the personal status law of modern (Muslim) nation-states. Amira Sonbol, for instance, shows how in the process of codification of the sharia, rulings were narrowed down and became less flexible (Sonbol 1996).

---

13   For more information on sharia, see Josef Schacht, *The Origins of Muhammedan Jurisprudence* (Oxford: Clarendon) (1982).

Marriage and Dowry (*Mahr*) in Islam

The law of freedom of religion is regarded as an individual as well as a collective right in multicultural society. In Sweden, the religious marriage ritual is one of the collective rights afforded religious minorities. The legal right to marry couples in religious congregations is built upon a Christian understanding of marriage, in which the marriage ritual is a sacrament ordained by God. This legal right was instigated due to the fact that, particularly after the Reformation in the 18th century, nuptials performed in a church became the only valid form of marriage in Sweden. At the same time, independent churches were established, and these Christian denominations outside the Lutheran state church of Sweden were thus in need of official acceptance of their own religious marriage rituals. In contemporary times, however, with the introduction of civil marriage and the fact that it is the Swedish state that legislates the Marriage Act, and not the church, *vigselrätten* does not have the same function it used to have. Instead, it seems to have become a symbol for religious freedom in Sweden.

Islamic marriage is different from Christian marriage. Marriage in Islam is not a sacrament, although it is regarded as an act of worship. Theologically, the idea is that marriage prevents sexual immorality and is thus a means to keep up the moral standard in Muslim society. Legally, the act of marrying is circumscribed by religious rules and regulations, but at the same time the marriage contract is secular in the sense that it is a contract between two people and the contract can also be dissolved, in contrast to the Christian notion of 'not dividing that which God has united'.

When a Muslim couple marries, the man offers the woman a dowry (*mahr*). The dowry varies from place to place and from one social class to another. The dowry is often divided into two portions: one a gift (money, gold, etc.) paid at the time of the marriage and the other a later dowry (*mahr al-muttaakhir*) to be paid if the man divorces his wife. If the woman sues for divorce, she has to pay back the dowry she received at the wedding if her reasons for doing so are not 'acceptable' according to sharia rules, i.e., the husband's sexual impotence, physical abuse, etc.

In countries with Muslim majorities and in Muslim-minority communities in Western countries, there is a conception that the higher the dowry offered to the bride, the more value she has as a woman. The consequence of this initial boon, however, could be that a woman getting a large dowry has difficulty paying back the dowry if she instigates a divorce. Muslim men have the right to marry more than one wife, both according to the law-school system and according to the personal status law in most countries with a Muslim-majority population. It is thus religiously, but also socially, acceptable, with polygyny occurring in Muslim-majority populations as well as in Muslim minorities in Western countries. This acceptance makes it possible for a man who wants to divorce his wife, but does not want to pay the late dowry stipulated in the marriage contract, to leave the wife or treat her unfairly without offering her a divorce. He can even remarry officially (in Muslim countries) or marry a new wife unofficially without divorcing his first wife, simply by making an Islamic contract (in Western countries). By acting in such a way, he can implicitly force his first wife to sue for divorce, with the result that the woman has to pay back the dowry she got at the time of the marriage in order to get her husband to divorce her. It is interesting to note that Jewish women might similarly have to pay their former husbands in order to get a divorce document, or *get* (Groth 2005: 146).

In my discussions with Islamic leaders in Sweden, they explained that one of the main reasons that a Scandinavian divorce does not automatically become an Islamic divorce is the matter of the dowry.[14] Thus, the concept of dowry, which supposedly benefits women, might be disadvantageous in case of divorce. If a woman pleads for a divorce and the judge does not accept her complaints as valid reasons for divorce, the woman has to pay back the dowry, money which she often does not have at the time of divorce. It is interesting to note that in, for instance, Bosnia, the dowry is a small symbolic sum, a custom that comes from the time of Tito.[15] This makes divorce a less complicated matter among Bosnians in exile than Muslims coming from countries with Islamic legislation, as the amount a woman has to pay back if she wants a divorce is small. This might be an indication that dealing with the matter of the dowry might make it easier for Muslims to equate a Swedish state divorce with an Islamic divorce.

Divorce in Islam

According to the Islamic law-school system, a man can obtain a divorce (*talaq*) from his wife without any reasons. In most Muslim countries there is a need to register the divorce, but securing a divorce instigated by the male partner is unproblematic. Divorce instigated by women, who can only obtain a decree on two conditions, is a different case altogether. Firstly, according to the law-school system and most personal status law systems in Muslim countries, a woman can request a withdrawal (*khul'*) from her husband.[16] Included in this form of divorce is an obligation that the woman provides economic compensation to her husband; she either pays back her dowry or the couple agrees to an amount to be paid by the woman to the man. However, in the law schools and in personal status law in many countries with Muslim majorities, the *khul'* becomes a divorce only by the consent of the husband. The second possibility for women trying to obtain

---

14   The second reason, they stated, is the matter of custody of the children. The rules regarding custody   differ in the Islamic law-school system, in which the children are the responsibility of the fathers, and the Scandinavian legal system, in which the custody usually goes to the mothers or is shared between the parents.

15   Personal communications with Bosnian scholars.

16   al-Sayyid Sabiq, *fiqh al-sunna* Vol. II, (Beirut: Dar al-Kitab al-Arabi) (1985), 246–54.

a divorce is to request that the judge proclaims a divorce (*tatliq*). If the husband has abused his wife, is sexually impotent, or does not fulfil his economic duties of supporting his family, the judge could decide to give the woman a divorce. In this form of divorce a woman is not obliged to pay economic compensation to the husband. However, in the personal status law of many countries with a Muslim-majority population, women have to support such claims with strong evidence. This implies that women who have been psychologically harassed by their husbands or who have been physical abused but not reported the abuse to the police or to a physician would not have sufficient proof to obtain a divorce through a judge. In non-Muslim Western societies there are few or no Islamic judges to whom women who want an Islamic divorce can turn. A woman suing for divorce might turn to the local mosque in order to get support for her plea, or she might turn to the court in her home country if her marriage was conducted there. Both options give women limited possibilities for obtaining a divorce, firstly, as few Muslim leaders in Muslim-minority communities in Western countries have the power to grant divorces and, secondly, as courts in the Muslim world rarely give a woman a divorce against her husband's approval.[17]

The issue of female-instigated divorce has in recent decades been highlighted in the 'Women in Islam' discourse. Many courts in countries with Muslim-majority populations impede female divorces despite the fact that, on the one hand, both the Koran and the hadiths talk about female divorces[18] and, on the other, that the traditional law-school legislation in certain cases allows a woman to divorce against her husband's wishes. That codification of sharia/fiqh (jurisprudence) legislation into modern personal status law has limited a woman's right to be granted a divorce in sharia courts might be illustrated by Sonbol's example of two different divorce cases in the Egyptian courts (Sonbol 1996: 1–2). The first case, in which a woman demanded a divorce from her husband, took place in 1857. Previous to their marriage, the husband had divorced his first wife and had made a verbal promise to his second wife never to remarry the first. When, despite this promise, he did remarry his first wife, the second wife came before the court bringing witnesses to his oral promise to her. The judge granted her divorce and full economic compensation. Sonbol's second case took place in 1959. A woman demanded divorce from her husband as he had allegedly been beating and abusing her. She did not request economic compensation from her husband. On the contrary, her husband was the one who claimed compensation, and he even demanded a higher sum of money for accepting and granting her a divorce

---

17   For more information on divorces in countries with Muslim-majority populations, see for instance the documentary film of Mir-Hosseini and Longinotto (1998), *Divorce Iranian Style*. See also Sonbol (1996).

18   Koran 2: 229. For hadiths, see for instance Bukhari, Book of Divorce no. 4867. These texts are used by Muslim activists in Sweden and by Islamic scholars I have interviewed in Europe and in the Middle East in order to claim that women have the right to divorce in Islam.

than he was entitled to according to the marriage contract. The judge accepted the husband's claim, as the Egyptian nation-state's legislation at that time granted men almost exclusive right to divorce. With these two divorce cases in mind, we can turn to recent legal changes in personal status law in Egypt, Morocco and Jordan. In the year 2000 a new divorce law, the so-called *khula'* law, was introduced in Egypt. The *khula'* law makes it possible for women to obtain a divorce without the intervention of a judge and without the consent of their husbands; they can do so instead by economically compensating the husband. A similar change in the Moroccan Family Code was enacted in 2004 (see Elliot 2009; Clark and Young 2008). In contrast to both Egypt and Morocco, where Islamists approved the legal changes, in Jordan, the change in personal status law was refused by the Islamists in the Parliament. It is, however, important to point out that the Jordanian Islamists wanted only minor amendments to the *khula'* law, such as the need for a judge to be involved in the process, whereas most conservative nationalists in the Parliament rejected the law *in toto*.[19] However, as the new law was passed by the Senate, the law is now in place in Jordan, waiting for a joint discussion between the Senate and the Parliament.

It is necessary to look further into this change of law in Egypt, Morocco, and Jordan. According to a human rights perspective, it seems that the new legislation will favour a woman's right to obtain a divorce. However, the main criticism against the law reform is that women of poor means have few possibilities to divorce due to the obligation of paying back the dowry, money that more often than not has disappeared into the housekeeping economy. Thus, the right to divorce is mainly a privilege for elite women and not for commoners. In my interview with the then Jordanian Member of Parliament, the Islamist Hayat al-Masimi, she voiced a similar criticism of the new law, but added that a judge could be a protector for women in such cases. 'A judge,' she claimed, 'can give the woman a divorce (*tatliq*) and she will not have to pay any economical compensation.'[20] It seems that even in countries with sharia family law, women would benefit from a system with small (or no) dowries. However, in those countries where women, according to sharia law, have no right to economic support (after the three first months of the *idda* period, i.e., the waiting period before the divorce is finalized) from the former husband, many women from the lower classes would still be forced to remain married to men they would prefer to divorce. Moreover, the fact that in sharia the children have to go to their fathers after a certain age (ranging for instance from two years old for boys in the Ja'afari law school to between seven and 13 years in the four Sunni law schools), women with little financial means who prefer to stay close to their children would also have limited possibilities to use their 'right' to divorce.

---

19   Interview with Hayat al-Masimi, member of the Islamic Action Front (IAF) and Member of Parliament in 2007, in Amman, August 12, 2007.

20   Interview with Hayat al-Masimi, member of the Islamic Action Front (IAF) and Member of Parliament in 2007, in Amman, August 12, 2007.

Islamic Divorces in Muslim Communities in Sweden

Whereas the issue of female-instigated divorce in Muslim communities in, for instance, its neighbouring country, Norway, has been highlighted in the last few years,[21] the topic has until recently been less discussed in Sweden. There has, however, according to Muslim leaders in this study, been an increase in divorce cases in Sweden due mainly to the increase of Muslim immigrants. It is nearly impossible, though, to trace the exact number of divorces in Swedish Muslim communities, as religious affiliation is not stated in statistical data. The Muslim leaders pointed further to two main interlinked reasons for this increase in divorce cases. Firstly, the changes in the family structure, where men are unemployed, 'staying at home and nagging their wives,' have destabilized the relations of Muslim couples. Secondly, Muslim women coming to Sweden become aware of their rights in society, particularly the economic possibilities of living without a man, and they tend to rebel against nasty treatment in a different way than they would have done in their countries of origin.

There are three main concepts of divorce in Muslim communities in Sweden. First, there is *talaq*, instigated by the man or the couple together. This form of divorce entails few problems, other than the psychological, for all parties – the spouses, the children, and other close relatives – involved in the process. Secondly, some Muslim couples tend to obtain (deceptive) divorces in order to increase their state allowances: they get a divorce according to the state's legal system, but remain married Islamically. The main procedure has been that one of the partners gets custody of the children and the other partner has low income or lives on social benefits; thus the allowance which should be paid by the partner is instead paid by the state. It might therefore be profitable for a family with many children to make such an arrangement. The third concept of divorce is the female-instigated divorce. As each individual's equal right before the law is the rule in Swedish secular legislation, some Muslim women living in Western countries plead for a divorce at the national court and use these divorce papers to try to obtain an Islamic divorce. However, if the husband has not signed the state's divorce documents and refuses to accept the divorce, the result would be a woman living in a 'limping marriage,' i.e., divorced according to the non-Muslim state system and married according to the Islamic system or according to her Muslim country of origin's state system. The number of women living in such 'limping marriages' is on the increase as reported by media and institutions working with Muslim women in Sweden.[22]

---

21   Norway has a similar legal right to marry couples afforded religious denominations as that in Sweden. See, for instance, Ferrari de Carli (2008: 5).

22   See the Swedish newspaper *Dagens Nyheter* (DN) 05/02/2007 'Svårt få muslimsk skilsmässa' (Difficult to Obtain an Islamic Divorce); *Dagens Nyheter* (DN) 06/02/2007 'Imam behöver samhällsstöd' (The Imams are in Need of Support from Society).

In the case of a woman who marries her husband in a country with a Muslim-majority population, and then remarries without obtaining an Islamic divorce document, she might be accused of bigamy or adultery (*zina*) if she returned to her native country. Moreover, if a woman is a believing/practicing Muslim, remarrying without having obtained an Islamic divorce could also affect her psychological health. A third aspect is the social environment. If a woman remarries without an Islamic divorce document, she might even be excluded from her community and be deprived of a social network.

Few Muslim leaders grant an Islamic divorce to a woman without the consent of her husband; i.e., either the husband has indirectly accepted a divorce by signing the state's divorce documents or he has directly consented to a divorce by signing the Islamic divorce documents. In 2004, according to my investigations, only three leaders in Sweden would consider doing so.[23] All the leaders explained, however, that they had granted divorce documents to women against the will of their husbands in the last few years, but had recently received both verbal and written threats and had therefore considered stopping these activities. One of the leaders was even abused in the street, and stated that 'as long as the authorities do not protect me for the work I am doing in helping women to get out of difficult marriages, I cannot risk the security of me or my family.'

It is particularly the cases of women living in 'limping marriages' that have recently kindled the new debate on Muslim divorce both on a macro and a micro level in Swedish society – in the Muslim communities as well as at the state level. One of the issues at stake is whether a state divorce should lead automatically to an Islamic divorce. This has been discussed, for instance, in the European Council for Fatwa and Research, based in Dublin and headed by the well known Egyptian-Qatarian Islamist, Yusuf al-Qaradawi. Another pressing issue is the question of the role the state should play in securing each minority member his or her individual rights. Does the legal right of religious associations to marry couples not give Muslim communities ambiguous signals as to the nature of their minority position within majority society? As long as a marriage contract conducted Islamically automatically becomes a legal marriage according to the state system, Muslims could understand this to be a sanction of keeping family legal affairs within the community, indicating that even divorce cases have to be handled within an Islamic framework.

---

23   As for case of Norway, Ferrari notes that there is one Shi'a organization that agrees to grant a divorce if a Norwegian legal divorce is in existence. However, she does not mention whether the husband's signature on the divorce document is required. If the husband has signed the legal state document, many of the religious organizations will grant a divorce to the woman. It is the case of the man's signature being lacking that is of importance to this study. See Ferrari de Carli (2008: 11).

Marriages and Divorces Abroad

Swedish authorities recognize divorces obtained in foreign countries on condition that one of the spouses lived in that country during the time of the divorce. Countries with Muslim-majority populations, however, have no general acceptance of divorces obtained in foreign countries. This probably has to do with women's restrictions in divorce cases, but it is the matter of dowry, or *mahr* that Muslim leaders in Sweden regard as the main obstacle to such bilateral cooperation. As Islamic legislation has detailed rules for dowry in case of divorce, it is necessary to establish the exact details of the divorce – who demanded the divorce and on what grounds – in order to fix accurate financial procedures. In some countries, such as Pakistan, for instance, there is a technical possibility for a woman to register a Swedish divorce, although in practice it is not always easy.[24] In other countries, however, such as many of the Arab countries and Iran, there is no such option. Divorce documents issued in Sweden for couples married in a country with a Muslim-majority population might not be accepted by the authorities in the country in which the marriage was conducted.

Majority versus Minority

Whereas the Swedish state has not yet paid much attention to 'limping marriages,' Norwegian authorities have tried to find solutions to this phenomenon. The difference in approach might be a result of the difference in the constitution of the migrant communities, the Pakistani community being the biggest and among the oldest immigrant communities in Norway (dating from the 1960s and 1970s), whereas the immigrant groups coming to Sweden in the 1960s and 70s comprised mainly people from Turkey and Yugoslavia. In these latter communities women in 'limping marriages' are not common, as was also confirmed by Turkish imams in Sweden, who claimed that they rarely dealt with divorce cases. According to them, fewer individuals of Turkish origin in Sweden have pled for divorce than, for instance, those in the Arabic-speaking community. There is more reason, however, to believe that the differences existing among the various ethnic communities have to do with variations in family legislation in the two regions. Whereas countries with an Arabic-speaking majority have sharia family courts, in Turkey family legislation, along with the rest of the legal system, has become secularized over the last decade.[25] Moreover, Muslims coming from the former Yugoslavia were familiar with personal status law in a secular state and therefore had less difficulty adjusting to the secular Swedish law system.

It is interesting to note that the Norwegian authorities introduced a change in the law on divorce in June 2003. In marriages between a Norwegian citizen and

---

24   See Human Right Service's webpage www.rights.no for further information.

25   See for instance 'Turkish Law Recognizes Women, Men as Equals' (accessed 14/10/2008) at www.womensenews.org/article.cfm/dyn/aid/777.

an immigrant, both parties were required thereafter to sign a declaration that they recognized each other's right to divorce. The change was aimed at helping women, presumably Muslims, living in 'limping marriages.' However, the opposition to the law was strong; it was particularly the Catholic Women's Association that lodged the strongest criticism against the Norwegian state. The tension between the right of freedom of religion on the one hand and gender-equal opportunity policy on the other became clearly visible in the ensuing discussion, with most religious associations critical of the amendment to the divorce law. The Catholics regarded their position as special due to the fact that their marriages would not be valid if they had to sign a paper of mutual right to divorce, which is forbidden in the Catholic Church. Most other religious associations, however, discussed the matter in terms of the right to freedom of religion. It is interesting that although Muslims are able to include in their marriage contracts certain conditions, such as the woman's right to obtain a divorce, Muslim organizations in Norway criticized the new law, seeing it as a violation of the right to freedom of religion.

Reflections

Multiculturalism is a struggle for justice, equality, and representation, but with regard to gender it becomes obvious that its stress on everybody's right to culture implies a traditional culture that is often based on gender-biased conceptions or gender blindness, such as the example of divorce in Muslim communities indicates. The question to pose is: who defines which part of a minority's system of meaning should be incorporated into a multiculturalist legal system? Sweden does not have a multiculturalist approach, but *vigselrätten,* the religious organizations' legal right to marry, could send multiculturalist signals to Muslim communities in the country. In Sweden, Muslim organizations are to a great extent run by first-generation Muslim immigrants who tend to promote the traditional law-school understanding of Islam. Community and religious leaders are to a great extent interested in the survival of the group, and thus endorse restrictions for members to withdraw from or leave the group. Traditional Islamic rulings are more suitable for securing the survival of the group than more gender-equality-oriented interpretations of the Islamic sources. For instance, the prohibition against Muslim women marrying non-Muslims is instrumental in keeping children within the group via the patrilineal descending principle in Islamic law, together with the notion of the man as the manager of the family. The idea is that if women marry outside the community, the group will decrease in number, as the children will belong to their non-Muslim fathers. As Muslims in Sweden have the option to live partly according to traditional family legislation system due to *vigselrätten*, they might also understand the divorce process as being a matter for the Muslim community instead of what it really is – a matter for the state. The Muslim understanding of a partial state acceptance of sharia through the marriage system could lead to an impediment in the process of integrating Muslim immigrants into the Swedish family legal system.

Another issue important to draw attention to in the multiculturalism debate is how the acceptance of various cultural traits implied in the notion of a multiculturalist as well as in a multicultural society could contribute to a cementing of minority cultures. The common hegemonic cultural content promoted by many Muslim leaders does not comprise the whole group's intellectual and religious development. For instance, in the last decades many alternative understandings of the Islamic sources have blossomed. These new interpretations indicate the multitude of minority sub-cultures that has to be taken into consideration while dealing with Muslim communities. It is important to view culture and religion in terms of processual change. But a multicultural or a multiculturalist approach could lead to a rigid view of what 'Islam' is, and fix this view in time and space. A promotion of the patriarchal law-school understandings of Islamic texts will weaken vulnerable sections of the community, such as women, children and homosexuals, as well as generate an in-group dynamic of disassociation from majority society and other religious and ethnic minorities. Perceptions of gender relations in the Western world have changed dramatically with the changing socio-economic conditions of the last two centuries. It might even be possible to predict a similar change in Muslim communities in Western society as time passes, with cultural and religious narratives being in a constant flux due to encounters between Muslims and non-Muslims, as well as encounters between Muslims from various cultural contexts. The migration process might thus be regarded as the ultimate example of how intercultural and interreligious exchanges result in something 'in-between' the old and the new. One consequence of the policies of multiculturalism, however, is that they could impede this development within Muslim communities by contributing to a fixing cultural and religious understanding in time and place.

As multiculturalism is about avoiding the hegemonic majority's discarding of minority positions, it is just as important to find ways to prevent the hegemony *within* the communities from taking charge over opposing members. What possibilities do members of minority cultures have to belong to more than one cultural community? For instance, what about homosexuals with religious directions in life who want to be part of a religious minority community, but are not able to do so due to biases within the community? And what about Muslim (and Jewish) women with religious outlooks who are divorced according to state law, but married according to Islamic (Jewish) law, and want to remarry? Or religious Muslim women who want to marry non-Muslim men, and who want to belong to both the religious community and the broader majority society? These are all issues that need to be resolved in a multiculturalist as well as in a multicultural society. Although the protection of cultural rights is an important task for modern society, it is the protection of every individual and every individual's freedom of choice to belong, that in the end is the ideological base for Western society.

A last issue of importance is the discrepancy between Swedish legal marriage contracts on the one hand and religious contracts on the other. In religious marriage contracts there are certain underlying assumptions of gender inequality, whereas majority society's secular marriage contracts presuppose gender equality – men and women's equal rights to decide to marry and to divorce. Without particular conditions in the marriage contract, such as both genders' right to divorce, prohibition of polygyny, etc., the secular legislation's acceptance of religious marriages implicitly signals an acceptance of gender discrimination within religious minorities. By accepting marriages in religious organizations with different gender policies than majority society, the authorities encourage religious legislation based on collective rights built on gender inequality. Thus, multicultural policy could cause injustice towards weak members in minority communities.

References

Al-Bukhari (n.d.) *sahih al-bukhari*, system *al-'alami*, CD-ROM, Jeddah: Company Sakhr al-'Alami.

Baumann, Gerd (1999), *The Multicultural Riddle: Rethinking National, Ethnic, and Religious Identities* (London: Routledge).

Becket, Clare and Macey, Marie (2001), 'Race, gender and sexuality: The oppression of multiculturalism', *Pergamon Women's Studies International Forum*, 24(3/4): 309–19.

Bhabha, Homi K. (1999[1997]), 'Liberalism's Sacred Cow' in J. Cohen and M. Howard (eds) *Is Multiculturalism Bad for Women?* (New Jersey: Princeton University Press). Available online at http://www.bostonreview.net/BR22.5/bhabha.html (accessed October 19, 2009).

Carlbom, Aje (2003) *The Imagined versus the Real Other* (Lund: Lund Monographs in Social Anthropology).

Clark, Janine A. and Young, Amy A. (2008), 'Islamism and Family Law Reform in Morocco and Jordan' *Mediterranean Politics* 13(3): 333–52.

Cowan, J.K., Dembour, M.-B. and Wilson, R.A. (eds) (2001), *Culture and Rights: Anthropological Perspectives* (Cambridge: Cambridge University Press).

Dagens Nyheter (DN) 05/02/2007 'Svårt få muslimsk skilsmässa' (Difficult to Obtain an Islamic Divorce).

Dagens Nyheter (DN) 06/02/2007 'Imam behöver samhällsstöd' (The Imams are in Need of Support from Society).

Elliot, Katja Zvan (2009), 'Reforming the Moroccan Personal Status Code: A Revolution for Whom?' *Mediterranean Politics* 14(2): 213–27.

Eriksen, Thomas Hylland (1997), 'Multiculturalism, Individualism and Human Rights: Romanticism, the Enlightenment and Lessons from Mauritius' in R.A. Wilson (ed.) *Human Rights, Culture and Context* (London: Pluto Press).

Eriksen, Thomas Hylland (2001), 'Between universalism and relativism: a critique of the UNESCO concept of culture' in J.K. Cowan, M.-B. Dembour and R.A. Wilson (eds) *Culture and Rights: Anthropological Perspectives* (Cambridge University Press), 127–48.

Ferrari de Carli, Eli (2008), *Religion, juss og rettigheter: Om skilsmisse, Polygamy og Shari'a-råd* (Oslo: Institutt for Samfunnsforskning).

Fink, Carole (1995), 'The League of Nations and the Minorities Question', *World Affairs* 157, No.4 (Spring 1995): 197–206.

Groth, Bente (2005), 'Mann og Kvinne skapte Han dem. Ekteskapets betydelse i jödisk tradisjon', I.B. Thorbjörnsrud, (red.) *Evig Din? Ekteskaps- og samlivstradisjoner I det flerreligiöse Norge* (Oslo: Abstrakt Forlag).

Kymlicka, Will (ed.) (1995), *The Rights of Minority Cultures* (Oxford and New York: Oxford University Press).

Kymlicka, Will (1999 [1997]), 'Liberal Complacencies' in J. Cohen and M. Howard (eds) *Is Multiculturalism Bad for Women?* (New Jersey: Princeton University Press). Available online at http://www.bostonreview.net/BR22.5/kymlicka.html (accessed October 20, 2009).

Merry, Sally Engle (2001), 'Changing rights, changing cultures' in J.K. Cowan, M.-B. Dembour, and R.A. Wilson (eds) *Culture and Rights: Anthropological Perspectives* (Cambridge: Cambridge University Press), 31–55.

Mir-Hosseini, Ziba (2000 [1993]), *Marriage on Trial: A Study of Islamic Family Law – Iran and Morocco Compared* (London: I.B. Taurus).

Mir-Hosseini, Ziba and Longinotto, Kim (1998), *Divorce Iranian Style*, TV-film.

Modood, Tariq (1997), 'Introduction' in T. Modood and P. Werbner (eds) *The Politics of Multiculturalism in the New Europe: Racism, Identity and Community* (London: Zed Books Ltd).

Okin, Susan Moller (1999), *Is Multiculturalism Bad for Women?* (New Jersey: Princeton University Press). Available online at http://www.bostonreview.net/BR22.5/okin.html (accessed October 20, 2009).

Parekh, Bhikhu (2000), *Rethinking Multiculturalism: Cultural Diversity and Political Theory* (New York: Palgrave).

Roald, Anne Sofie (2001), *Women in Islam: The Western Experience* (London: Routledge).

Sander, Åke (1996), 'The Status of Muslim Communities in Sweden' in G. Nonneman, T. Niblock, and B. Szajkowski (eds) *Muslim Communities in the New Europe* (London: Ithaca).

Sander, Åke (1997), 'To what extent is the Swedish Muslim religious?' in S. Verivec and C. Peach (eds) *Islam in Europe: The Politics of Religion and Community* (Warwick: Centre for Research in Ethnic Relations, University of Warwick).

Schacht, Josef (1982), *The Origins of Muhammedan Jurisprudence* (Oxford: Clarendon).

Shachar, Ayelet (2001), *Multicultural Jurisdiction: Cultural Differences and Women's Rights* (Cambridge: Cambridge University Press).

Sonbol, Amira El Azhary (1996), *Women, the Family, and Divorce Laws in Islamic History* (New York: Syracuse University Press).

SOU (Statens Offentliga Utredningar) (1974), *Investigation of Immigrants 3* (Stockholm: Regeringskansliet).

Steinsalz, Adin (1976), *The Essential Talmud* (New York: Basic Books).
Wadud, Amina (1999), *Qu'ran and Women: Rereading the sacred text from a woman's perspective* (New York and Oxford: Oxford University Press).

Internet sources

Human Right Service's webpage www.rights.no.
'Turkish Law Recognizes Women, Men as Equals', accessed October 14, 2008 at www.womensenews.org/article.cfm/dyn/aid/777.

Chapter 6
Iranians in Britain

Vida Nassehi-Behnam

Introduction

The immigration of Iranians to Britain began years before the 1979 Islamic Revolution. A number of retired civil servants, industrialists and Westernized elites with financial resources came to England in search of a better life and a higher standard of education for their children before that time. Holding a permanent residency card, some could, if they wished, continue to work in their fields of expertise in exile; others lived on the revenue of investments they had made in Iran or in England.

It is not an easy task to define this community, as most of its members, especially the new generations, have become immersed in British society. However, they too have played an important role in the adaptation process of post-revolutionary Iranian exiles.

The profile of post-revolutionary immigrants, on the contrary, is easier to procure. The composition of this diaspora is quite varied, and depends largely on when and why the people in it left their homeland. Generally speaking, there are three types of post-revolutionary Iranian immigrants: political; socio-cultural; and economic.

Among political exiles, one must make a distinction between two main groups – those who left the country before the collapse of the government of President Bani-Sadr and those who left after this event.[1] The first category consists mostly of upper-class families, hostile to the revolution, who held key positions during the Pahlavi regime, a well-educated and Westernized elite with substantial financial resources. Most of these people chose Britain because of their familiarity with British culture. The second group consists of disappointed revolutionaries, hostile to both the Pahlavi and the Islamic regimes, politically engaged, of a younger generation, educated but not necessarily Westernized. Britain was not always the country of their choice. Many went there because they had no other option.

Parallel to these asylum-seekers, a second type of exile is composed of Iranians who were not politically active to any great extent, but left the country due to the socio-cultural upheaval and the morose atmosphere that prevailed in Iran,

---

1 Abo'l Hassan Bani-Sadr was elected as the first Iranian president in January 1980 and was dismissed by A. Khomeini in June 1981. Since then, all parties in Iran except the Republican Islamic Party have been banished and their followers arrested.

especially with regards to women and youth. Contrary to political immigrants, these people left the country with their families. This category consists mostly of upper- and upper-middle-class urban individuals who could afford the cost of such a displacement. Soon after the revolution, two groups of youth were especially affected – those who left Iran to continue their education after the universities closed as a consequence of the regime's Cultural Revolution, and those who fled in order to escape the draft during the Iran-Iraq war.

During the 1990s, a third, economic type of immigrant was added to the previous list of Iranian émigrés as the post-war economic situation and growing rate of inflation forced many more to leave the country. Their first destination was Sweden, but because of some restrictions and the racial problems that arose there due to numerous incidents, the flow turned to Britain.

Today, however, the profile of young Iranian immigrants has totally changed. It encompasses all the categories mentioned, both sexes and different educational levels. Recent émigrés flee the undesirable socio-cultural atmosphere and, above all, the unpredictable socio-economic and political situation that still prevails in Iran.

A Demographic Portrait of Iranian Immigrants and Families in Britain

The demographic data available on the Iranian population in Britain is not very precise. The lack of information could be due to a number of reasons, including the small number of Iranians in Britain and the fact that Iranians do not live in a concentrated area, which is the case of many other minority groups in, for instance, London. Many do not appear in the census records because they have obtained British citizenship.

The first source of demographic characteristics comes from the 1981 population census, which found a total of 28,617 individuals who were born in Iran and living in Britain (18,132 males and 10,485 females). The noticeable difference between the number of males and females in this breakdown lies in the fact that right after the revolution, Iranian immigrants consisted mostly of male political personalities. Figures based on a research paper published by Refugee Action, a charity organization in the UK, stated that the population of Iranians in Britain increased from 8,205 to 28,608 between 1971 and 1981. Between 1979 and 1984, 8,000 Iranians arrived in Britain, generating the largest percentage of asylum-seekers in the country.[2] This period marks the dissolution of all opposition political parties, one after another, in Iran.

According to other figures from the 1991 census, 32,262 Iranian nationals were then resident in Britain; among them, 16,856 lived in and around London.

---

2   The Iranian Community Centre Annual Report for March 1988, 266–268 Holloway Road, London N7 6NE.

Attention should be paid to the fact that the figures listed above do not include the children born to Iranian parents, nor those whose immigration status is unclear.

The Home Office has also released figures estimating that 16,000 to 20,000 temporary visas have been extended to Iranians every year since 1990. If this estimation is accurate, there are many more Iranians in Britain than indicated by the census data (Spellman 2004). According to the Iranian consulate in London, around 35,000 Iranians were registered at the consulate in 1999.[3] In 2004, the same source states the number of Iranians as 75,000. The latest British Census (2001), recorded 42,494 persons born in Iran and the Office for National Statistics estimates the number of Iranian-born living in the UK at 60,000 in 2008.

Place of Residence

According to the available data on place of residence, British regions with significant Iranian-born populations, in descending order, are: London; Manchester; Bradford; Leeds; Glasgow; Newcastle; and Southampton. Iranians in London reside mainly in the following boroughs: Brent; Barnet; Ealing; Hammersmith and Fulham; Kensington and Chelsea; and Westminster in the inner city.

Most of the first group of Iranians who arrived in London just before and at the time of the revolution live in affluent areas, including Kensington, Chelsea, Knightsbridge, Richmond, Hampstead and Swiss Cottage. The second wave of Iranians seeking asylum and settlement in Britain were often from more modest socio-economic backgrounds. They were dispersed in different areas of London based on socio-economic background and political affiliations.

Immigration Process

Of the total respondents, 20 per cent came to Britain before the revolution. Among them, some emigrated with their families for various reasons, some were government employees who decided to remain in Britain after the revolution, and some were students who did not return home after finishing their education. A small percentage came in 1979, just before or soon after the revolution. This group mostly represents high-ranking officials of the previous regime.

The largest percentage (one-third) came during the 1980s, which is the most critical post-revolutionary period, when all non-official parties were banned by the government and their members persecuted. During the 1990s the percentage of immigrants decreased for a while, but took off again by the beginning of the year 2000. That is when waves of economic asylum-seekers began to arrive in Britain. For this category of immigrants, reaching the British Isles was not easy. They usually first made their way to France,[4] passing a number of frontiers with the help

---

3 Interview by K. Spellman with Iranian consulate member in December 1999.

4 Sangatte camp existed in Calais (in the north of France) until 2003. Since then, asylum-seekers live in a self-made camp in catastrophic sanitary conditions. Every now

of well-paid guides, and then crossed the English Channel illegally in trains or trucks, confronting serious danger to their lives.

Although a considerable number of them were captured and sent back, thousands managed to arrive in Britain, find jobs, obtain refugee status and bring along other members of their family under family reunion laws.[5] Here is one of them, a 32-year-old woman,[6] describing her perilous journey:

> I first came to Turkey with my children; then I contacted the smuggler my brother had found for me. We were around 60 persons at the designated site. We passed the Turkish frontier until we reached Italy. He took us to a sort of a den [cave] where he used to hide his passengers. It took us 25 days and three attempts to pass the frontier. To catch the train we had to jump over the barbwire wall. I was a small woman with bags and two children; it was very hard but with the help of young men I finally did it. Then we had to jump on a train that passed the station at a slow speed. Everybody got on the train, except for me and my children. We were arrested by the police. They took us to a hotel and deported us the next morning. I called the smuggler and asked him for help. This time he took us, around 20 persons, to a waterfront... I don't know where. We went on a boat which had a hole and water was penetrating inside. To make it short, we arrived in trucks, paid [for] by the smuggler, at the refugee Camp at Calais, Sangatte. It was a horrible place. My children called it the bottom of hell. They bit each other over anything: women, drugs. I was very ill and was bleeding like hell. There I met people who had been waiting for months to pass the channel. This time we had to squeeze in on a truck and remain there in dead silence until we were sure that we had entered British soil. It was very cold. We had to wait in the parking area to take advantage of an occasion [to head out]. That's what I did with the help of the smuggler and after many attempts. We got in a truck that was carrying cartons of eggs. We had to sit at the very back of the truck in the dark. I am claustrophobic and feel suffocated in such places. I started to cry, took a piece of paper, wrote our names and address on it so that if I die my children could be saved. After a while I felt that the truck was getting into the ship and later left it. Our smuggler had told me that if the journey takes long, cry as loud as possible; and that is what I did. Then I heard the driver say, 'Shut-up', A sound I was delighted to hear.

---

and then French police evacuate the camp and send its inhabitants back to their countries of origin. But the human traffic goes on and on.

5   According to a French TV programme called 'Les émigrés Clandestins', broadcast on the Paris Première channel in April 2000, every year approximately 80,000 immigrants manage to cross the channel. Among them, 70,000 are captured and sent back; the rest disappear into British society.

6   A 32-year-old, separated woman with two children who came to London in 2000 and was accepted nine months later as social refugee.

Among the respondents in our study, 60 per cent were British citizens. This percentage also covers those who have dual citizenship (British-Iranians) and those who came to Britain before the revolution. About 25 per cent were convention refugees or refugee claimants; 13 per cent were permanent residents and 2 per cent had illegal status.

Obtaining refugee status, however, is not an easy task. A famous British-Iranian lawyer told me in an interview: 'I receive between 250 and 300 Iranian refugee claimants every year but only 10 per cent of them are accepted on the first attempt. And it is becoming more and more difficult. For example, in 1998 70 per cent of demands were accepted, whereas in the year 2000 the percentage dropped to 12 per cent.'[7]

As for reasons for immigration, let us begin with the results of a survey in 1982 among Iranian female refugees. Among the respondents, 40 per cent gave political reasons, 10 per cent cited family difficulties and the rest socio-cultural reasons such as Islamization of daily life, compulsory hijab and limited access to education for girls (Shafiï Roohi 1992).

Nearly 20 years later, the results of our survey are not far from the one carried out in 1982. Forty-eight per cent of men and 38 per cent of women provide political reasons for having left Iran. A middle-aged man from Ghazvine, a town not far from Tehran, gives his version of why he was forced into exile:

> Before and after the revolution, I was politically active in the workers' movement. Once I was caught and spent five years in the prison of the Islamic regime. In 1994 almost a second revolution took place in our town. Hundreds of rebels were imprisoned and a considerable number were executed. I was well-known as an activist all my life; therefore, I was in danger. I went into hiding until I could get out and I left the country illegally.

A young male student from a small town in the northwest of Iran says:

> I was born in a backward traditional and religious family. We were eight brothers and sisters. One of my brothers hanged himself. He could no longer tolerate the burden of his family and the society he lived in. I can tell you about cases of young girls who committed suicide by burning themselves. I remember on the way to our school, there was a place called Jelo-khan, where we could see officials hanging so called 'criminals' but the fact was that most of them were political activists.

Among non-political respondents the following reasons were mentioned, in order of importance, for leaving Iran: education of children, especially girls; pursuit of university education; difficulty tolerating the socio-political atmosphere (war,

---

7   Interview with solicitor Ali Rahimi, London, March 2003.

religious and gender discrimination); domestic violence; and, finally, difficulty finding and even searching for a job.

A young woman from Masjed-e Soleiman (in southern Iran) told me about her reasons for seeking refugee status in Britain:

> I left the country to get away from my violent husband. He had sexual problems but would not go to see a doctor. You know how men are! To see a doctor hurts their pride. He, therefore, took his revenge on me. But what finally persuaded me to leave the country was to save my children.

A young Kurdish girl talking about her exile says:

> In Sanandaj life was hard. For me, with only a high school diploma, there was no job. Even if I could endure all the problems and obtain a university degree, there would be no job. My sister had passed the entrance exams to get into university but they did not let her in as our family was known for being politically involved. Before interviewing the candidates, they already have their family and socio-political backgrounds. My brother was not admitted to a public university either. My father had to pay his tuition to go to a private college, although it was a real burden on the family. So, I had no future in my country!

Many single women also left the country with the idea of reshaping their lives. Among them are young divorcees and widows for whom the intolerable post-revolutionary atmosphere became a pretext to break with family-network supervision, despite its advantages. We can also distinguish disappointed ex-militants, in ideological disagreement with their spouses and in search of new identities, who wish to change their lifestyles and liberate themselves from the marriage bond. In fact, once they get through the adjustment process, displacement may present a positive experience for this group.

Characteristics of the Respondents

Both sexes were represented in the sample surveyed. The percentage of women who agreed to fill out the questionnaires was larger than that of the men. Men were often sceptical about field research and did not trust researchers. Consequently, the percentage of women, in spite of our efforts, exceeded that of men.

Most of the respondents (2/3) were between 30 and 60 years of age, which means that they migrated to Britain while still young. Among the elderly, two-thirds were men, which is probably due to the immigration of political elites during or just after the revolution.

In the sample, we had a range from highly educated to completely illiterate individuals. But it is important to note that among the respondents, three-quarters of the women and half of the men said that they took advantage of the British government's educational opportunity programme in order to study and promote their socio-economic position.

From well before the revolution, higher education had become a key factor in upward social mobility in Iran. Consequently, parents went to great lengths to send their children to university. In exile, this attitude is still rooted in their minds. A woman I interviewed in one of the Iranian community centres told me:

> Today a considerable percentage of British university students are foreigners and especially those coming from developing countries, Iran included, for whom higher education has an ultimate value. Until lately, refugees could benefit from British grants and they did not have to pay tuition. Today they can obtain long-term loans. Although famous universities are very selective, numerous young Iranians attend British universities right now.[8]

This is true in France as well, especially because state universities there are free of charge.

On the whole, the men in our study come from more highly educated families than the women. But as far as their place of birth is concerned, the men are mostly from the provinces and the women from Tehran.

Their occupations before the revolution covered a variety of spheres, from high-ranking positions to skilled labour. But the result of the survey shows that the higher their position before exile, the less opportunity they had to continue their professional life in Britain. That is probably why we find 30 per cent unemployment among male respondents.

The gender ratio in the working group is about equal, despite the lower professional qualifications of the women.

Survey results indicate that one third of the respondents were working in professions such as law, medicine, engineering, and architecture. The next considerable percentage covers civil servants, a type of work which seems to suit mostly women (15 per cent of women and only 3 per cent of men). This is probably because women, whether working outside the home or not, are responsible for household chores and the care of children. Consequently, they prefer government office work, which is less time-consuming, has more predictable hours and less risk of layoffs. The rest of those surveyed are in administrative and service employment or non-professional work (student, unemployed and retired). As for the unemployed respondents, they all said they could find a job if they were willing to work in fields inferior to their competence and/or accept being underpaid. A newly arrived immigrant says:

> The only job we can find is in the services sector, such as food delivery. In such a job we must work at least 60 hours per week to be able to survive and have a roof

---

8   Interview with Roya Amir Ebrahimi, in charge of the women's section of the Iranian Community Centre in London, March 2003.

over our head. I know Iranians who work up to 80 hours per week for two and a half pounds per hour, whereas the minimum wage is five and a half pounds.

Consequently, the unskilled refugees covered by the social security programme prefer to study or live modestly on government benefits rather than work. A young refugee who was active in an Iranian association said: 'What is important for me is to be politically active and help Iranian refugee claimants. Many of them live in isolation and some commit suicide. These are my problems. My aim is to help them get out of their horrendous situation.'

The least frequently answered question in our survey was the one dealing with the income of the respondent and his or her family. It remains, therefore, an ambiguous subject matter.

Islam is the predominant religion of Iranians in Britain, although many claim to be non-religious. Smaller minorities, such as Zoroastrians, Jews, Baha'is and converted Christians should also be mentioned as part of the Iranian community in Britain. In London, there are also Iranians belonging to the Sufi order (for more information on the subject, read Spellman 2004).

To the questions concerning ethnic and Islamic beliefs, respondents on the whole showed no strong tendency towards religious practices; only about 10 per cent wished their children could take Koran lessons, or wanted them to marry someone within the Islamic faith. To the question concerning September 11 and its consequences, respondents said that it did not have an important impact on the behaviour of English people towards Iranians.

Family Typology

According to the data obtained from the sample, 60 per cent of the respondents were married and the most frequent age at marriage was between 20 and 29; 33 per cent of the men and 8 per cent of the women were single and the rest were divorcees, widows or separated. Family size, compared to the pre-revolution period, has been reduced, and 53 per cent of the respondents had between one and three children.

The data also point to a number of broken families. The single-parent Iranian families living in London are mostly among the economic type of immigrants who left Iran during the 1990s and could not afford the expenses of a whole-family displacement. That is why, among them, there are more males than females.

Extended families have become scarce. Forty-two per cent of male respondents and 38.5 per cent of females said that they lived in large families (conjugal plus father, mother or other relatives of husband or wife) while in Iran, whereas this percentage drops to 3 and 5 per cent, respectively, in exile. Nevertheless, 15 per cent said that they provided shelter to new families arriving in Britain and/or intended to help them out until they could find a residence.

Age at marriage has increased, especially among the middle- and lower-middle-class young exiles. The main factors behind this phenomenon are the desire to attend university and to be able to live independently. Leaving one's parental home has become possible, especially for women in exile. In Iran, it was not an easy task for a young girl to live alone. Thus, many single women left the country with the idea of reshaping their lives and breaking with the supervision of the family network. Once in exile, they can work, rent a residence, have relations with the opposite sex and receive financial help, if needed, from social institutions. Consequently, they can afford to postpone marriage if they wish to do so.

The young generation is much freer to choose their future spouses from a much broader circle than in Iran. Love and sexual compatibility have appeared as prominent factors in marital choice. Parents (the first generation), believing in traditional Muslim culture, do not approve of premarital sexual relations, especially for their daughters, but at the same time they want them to live like their peers. In an interview, a mother told me:

> When my daughter reached the age of 17 and she still did not have a steady boyfriend, I became worried. But as soon as she found one, I was constantly concerned about her future and could not get the problem of virginity out of my mind... and didn't dare to talk to her about it.

Endogamous marriage among cousins is practically non-existent among emigrants, but marriage inside the broader kinship network is still functional, especially among well-to-do families that prefer to keep their privileges intact. But Iranian families are so scattered around the world that we can easily say that, even among marriages inside kinship networks, the circle of mate selection has become as wide as the world.

Nevertheless, the first-generation immigrants surveyed are not very keen about mixed marriages. In 80 per cent of the cases, parents, when asked their opinion on this matter, said that they preferred marriage among Iranians. The reasons they provided were a lack of relationship between the families involved and language barriers.

Marriage through correspondence can be considered as a new type of mate selection for Iranians in exile. These marriages are normally arranged by relatives or friends and are held without prior meeting between a young woman living in Iran and a middle-aged man residing in a Western country.

Results of studies on immigration have shown that marriages that have as their main target a residency permit outside Iran are seldom successful and end up in domestic violence or divorce (Mahtab 1999). But divorce in these cases does not seem an easy solution since in most Western countries the bride's residency permit depends on the husband's.

Speaking of polygamy and temporary marriage may seem out of place for discussion here, but these issues did reappear in Iran's post-revolutionary period and had consequences for families in exile. These practices have never been prevalent in Iran's urban areas (Nassehi-Behnam 1985), but since the revolution, although limited in number, they have recurred among single bachelors who could not date members of the opposite sex. After a while, however, men whose wives, upon mutual decision, had left Iran with their children also took advantage of the situation. When these men married a second wife, the situation became a serious source of economic and affective family conflict, one in which women were the main victims.

Changing Roles and Status among Family Members in Exile

Spousal Relations

The implications of gender within Iranian families in exile may be treated on different levels. According to Athias (1998), we should explore how the social and economic positions of men and women are partially determined by the ways in which gender relations within the ethnic culture and within the host society interact with one another. We should see, furthermore, if and to what extent this cultural and structural shift has produced liberating experiences for women. In other words, see if this shift has modified relations among family members (Athias 1998).

Iranian female immigrants seem to have escaped the general stereotype that among the Middle Eastern diaspora, women are in a subordinate position to hegemonic men (Kandyoti 1991). Unlike women from Middle Eastern societies who are expected to follow their husbands into immigration, many Iranian women were instigators of family displacement. Thus, they felt responsible for the consequences and subsequently tried to make up for them by heading their exiled households effectively.

In general, Iranian women in exile have proven to be more realistic than Iranian men. To manage and protect their families, they take the harsh reality of exile and turn it to their advantage, improving their status within the family and within the ethnic group. This has also been demonstrated in other studies on Iranian communities.[9] The reasons can be found in the following evidence.

The existence of a considerable number of single-parent families, especially at the beginning of exile, gave women the obligation of playing both masculine and feminine roles at the same time. Once couples were reunited, many of these women refused to go back to their previous status. This situation forced family members to renegotiate family and, especially, gender roles. In cases of failure, this became a source of conflict.

This new situation among broken or reconstructed families, especially those with low incomes, forced women to support the family alone. More practical and flexible, they accepted jobs inferior to their competence, whereas for many men it was hard to engage in degrading jobs, and they chose to stay home and look after

---

9   See Mahdi (1999) and Darvishpour in *Nimeye Digar*, op. cit.; Hosseini-Kaladjahi, *Iranians in Sweden*, University of Stockholm, Gotab AB (1997).

the children. This situation changed the traditional symbolic image of a tender, ever-present mother and an often absent paternal breadwinner authority in the family.

According to the results of a study of immigrants in France and Britain, a relatively high percentage of Iranian women are now (compared to the pre-revolutionary period) financially independent, either because they work (47 per cent in France and about 50 per cent in Britain) or because they are covered by the social security system, especially those who belong to the single-parent family category. And many, especially in the younger generation, are socially active and interested in political issues.

A young, divorced social refugee talks about her independent situation once in the host country:

> First I came here because of my daughter's health problem and that was the reason why they gave me a visa. But after some time in London, I became aware of my situation as a woman and a wife. I always thought the women's right movement was just 'talks,' but here I became conscious how in the Islamic Republic men have all the rights and can make you do whatever they want. In Iran I could get a divorce if I persisted but had to deny all my rights as a mother. But here I went to see a social worker who sent me to a lawyer. I asked for a divorce and got it after all and obtained the guardianship of my children.

The degree of cultural adaptability is also an important factor in changing roles among exiled family members. Women in Middle Eastern countries are taught to adapt themselves to new situations. In exile, this habit serves mothers to adapt themselves more easily to the new cultural codes of conduct. As for their education, which is an important key to adjustment, 67 per cent of female respondents in the London survey pursued their education in the UK, whereas for men the percentage dropped to 45.5.

More evidence of the willingness and flexibility of women to adjust to their host society is demonstrated by the fact that although most Iranians in the UK regard Iran as their 'home country,' among those who regard both Iran and the UK as their home countries, females account for three times more cases than men.

Replies to the question regarding media coverage of the Muslim community show that women are also more positive in that area than men. The percentage of men who think the media treat the Muslim community unfairly is three times that of women.

This openness towards the outside world, along with day-to-day contact with it, has given women the opportunity to adapt more easily to the traits and lifestyles of host cultures than men. It has allowed them to take part in the public domain and also, consequently, to better understand their children who live between two cultures. The women we surveyed said that they often had to play the role of mediator between children and their father.

All of these factors have totally changed the marital relations of Iranian immigrants and forced couples to accept more egalitarian attitudes. But these initiatives, which liberate the father from a segment of his responsibilities, can gradually reinforce his feelings of degradation as well (Anton and Scotto 1989), and may end in domestic violence. This situation occurs quite frequently among economic migrants, who often come from traditional, lower-income families. In these cases social institutions protect women who, in turn, take advantage of the situation to liberate themselves from authoritarian husbands who cannot change their patriarchal attitudes and behaviours (Darvishpour 1999; Mahdi 1999; Khosravi et al. 1997).

Parent-child Relations[10]

Among Iranian exiles, the more the parents are initiated into Western culture and open to the world, the better the child learns to accept and live with these differences. The parent-child relation in these families may only suffer from the generational gap that all families go through. On the contrary, in families that are not familiar with the culture of the host society, children undergo a more intense conflict situation between the two disparate worlds. Here both generational and cultural gaps come into play. Parents whose authority has become increasingly questioned through an extreme change of lifestyle are no longer able to practise their child-rearing methods or discipline. Faced with such incompetence, children who learn through their own initiative become, in a way, the educators of their parents.

Children not only transfer the prevalent way of life to their parents, but, as they grow older, also become the guardians of family ethics. For example, they encourage their mothers to divorce abusive fathers, guaranteeing her expenses, and interfere in parental relations. A middle-aged mother who came from a traditional family said the following about her children: 'My daughter often accuses my husband of lack of attention towards me. She criticizes her father's negligence for not offering me flowers for my birthday.'

This inversion of roles can at times become a source of conflict between two generations or, on the contrary, lead to a more egalitarian relationship and a more positive exchange of ideas. Thus, in the course of an instructive game, the child initiates his parents into Western values in exchange for their knowledge of an Iranian cultural heritage that is dear to them. Iranians are very proud of their heritage, and place strong pressure on their children to retain their native language and identity. However, this attempt at a harmonious synthesis of the two cultures is not always successful. A middle-aged mother who has lived in London since 1987 and feels guilty about the loss of heritage in her family, says:

10   Nassehi-Behnam (2005).

Unfortunately my children don't have any knowledge of the Persian language. They were both born in England and their father sent them to a boarding school very early to place them in an English atmosphere. Therefore they only have English friends. I tried very hard to teach them Farsi; I even forced them in a way to follow Persian classes. But they hated it, as Saturday was their only free time and they wanted to spend it with their friends. Now that they have grown up and do understand oral Farsi, whenever I get a chance I talk to them about Persian culture and Iran's socio-political problems, but no use. However, I don't give up, for this is very disappointing to me. I would like to believe that deep down in their minds there certainly is a place for Iran.

Others manage to remove the borders between the host culture and that of their native land, between home and the society at large. Here is the reflection of a political refugee who came to London in1998 and is satisfied with the cultural education of his children:

We try to teach both cultures to our children and encourage them to have a good relation with Iran and Iranians, even though my life was in danger while I was at home. Our children speak the Persian language well, and both have Iranian and English friends. They are very well adapted to the English culture and feel at home here. I am also accustomed to my life here; I have a good job and I am happy.

What was said here concerns relations between the first and second generations. As for the third generation, the situation has changed, since they are being educated by parents who were born and brought up in exile.

Family Disorganization

A rise in marital instability in exile has been demonstrated in several studies on Iranian communities in diaspora. The reasons can be summarized as follows: first, the migration alone of politicized men at the beginning of the revolution and the later joining of children and wives, who lived for years far from their spouses; secondly, and often resulting from the first factor, is the cultural gap between women's new attitudes and behaviour and that of men, especially in middle- and lower-middle-class exiled families; and, finally, the existence of societal institutions that advise, help and protect women who wish to seek divorce and independence. I must add that the degree of adaptability of migrants belonging to less fortunate social strata and not acquainted with Western values is less functional in exile. Their families are therefore more prone to disorganization.

Socialized at home and through educational institutions to have a discriminatory image of women, Iranians learn to accept the practice and transfer of traditional gender roles, and maintain patriarchal norms and attitudes (Taleghani 1994; Nassehi-Behnam 2005). Once in exile and confronted with new codes of conduct, they may change these attitudes after a fairly short time, but the behaviours associated with them linger, causing situations that may end in domestic violence and divorce. Results of sociological research in Germany, Sweden and England[11] are witness to many such cases of domestic violence among Iranian couples suffering from conjugal conflict.

According to the London survey results, the question 'Does fear of anti-violence law and rules result in non-violent behaviour?' had an affirmative response in 40 per cent of both sexes. Their answers to the next question suggest that they are right. In response to the question 'Do arguments ever result in physical violence?' only 4 per cent of Iranian women in the UK said that they were targets of physical violence.

Results of a field study in Sweden revealed a very high rate of divorce among Iranian couples, usually initiated by the women. One of the counsellors at Jame'ye Iranian (The Iran Society) in London told me in an interview:

> The section for family problems is the most active section of this association. We receive a considerable number of people, mostly women. In the West the situation becomes more favourable for family disputes, since in exile the usual barriers that dissimulate marital problems no longer exist and pre-immigration conflicts resurface. In exile, women are able to obtain their lawful rights and are not forced to submit to spousal violence. When I asked a violent husband, who had been summoned by the police before, why he was abusive towards his wife, he said: 'We lived together for 13 years in Iran and we used to quarrel now and then, but she never said a word and we would forget about the problem. I never imagined that my wife would dare to call the police on me. If I knew such a thing would happen here, I would have never left my country!'[12]

According to the results of the above-mentioned series of interviews in Sweden, a 50-year-old man who due to his violent behaviour had been forced to leave his family, says:

> Since our separation I feel very lonely. Experience has shown me that you should never give women a break. Here, instead of giving women so many possibilities, if they would find men decent jobs, families would not be dissolved.

These men, who have not been able to adjust to new gender roles, will remain marginal in their new social setting. According to the Iran Society counsellor, so called 'mail brides' are often the targets of men's brutality. She says:

---

11   Darvishpour, in *Nimeye Digar*, op. cit.; Hosseini-Kaladjahi, op. cit.; Khosravi, S. and Graham, M. (1997).

12   Interview with Fowsier Karimi, London, March 2003.

A number of women who visit us for divorce counselling are young women who have been sent from Iran to marry exiled men. Their husbands are usually much older; they came to England a long time before and have had all kinds of sexual experiences. But when they wish to get married, they go after a young, virgin girl. These young women either want to come out of Iran at any price or they are innocent teenagers who look for a nice man and a comfortable home abroad. But they are often badly treated. Afraid of losing them, husbands force them to stay at home, [and] don't give them permission to have a social life or follow English courses, which is the key element to their adaptation process. But sooner or later, they find our address and come to see us for a possible separation or divorce.

But the main problem these women are confronted with is their dependent status in the host country. Consequently, they tolerate their husbands' assaults as long as they can. In England since 1996, because of activities of refugee associations, women asylum-seekers have gained the right to be heard as well as men, and their status is no longer dependent on their husband's. But most Iranian women prefer to stay dependent on their husbands so as to be able to travel to Iran. If they ask for a divorce, they can no longer return.

And even if their situation permits a demand for divorce, they must go through a number of bureaucratic and time-consuming procedures demanded by government agencies and the Iranian embassy, which will not grant a woman a divorce without the consent of her husband. Consequently, these women can no longer go back to Iran, since they cannot leave the country without their husband's permission. And if they have children, the situation becomes even more complicated (see M. Kar 2003 for more details).

New Family Networks

The Iranian Revolution and the immigration of numerous Iranians into the West have split up family networks altogether. But during nearly three decades of exile, these émigrés have encouraged other family members to immigrate, and have helped them to settle. As a consequence, new family networks have been constructed, in time giving birth (through mixed marriages) to a multinational kinship system outside the home. These networks operate beyond national borders and are quite functional for exchanges regarding jobs, housing or housing-guarantee offers. For example, the findings of the London survey show that Iranians mostly resort to relatives for help and support (47 per cent) and spend their leisure time with them (50 per cent).

Among the new generation, face-to-face relations have been replaced, due to long distances, by electronic connections. This new medium seems especially suited to the needs of communities in exile, as it has the capacity to facilitate ongoing communications between the scattered diasporas and the homeland. Being relatively inexpensive, uncontrolled and easy to operate, it has become an appropriate means for Iranian youth to get in touch and maintain a sort of solidarity, in spite of their differences.

Nevertheless, family reunions are also taking place at regular intervals in countries such as Turkey and Cyprus, which are convenient for all family members and do not require visas for Iranian nationals. This is a way to get to know the newcomers with hyphenated nationalities and double nicknames.

A series of genealogies of several kinship networks that I have gathered show how widely scattered some Iranian families have become. They also reveal a considerable number of mixed marriages. In some of my cases, members of the kinship network consist of up to 17 nationalities living in four continents and eleven countries.

The Temptation to Repatriate

During my investigations in France in 1985, practically all respondents said they had left Iran unwillingly. But to the follow-up question 'Do you intend to stay here or go back home eventually?' they all responded that they would like to return to Iran, but only when there was a change in the country's socio-political conditions. However, after three decades of exile, they have lost that 'home fever' and have become more realistic. The following extract of an interview with a middle-aged, well-educated man talking about his attitude towards his family in emigration reflects the situation of Iranians of the first and second generations in exile:

> We don't want to go back any more. The only feeling that I have concerns my old [memories], which are too distant and colourless by now. All the people I knew are either dead or in exile. My sons have the same feelings. They have kept family relations alive. They are in constant contact with their grandmother and their aunts in Iran, and they come visit us quite often. When British citizenship was offered to us, my second son, who was ten years old by then, had hidden our passports and was screaming in tears that we were Persians and should stay that way. But by now, after nearly two decades, they are both well integrated in English society and speak to one another in English. As for us, all our close friends are Persians and we have created our microcosm, keeping our culture and identity intact.

And, finally, it is good to consider a second opinion. Here is the testimony of a woman who came to England 25 years ago with her child:

> One must become established somewhere, leave the nomadic situation and grow roots. Iran is my motherland but here is the country I have chosen to live in. When I obtained English nationality, I was really happy. I respect my new identity and I am grateful to English people who have provided me with this opportunity. Many won't express such an opinion. They are not even willing to hear it. But I have made my decision sincerely. For Iran, I am ready to do anything I can if

need be, but I had to make up my mind once and for all about where I belong. I said to myself, this society has accepted me with all my troubles and has given me opportunities. If a foreigner came to Iran, he would have to go through a lot more hardships than I did. I know how lucky I am. I strongly feel that I am cosmopolitan and multicultural. I assume that I am an Iranian, a Muslim, and an English citizen. I am modern and I think that British Muslims should come out of their marginal attitudes and be modernized.

References

Anton, M. and Scotto, J.C. (1989), 'Indispensable aventure de l'adolescence', *Revue Migrations Santé*, No. 78.

Athias, F. (1998), 'Evaluating Diaspora: Beyond Ethnicity?', *Sociology* 32(3): 557–580.

Darvishpour, M. (1999), 'Violence against women in the family', in V. Nassehi-Behnam (ed.) *Nimeye Digar*, Vol II, No. 5, 178–192 (in Persian). (Chicago: Midland Press).

Hosseini-Kaladjahi, H.(1997), *Iranians in Sweden*. (Stockholm: Gotab AB Publisher).

Iranian Community Centre Annual Report (March 1988), London.

Kandyoti, D. (1991), *Women, Islam and the State*. (Basingstoke: Macmillan).

Kar, M. (2003), *A Research About Violence Against Women in Iran* (in Persian). (Tehran: Rochangaran Publisher)

Khosravi, S. and Graham, M. (1997), 'Home is where you make it: Repartition and diaspora culture among Iranians in Sweden', *Journal of Refugee Studies* 10(2): 115–133.

Mahdi, A.A. (1999), 'Trades and places: Change in gender roles within the Iranian immigrants', *Critique* 15, 51–75.

Mahtab, M. (1999), 'Women Speak', in *Nimeye Digar*, op. cit., 153–178.

Nassehi-Behnam, V. (1985), 'Iranian Family: Change and Continuity', *Current Anthropology* 5, 557–563.

Nassehi-Behnam, V. (2005), 'Transnational Identities: A generational study of Iranian immigrants in France', Osaka, JCAS Symposium, Series 17, 251–267.

Nassehi-Behnam, V. (2005), 'Domestic violence: Iran and Afghanistan', *Encyclopedia of Women and Islamic Cultures* (EWIC), Vol. II, 117–119.

Shafiï, R. (1992), 'The situation of female refugees in England between 1982 to 1992', *Ârash Review* No. 36–37, 30–32, (in Persian).

Spellman, K. (2004), 'Persian Community in Great Britain', *Encyclopaedia Iranica*, Vol. VI, 273–275. (New York: Bibliotheca Persica Press).

Spellman, K. (2004), *Religion and Nation: Iranian Local and Transnational Networks in Britain, Forced Migration*. (Oxford: Berghahn Books).

Taleghani, M. et al. (1994*), Portrayal of Women in Primary School Text Books Before and After the Revolution.* (Paris: UNESCO publication).

Chapter 7

Changing Spousal Relations in Diaspora: Muslims in Canada

Haideh Moghissi

In my opinion, women can adjust and adapt to the society, when they immigrate, better than men. I think men try to avoid adjusting and they cannot cope with the changes in the society and environment (Iranian female in Toronto).

I believe that [my husband and I] get even closer to each other in Canada as we only have each other here… (Palestinian woman in Toronto).

Introduction

Muslims are relatively new in Canada. Before 1961, the Muslim community in Canada constituted a small minority. The rate of immigration from Muslim-majority countries was also negligible. Beginning in the 1980s and particularly in the 1990s, the picture changed. Over 66 per cent of the population of Muslim cultural background immigrated to Canada between 1991 and 2001, and it is now the fastest growing religious and ethnic group in the country, as within only a decade this population had grown by 128.9 per cent. According to the 2001 Census of Canada, when for the first time religious identification was included in census questions, about 2 per cent of the total Canadian population, or 579,600 individuals, identified themselves and their children as Muslims. Of the total Muslim population, only 137,800, or about 23 per cent, are Canadian-born, making the vast majority foreign-born; over 91 per cent of Muslims 15 years of age and over are first-generation Canadians; about 7.7 per cent are second-generation and only 0.8 per cent are third-generation. Almost all of the Muslims in the country live in major urban areas. Their median age is 28, well below the Canadian median of 37. The vast majority (59 per cent) are married, and there are more Muslim men (over 52 per cent) than women.[1]

Muslims in Canada are well-educated. While about 25 per cent of persons 15 years of age and over have less than high-school education, over 28 per cent have a university degree. This figure is higher for men, with 33 per cent, compared to women, with about 23 per cent. Over 26,000, or 6.4 per cent, have a master's degree,

---

1 The statistical profile of Muslims in Canada in this section is taken from Diaspora, Islam and Gender Project, York University (2005), *Selected Communities of Islamic Cultures in Canada: Statistical Profiles.*

and over 6,000 have earned a doctorate. Given a relatively youthful population, 22 per cent of self-identified Muslims 15 and older attend school on a full-time basis, and 7.4 per cent attend school part-time. The distribution of school attendance is more or less similar for both sexes, with women having a slightly higher level of full-time attendance (23 per cent). Muslim women's level of schooling, while lower than Muslim men, is nonetheless quite high. Over 44,000, or about 23 per cent, have a university degree. This percentage is much higher than the national level of university-educated women in Canada, which is 14.8 per cent. It is also higher than the related percentages for women of a few other religions, including Roman Catholic (13.4 per cent), United Church (14.2 per cent), and Sikh (16 per cent). However, while this percentage is comparable to others, including Hindus (23.8 per cent), it is much lower than Jews (36.3 per cent). Overall, the level of post-secondary education of Canadian Muslims, both male and female, is higher than the national level. Despite a high level of post-secondary education (almost double the national average), however, Canadian Muslims have a very high level of unemployment, which is almost twice the national average of 7.4 per cent. The 14.3 per cent Muslim unemployment level is much higher than the percentages of all other major religions, for example: Roman Catholics 7.4 per cent; Baptists 7.1; Buddhists 8.9; Jews 5.3; and Hindus and Sikhs about 9.5 per cent each. The unemployment rate of Muslim women, despite their relatively high level of education, is 16.5 per cent.

Family as the Zone of Comfort or Conflict[2]

As in other parts of the world, Canadian Muslims are not a homogenous or unified group, and the level of their participation in social and political life and adaptation to the civic and cultural norms of the country differ from one community to another. This reality makes futile any generalization about Muslim experience in Canada, for the social and economic conditions of life both pre- and post-migration and the levels of attachment to the cultural norms and values of the original country play an important role in the process of adjustment and the level of integration.

---

2   Throughout this chapter the identifier 'Muslim' is used to refer to persons self-identified as such in the survey, for practical reasons, to avoid using identifiers such as 'people from Muslim cultures', 'individuals from Muslim-majority countries', 'people from Muslim Middle East' and the like. One must emphasize that the identity markers 'Muslim' or 'Islamic', rigidly assigned to diaspora coming from Muslim societies, have far-reaching, practical consequences for the day-to-day life of the population. Their immediate impact, albeit not obvious to outsiders, is to promote cultural and social exclusion and inevitably leads to discrimination in equal access to jobs, housing, schooling and health-care facilities, diminishing the sense of entitlement, guaranteed under Canada's Charter of Rights, that is taken for granted by other citizens. This chapter draws upon my 2009 monograph.

Until a decade ago, one could more confidently argue that age would also define the level of attachment of Muslims in the West to their formative cultural practices and mores and, hence, the level of integration. But the growing radicalization of a relatively large number of second- and third-generation individuals among the Muslim populations cautions us from such generalizations. Nonetheless, it is safe to argue that the younger generations gradually become more selective in engaging with their ancestral cultures than the first generation, and that they are more prepared to integrate into the social and cultural practices of the larger society. The extreme cases of violent clashes between parents and children, particularly girls, with a few cases ending in a tragic loss of lives, might speak to generational differences in the level of separation from the old cultures.[3]

Nonetheless, for Muslims as for other marginalized migrant populations, internal factors, most notably family and spousal relations, play a crucial role in their sense of psychological security and confidence, as well as their will to adjust to or resist adjustment to new ways of life. Family can represent either a comfort zone or a conflict zone to the individuals involved. It depends how the inevitable changes associated with spousal responsibilities, interactions within the conjugal unit and perceptions of legal rights and obligations arising from life in the new country are processed and absorbed. These changes can turn into a continuing source of contestation and add to the burden of adjustment to the new socio-cultural milieu or they can assist the process.

Studies of various migrant communities point to the negative impact on spousal relations of the day-to-day struggles of life in the new country, compounded by the absence of the support network of extended family and friends, social isolation and a sense of loneliness. It is suggested that men and women process the experience of migration and resettlement differently, and that these differences become a continuous source of tension within the diasporic family (Grmela 1991; Nassehi-Behnam 1991; Kocturk 1992; Afshar 1994; Eastmond 1993; Buijs 1993; Moghissi 1999; Moghissi and Goodman 1999; Hojat, Shapurian, Foroughi et al. 2000; Ashrafi and Moghissi 2002; Husain and O'Brien 2000, among many). The idea, also discussed by Vida Nassehi-Behnam in Chapter 6 of this book, is that women, generally, more readily, or at least less painfully, accept the reality of relocation and try to adjust to it. Once the reality of exile and the need to adjust to new conditions has been established, it is argued, women may welcome the change from strictly controlled gender roles within the family and the reduced pressures coming from the extended family and from society at large. These ideas also informed the research project among the four communities with whom we worked.

---

3   The most highly publicized and debated case was that of Aqsa Pervez, a young Muslim girl in Toronto who was killed in December 2007 by her father in a rage over her refusal to wear hijab. Another case was the July 2009 drowning of three young girls and their stepmother, all of Afghan origin, in Kingston, Ontario, over one of the girls' conduct, which the family had found contrary to their moral expectations.

Examining changing family dynamics within these groups, we focused on exploring two major interrelated questions. The first was whether men are indeed more predisposed than women to be stuck in nostalgia for their known and familiar culture, with its clear-cut gender roles and sex and age hierarchies, and, if so, whether religion plays a disproportionate role in supplying energy to these conservative attitudes. The assumption was that among migrant populations, women's and men's attitudes within the family unit can be different in dealing with the stresses of the migration and resettlement process. Many men, particularly those who have left a productive and rewarding life behind and are unable to pick up from where they left off or start a different but equally satisfying life in the new country, experience nostalgia and embrace a glorification of the past life and cultural values and practices that is in some cases also expressed in a turn or return to religion.

Our second area of investigation posed the question, what are the social, economic and cultural pressures that can lead individuals to barricade themselves behind ideas of 'cultural difference' and 'Islamic tradition', resisting the changes, particularly in gender roles, which the new setting demands? The idea was that a decline in the family's socio-economic status or cultural pressure felt from the larger society can become sources of tension at home.

What the statements of men and women from the four communities illustrated first and foremost was the significant diversity in their perspectives and social values even though they all originated in countries dominated by Islamic laws and religious practices. That is, challenges to older ideas seemed indeed to be processed differently, not only by women and men, but also in different communities and in different settings. But these differences may reflect the influence of external factors that help frame people's images of proper gender relations and gender roles. In other words, efforts to return to a pre-given culture, with an associated social conservatism that is often justified through religion, are not the inherited values of Muslim men. They rather might be a reaction, at least partially, to the greater difficulty they have in adjusting to a new society or new conditions of life. That is, the difficulty of finding satisfying jobs in the new country and the pressures arising from normative expectations regarding gender roles are stressors that can take away men's sense of masculine authority and power within the family, disrupting the clear-cut gender roles that are assumed to be part of the 'Muslim culture.' Hence, conservatism in the family reflects not only the ways females and males traditionally relate to each other in their original cultures, but also stems from how readily the larger society makes room for immigrant women and men.

A few examples from oral interviews and focus groups illustrate the diversity of views and their underlying reasons.

> I believe the unsuccessful marriages of immigrants all have their roots in the past
> and back home. For example in Iran, because of the social situation, women put
> up with a lot of things. This is either because of their children or because of their
> financial dependence on their husbands. However, the Canadian government

supports single mothers. Other than this, some women fall for the superficial freedom that they see in the Western world. These are the women who were too limited and felt too much pressure in their family in Iran. In my opinion, women can adjust and adapt to the society when they immigrate better than men. I think that men try to avoid adjusting and they cannot cope with the changes in the society and environment (Iranian female in Toronto).

With my husband, thank God, it is a special relation. My husband is a very understanding person. But life in Canada is totally different than our life back home. There are no changes in our relationship since we moved to Canada, but there are many things that we need to get used to. I believe that we even get closer to each other in Canada, as we only have each other here. Our relation with our children is also fine (Palestinian female in Toronto).

I met my husband in Afghanistan. He always felt good here despite the women's freedom. Compared to some other Afghan men, he is very open and wise. I once asked him, if Afghanistan went back to a normal, stable and peaceful country, would he go to settle there with his family? He replied that returning to one's homeland was very desirable but the womenfolk would never accept to return after living in Canada, and returning to traditional women's roles after getting the taste of a modern women's lifestyle such as getting access to disposable diapers for a baby and such other luxuries (Afghan female in Montreal).

I met [my wife] in the first term of our graduate studies in Tehran; we were class-mates... I think I should not have married at all because I am a very selfish person; I have a high self-esteem and this is not good for marital relationships. In marriage, both should step back a bit. But she is very tolerant and generally is a person who sacrifices a lot for her family [sisters and brothers] as well as for me. I expect things to be taken care of at home. I know she goes out at the same time as I do and comes back with me, but cooking, for instance, must be done everyday; I don't eat leftovers. Some guys eat whatever is ready to eat. Not me... I know this is hard for her and she is as tired as I am but this is something I had told her from day one. I have tried to be good, and I have changed a lot I think. I no longer expect 100 per cent of her; but I do expect 50 to 60 per cent (Iranian male in Montreal).

My husband, deep down inside, is very traditional, even though on the surface he seems very integrated [into Canadian society]. If he had been more Westernized, I would have had to adjust to that too. My husband says that before, when he was a student, he was not that much middle-ground. He was a lot more Westernized. [Her husband did his undergraduate study in the US before he moved to Canada.] He says that he's older now, so his thinking has changed... We try not to be influenced by outside things. The society here is very different from

our [Pakistani] values. We try to keep our values because we want to raise our
children in a Pakistani atmosphere (Pakistani female in Montreal).

The question that would follow here is the influence of factors such as levels of
education, job satisfaction and the extent of religious commitment, as well as the
patterns of gender relations in the country of origin and in Canada, in the changing
dynamics of family and spousal relationships.

Relocation and the 'Quality' of Marital Life

The majority of those surveyed had married in their country of origin. In all four
communities the number of married women was much higher than that of men.
But sharp differences among the communities were observed in relation to the
question, 'Who decided whom you should marry?' Amongst Iranians, over 55
per cent had chosen their partners themselves. The figure was much lower for the
other communities (over 21 per cent of Palestinians, about 13 per cent of Afghans,
and 9 per cent of Pakistanis).

Declaring the existence of stress or violence within the family, or admitting to a
'low' quality of spousal relationship, also varied among the four communities, and
particularly between males and females. This may be related to real differences
between males and females in the experience of spousal relations across the
communities, or to differences in the willingness to declare openly a stressful
relation. Thus, males in each group were less likely than females to report a 'low'
quality of relationship; in each of the communities, comparing percentages for
males with those for females showed the existence of a substantial gender gap. As
an example, a 'low' quality of relationship is reported by 26 per cent of Afghan
females, but only by about 15 per cent of Afghan males, by 22 per cent of Iranian
females but only 16 per cent of Iranian males, and by 15 per cent of Pakistani
females but only 9 per cent of Pakistani males. Apart from these gender differences,
in comparing data for both males and females across communities, differences by
ethnicity are also substantial. Pakistanis and Palestinians are consistently more
positive than Afghans and Iranians about their marriages.

Males and females in the four communities did report increased tension
compared with what they had experienced in their countries of origin. None of
these groups had found family life less stressful in Canada – at least, no group
was prepared to testify to stress levels in their home countries that matched what
they had experienced in the new country. But tension estimated by males was
always less than the tension reported by females, fitting with the greater tendency
of males to report a 'high' quality spousal relationship. For example, about 15 per
cent of Afghan males remembered 'much' or 'some' tension in the home country,
compared with 29 per cent who report this in Canada; likewise, for Palestinian
males, the figures have gone up rapidly from 22 per cent to 46 per cent. Among
the groups reporting smaller differences, figures have gone from 31 per cent to

38 per cent for Afghan females; from 32 to 46 per cent for Palestinian females; from 44 to 55 per cent for Pakistani females; from 49 to 57 per cent for Iranian males; and from 63 to 65 per cent for Iranian females. Here again, differences in reporting tension between the spouses were observed among the four communities. Generally, Iranians, male and female, report a higher level of tension in Canada, followed by Pakistanis and Palestinians.

The difference between the surveyed communities in experiencing (or reporting) marital tension can be explained in several ways. It can be attributed, on one hand, perhaps, to the existence of greater inhibition in some cultures despite the existence of much public discussion in Canada about family tension and violence, an openness that is expected to make it easier for the individual living in a similar situation to speak out. It is also possible that the worries about more practical or material life-concerns does not allow spouses to just 'sit back' and think about the quality of their marital life, unless actual physical violence is involved. On the other hand, given that a much larger percentage of persons in some communities come from a more educated, middle-class background, the higher expectations for gender equality and greater emphasis on individual autonomy in Canada may stimulate greater sensitivity among members of this group to problems within the family, and thus an increase in showing feelings and speaking of tension. What is sure in either case is the reality of a more pressured and stressful way of life in Canada compared with life in the home county.

The last interpretation is supported by the following statements by Pakistani males:

>...Then she had the opportunity to work at a women's centre, and they are mostly feminists there. So, to be in the midst of these feminists, and then to have that background [of staying at home and raising children], I think her attitude changed. For example, take the issue of changing my daughter's diapers when she was a baby. It would feel odd to me to do this; this is not what men do. But my wife would say, 'Why won't you do this? You're her father. You should do it. Everyone does it here.' In traditional [Pakistani] culture, a man can take care of his son, but not his daughter. For the daughter, the mother is there; she'll take care of these things. This used to be very difficult for me to deal with. I was thinking, where have I come [to, here in Canada]? What kind of country is this? Everything has totally changed. So that is how there has been a change (Pakistani male in Toronto).

>With regard to how we live together, yeah, we are equals... [From my wife's perspective], it is like, my world is separate from your world. I will respect your world, and you respect mine. If I feel like it, I will respect it, if I don't, then I won't, because I am a different person. You can't impose anything on me. If you like something, it doesn't necessarily mean that I like it too. This was very difficult for me to digest, because how could I like something and she not like it? It was just assumed that the things I like, she will like them too,

wherever I go, she will go with me; she is my wife, she is part of me... This is where we have clashes. That concept of oneness that we have [in Pakistan], it disappears here. Here they have more of a concept of individuality (Pakistani male in Montreal).

As for the substantial differences in tension reported between males and females, one might conclude that there is a gender difference in terms of what constitutes tension or violence – something not specific to these populations. Also, a very rosy view of the spousal relationship is given by Pakistani and Afghan males. For example, to get a more detailed view of the specific tensions that develop within spousal relationships, respondents were asked about six aspects of their marriage: (1) how often they argued with their partner; (2) the difficulty with which partners 'solve problems when they arise'; (3) whether arguments 'ever resulted in actual physical violence'; (4) whether the arguments ever made her or him 'frightened' by what the partner 'says or does'; (5) whether the respondent was ever 'insulted' by the spouse, and; (6) whether the spouse 'made fun' of their 'actions or opinions.' Only 2 per cent of Pakistani and 5 per cent of Afghan men thought the relationship with their partners was very tense, the lowest estimates among the males interviewed. Presumably, the factors of nostalgia and of wanting to protect an idealized image of one's personal life seem to be at stake here. Should we conclude that where tension exists in the country of origin, it continues or perhaps increases as a result of dislocation and relocation, but that if relations are relatively amicable, they survive the pressures of migration? Perhaps. In other words, the roots of the problem may have already existed in the home county and are only amplified in the new country. The three following statements suggest that new stresses in Canada may help crystallize a difficult situation and the push for a resolution, or perhaps also that the changed legal environment makes a resolution possible:

Physical violence continued even after [our] arrival in Canada... When we were both working it became harder and harder to live together. My husband did not want to take care of the house or his family. I only called the police once and that was when he wanted to return home after being away for two weeks. He wanted the key to our car but I refused to give it to him and asked him to go. He forced himself in and wanted to beat me. I called the police and explained the situation [and they] in turn asked him to go away and leave me [alone]. That was the only time (Afghan woman in Montreal).

He was 12 years older than me. We didn't have a good relationship with each other. Tension, fighting, and beatings started immediately after the marriage. I knew that he had relationships with other women... After a while, I planned to come to Canada somehow and get [a] divorce... I got the Canadian divorce, not the *shari'a* one (Iranian woman in Toronto).

My fiancé moved to Canada a few months before me because his paperwork was ready sooner. During this time, I got the chance to think about my future and about my decision to marry this guy. I realized that he was not the right guy for me, and when I came to Canada, after a series of long fights and arguments, we finally broke up and went our separate ways (Iranian woman in Toronto).

Noting differences among female responses from each community in reports of 'happy' marriages, the experience of spousal tension and claims about sharing in decision-making, can we assume that in some communities more than in others there is a tendency to cover up difficulties or to keep silent about abuse or even ordinary troubles? Would admitting failure in marriage for a religious person from a tightly knit community be seen as somehow admitting to a failure in following prescribed religious obligations or even to an incipient breakdown of authority? Perhaps there is too much at stake in relations of intimacy to admit, even to oneself, that one is in a difficult or unhappy situation. Again, this is not a phenomenon unique to immigrants or to people from the Middle East. But given the political situation, the denial may be more stubbornly internalized as a protective shield as the couple, deprived of broader family ties, draws together because it feels socially isolated and vulnerable. The following testimonies are instructive in this regard:

I believe that [my husband and I] get even closer to each other in Canada as we only have each other here… We both believe that it is really hard to raise children in this country, as they have too much freedom. We do not want our children to sink into the Canadian culture (Palestinian woman in Toronto).

Our relationship is good. Since we are alone here and there are no other relatives around us, we lean on each other and we are much closer than before (Iranian woman in Toronto).

The refusal to acknowledge or report the existence of tension and violence can be motivated by a desire to protect community 'honour'. The perception of both men and women may be that by making a 'private' matter public, they expose the whole community to more abusive perceptions and stereotypes. But often men know and take advantage of women's hesitance to report violent or other abusive acts, as described by a female respondent who was repeatedly physically abused:

He was under the impression that I would call the police, so he would threaten me about how the family and the community would view the situation, the gossip that would take place and [how] the family's name would be tarnished due to my complaints. So I hoped that things would change with time, but they got worse, and it became too much for me to bear. So my husband left home and I did not stop him from leaving (Afghan woman in Montreal).

In fact, the need for community approval may affect many aspects of a woman's life, as reflected in this comment by another respondent:

> I would never accept my mother to marry again. She is young but there are many other young Afghan women that are widows, separated or in the same conditions as my mother that are not remarried. And even if she is special, I can't accept it. I have already given a [lot of] thought about it. Deeply, I would like her to remarry, but all my community will laugh at me and at us. My culture, my society does not allow it (Afghan youth in Montreal).

Education, Job Satisfaction and Spousal Relations

Dislocation and relocation might indeed create or accentuate tensions in the family. Yet we have observed gender and national-origin differences in experiences of family life and spousal relations or in willingness to give testimony about intimate relationships. It then follows that we need to examine the role played by external factors such as the respondents' class composition, levels of education or degrees of job satisfaction. To be sure, it is not unusual among ethnic minorities of different cultural backgrounds that a man feels the pressure of making a living in the new country at a job unbefitting his educational qualifications, and with fewer rewards. This economic decline, together with a loss of friends and social status, can provoke a deep emotional vulnerability, making him more dependent on family members, and particularly on his wife. In such a situation, the wife is expected to provide the previously expected domestic services along with, possibly, holding a job herself and catering to the man's wounded ego (Moghissi and Goodman 1999).

In our sample, not only did the respondents' levels of education in their respective countries of origin differ but also the education they had obtained in the new country. Some individuals did not augment their education in the new country, while others pursued post-secondary degrees at a college or university. Levels of education did seem to have an impact on the quality of spousal relations. For example, Iranian men and women with university degrees or higher report a 'high' quality of relationship, and the same is also true for the small number of Afghan males with Canadian degrees. Those with more education also tend to claim less tension at home, whatever is, in fact, the reality of the situation. This is the case for Afghan, Iranian, and Pakistani men and women, amongst whom those with degrees are consistently less likely to report 'high' tension than those without degrees. As well, there seems to be a correlation between obtaining a degree in one's country of origin and claims of a 'high' level of sharing in decision-making and household responsibilities.

Perhaps the most plausible explanation for this educational advantage is that those with degrees are more likely to obtain better jobs and a better economic status, and this in turn may contribute to a better spousal relationship, reducing tension and helping to foster equality in decision-making. However, such respondents represent a more privileged section of their communities, since the percentages obtaining a university degree in Canada are relatively small, and even those with degrees from their home countries may encounter difficulties when their credentials are not formally recognized and thus have difficulties in finding a good job. That is why despite high levels of post-secondary educational accomplishment (almost double the national average), Muslims in Canada generally have a high rate of unemployment. This sobering situation raises the possibility that dissatisfaction in the workplace or the problem of finding work may produce a general feeling of unhappiness that is echoed or reinforced by circumstances at home.

As might be expected, males in the four communities who felt that their job made good use of their education brought a more positive and less insecure tone to the reports. As well, Iranian, Pakistani and Palestinian females who were satisfied with the payoff of education for work were also more likely to find their home situation to be of 'high' quality. The effect is particularly strong for Palestinians, where 48 per cent of males and 28 per cent of females who feel their current job is 'much better' or 'better' than the one in the old country record a 'high' quality of spousal relationship, as compared with only about 8 and 10 per cent, respectively, among males and females whose job is judged to be 'worse' or 'much worse' than in the country of origin. For other groups, the corresponding estimates for a 'high' quality of spousal relationship are similarly tied to job satisfaction: 37 per cent for Afghan males who feel their current job is 'much better' or 'better', as compared with 9 per cent who report their job is 'worse' or 'much worse' (a 28 per cent difference); 39 per cent for Pakistani males who feel their current job is 'much better' or 'better' as compared with 26 per cent who report their job is 'worse' or 'much worse' (a 13 per cent difference); and 35 per cent for Pakistani females who feel their current job is 'much better' or 'better' as compared with the 20 per cent who report their job is 'worse' or 'much worse' (a 15 per cent difference).

The tendency of respondents to report equal sharing in power and household responsibilities is also more apparent for those among most of our groups who feel they have been 'treated fairly' on the job. For example, among Iranian females, 21 per cent of those who feel they have been treated fairly on the job score 'high' on spousal sharing of decision-making and duties, compared to 4 per cent who feel they have not been fairly treated, a difference of about 18 per cent. Among Afghan males, 49 per cent of those who feel they have been treated fairly on the job score 'high' on spousal sharing of decision-making compared to 38 per cent who feel they have not been fairly treated, a difference of about 11 per cent. As well, claims to share in decision-making are more evident among those who feel they have a 'much better' or 'better' job in Canada in relation to their job at home. The strongest effect is noted for Afghan males, where we also see a link between claims about sharing in decision-making and the perception that one has a job that 'makes good use of one's education', reinforcing connections for them between a positive job experience, a 'high' quality of spousal relations and 'low' tension at home. For this group in particular, leaving a deprived and often dangerous situation, the move to Canada appears to have become a shared family project for social ascent; similar patterns are also observable for the Palestinians in our study. Other factors can also play a part in shaping relations between spouses. For example, among Iranians and especially Iranian males who have suffered losses in economic status in making the move to the new country, educational achievement by itself seems to be important in its effects on the experience at home, while the 'gender gap' between males and females in their perceptions of fairness in decision-making is relatively small.

Religion and Spousal Relations

The level of respondents' reliance on their faith is another factor that might affect claims about the quality of spousal relations, the existence or non-existence of tension at home and decision-making in relations. We should keep in mind, however, that we rely on respondents' claims about marital experience, not on direct observations of behaviour.

Generally, the high scores on religious identification and religious practice are connected to the tendency to claim a 'high' quality of spousal relationship, and this claim is always stronger for males than for females. For example, 37 per cent of Afghan males who said they were 'strongly committed' to their faith reported a 'high' quality relationship as compared with 10 per cent of those who identified themselves as 'secular'. The percentages were 63 per cent as compared with 24 per cent for Palestinian males self-identified in those categories.

These data can be read in several ways, beginning with the recognition that communities of Muslim cultural background are remarkably different in their identification with religion. For example, it is possible that the 'happy' religious couple, fulfilling family duties they conceive of devoutly as religious prescriptions, may feel genuinely happier in their marriage, even though they experience more spousal tension in Canada than they did at home. For the 'strongly committed' man, the desired state would be one in which he feels secure, even if under pressure, while for the woman, it would mean accepting traditional ways without criticism. In a more active version reflecting such an attitude, the couple would go beyond the mere performance of ritual, trying to find in their beliefs and practices some degree of compensation for the demanding pace and ordinary troubles of life in the new country. This would mean 'working at' and nourishing the family relationship (or some ideological notion of it) which, for them, is seamlessly bound to religious devotion. However, it is also possible that they do not feel happy at all, but feel compelled to hide the truth about their relationship from themselves and from everyone else, denying major or minor tensions. To do otherwise, in their minds, would be an act of disloyalty to the faith and to the community of believers, and would stain their reputation.

The general conclusion is that claims to 'happiness', subjective as they may be, can be interpreted in a variety of ways, keeping in mind the complexity of measuring 'happiness' in any case, given that the term is generally an over-used and vague concept and that it tends to be based on context. Claims about one's 'happiness' can be closely bound to ideas and ideals concerning class, gender and culture. So we have approached the notion of 'happiness' cautiously in this study. We can assume, however, that to admit to having a troubled relationship is more acceptable among those who have a smaller stake in protecting their standing as Muslims in the community. Even so, this does happen – indeed, with substantial frequency but more among religiously committed females (including Pakistani women) than among males. By contrast, secular respondents, both male and female, are not subject to these religious obligations and thus are freer to describe what they feel regarding problems in their marriages. For them, home, religious piety and personal respectability are not so firmly fused.

Conclusions

The data on spousal relations in this study firmly confirm the flaws of essentializing perceptions when it comes to people of Muslim cultural background. Individuals in the four communities in this study show a remarkable lack of homogeneity in their self-identification and in their perceptions about their positions within the society and in the family. Indeed, the differences among the four communities in Canada challenge the appropriateness of the notion of a homogeneous 'Muslim' diaspora, pressing upon us the need to interrogate carefully the political import of the term and to ask why, how, and under what circumstances these particular diasporic groups are formed in the West. The findings also support the claim that external socio-economic factors are significant in shaping perceptions of one's place in the world. And despite gender differences in responses to questions regarding quality of spousal relations or the existence or non-existence of tension within the family, the data did not support the idea that there would be greater opportunities for women in the West. In the end disappointment on this score may have had a powerful impact on their readiness to confront existing structures and relations that are familiar and thus more secure than the unknown and challenging conditions associated with change. It also militates inevitably against women's self-perception and independent thinking. The fact that respondents in our survey who report tension and unhappiness in their marriage still said they would avoid divorce is quite instructive here. This must ring a bell for policy-makers and non-governmental organizations whose focus is the promotion of gender awareness, gender equality, and women's well-being that without providing actual, tangible and accessible social services and opportunities for economic independence for marginalized women, they cannot be convinced and encouraged to resist harmful masculine cultural practices within the family or ethnic community.

References

Afshar, H. (1994), 'Muslim women in West Yorkshire: growing up with real and imaginary values amidst conflicting views of self and society', in H. Afshar and M. Maynard (eds) *The Dynamics of 'Race' and Gender: Some Feminist Interventions*. (London: Taylor & Francis).

Ashrafi, A. and Moghissi, H. (2002), 'Afghans in Iran: asylum fatigue overshadows Islamic brotherhood', *Global Dialogue* 4: 4.

Buijs, G. (ed.) (1996), 'Introduction', in *Migrant Women Crossing Boundaries and Changing Identities*. (Washington, D.C.: BERG).

Eastmond, M. (1996), 'Reconstructing life: Chilean refugee women and the dilemmas of exile', in G. Buijs (ed.) *Migrant Women: Crossing Boundaries and Changing Identities*. (Oxford and Washington, D.C.: BERG).

Flynn, K. and Crawford, C. (1998), 'Committing "race treason": battered women and mandatory arrest in Toronto's Caribbean community', in K. Bonnycastle and G.S. Rigakos (eds) *Unsettling Truths: Battered Women, Policy, Politics, and Contemporary Research in Canada*. (Vancouver: Collective Press).

Grmela, S. (1991), 'The political and cultural identity of second generation Chilean exiles in Quebec', in S.P. Sharma and A.M. Irvine (eds) *Immigrant and Refugees in Canada: A National Perspective on Ethnicity, Multiculturalism and Cross-cultural Adjustment*. (Saskatoon, Saskatchewan: University of Saskatchewan).

Kocturk, T. (1992), *A Matter of Honour. Experience of Turkish Women Immigrants*. (London and New Jersey: Zed Press).

Moghissi, H. (1999a), 'Away from home: Iranian female diaspora in Canada', *Journal of Comparative Family Studies*, 30: 2.

Moghissi, H. and Goodman, M.J. (1999), '"Cultures of violence" and diaspora: dislocation and gendered conflict in Iranian-Canadian communities', *Humanity and Society: Journal of the Association for Humanist Sociology* (Special Issue on Gender and Violence) 23(4): 297–318.

Moghissi, H, Rahnema, S. and Goodman, MJ. (2009), *Diaspora by Design, Muslims in Canada and Beyond*. (Toronto: University of Toronto Press).

Nassehi-Behnam, V. (1991), 'Iranian immigrants in France', in A. Fathi (ed.) *Iranian Refugees and Exiles since Khomeini*. (Los Angeles: Mazda Publications).

Rahnema, S. (2005), *Selected Communities of Islamic Cultures in Canada, Statistical Profiles*, Toronto, Diaspora Islam and Gender Project/York University.

Chapter 8

Sexing Diaspora: Negotiating Sexuality in a Shifting Cultural Landscape

Fataheh Farahani

This chapter is about diaspora. Through an analysis of the narratives of first-generation Iranian women living in Sweden and by placing gender and sexuality at the centre of my attention, I seek to demonstrate how migratory experiences impact sexuality and how and in what ways sexuality is constitutive to migratory process. By discussing some of the key subjects raised by the interviewees, such as intimacy in the diasporic space, contradictory gender discourses, the dominating impacts of existing Orientalist stereotypes, and their sense of (be)longing or lack of (be)longing, I will examine how the women experience their sexuality through the simultaneous and sometimes contradictory discourses of dislocation, attachment, and relations in the diasporic space.

Diaspora and Diasporic Space

Increased migration across the world during the last decades has placed the concept of diaspora at the centre of theoretical and analytical scholarly discussions (Clifford 1999; Safran 1991; Vertovec 1997). This has made diaspora one of the most frequently debated terms within academic discussions on imposed dispersion, displacement, refugees, globalization, multiculturalism, (re)establishment of transnational communities and cultural politics. Consequently, 'diaspora' has turned into, as Paul Gilroy puts it, an 'overused but under-theorised' (1997:332) term. Furthermore, diaspora cannot stand as an epistemological category of analysis, separated and distinct from the stiflingly exchangeable intersectionality of race, class, gender and sexuality. A gendered understanding of the reasons, processes and consequences of migration, therefore, will undoubtedly offer new aspects for understanding and conceptualizing diaspora (Anthias 1998; Espín 1999).

While the word 'diaspora' literally means 'a scattering or sowing of seeds' or 'dispersion from,' which according to Avtar Brah (2002) implies a notion of centre, 'a "home" from where the dispersion occurs' (2002:181), the theoretical concept of diaspora challenges the discourses of fixed origins. By challenging the discourses of 'fixed origins', Brah not only defies the search for a genuine and authentic identity or unsullied glorious past, but also explains how 'the same' geographical place may stand for diverse histories and meanings. In her intersectional approach, not only do the circumstances of leaving play a central role but also important are the conditions of arrival and living. By focusing on the specificities of arrival and the existing social relations in the new circumstances, Brah introduces the concept of *diaspora space* in lieu of diaspora. According to her, the concept of *diaspora space* includes not only the immigrants and their descendants, but also those who are constructed and represented as local. Therefore, diasporic identities, as Brah declares, 'cannot be read off in a one-to-one fashion straightforwardly from a border positionality, in the same way that a feminist subject position cannot be deduced from the category "woman"' (2002: 207–8).

Sexuality and Intimacy in Diasporic Space

In spite of the relative newness of the Iranian diaspora, research on Iranian women and gender imbalance among Iranian families (with a handful of reflections on sexuality and sexual behaviour among other factors), has been the centre of several scholarly enquiries (Ahmadi Lewin 2001; Alinia 2004; Darvishpour 2003, which looked at Sweden; Mahdi 1999, 2001 which looked at the US; Nassehi-Behnam 1991, which looked at France; Shahidian 1999; Moghissi 1999, 2005, 2006, which looked at Canada; Bauer 1994, 1998, 2000, which looked at Germany and Canada).

The sample in my study consists of Iranian-born women who had left Iran after the 1979 Revolution. Most of the interviews were conducted in Persian except in the case of the youngest participants, who preferred to speak in Swedish. Except for one of the research participants, who was in her mid-twenties, all were between 38 and 51 years of age at the time of interviews. They had left Iran either on their own (in contrast to a generalized assumption that it is usually men who migrate first and that their partners join them later) or with their husbands and/or children. All the interviewees had lived in Sweden between 11 and 18 years at the time of the interviews. Except for the youngest participant, all were married when they came to Sweden. One woman was a widow who had lost her husband because of his political activities, and four had come to Sweden on their own (or with their children), with their husbands joining them later. Two of the participants came to Sweden by marrying a male already resident in Sweden.[1] Two women live with European men, five live alone or with their children, and one is attracted to both women and men. Except for her, all the other women who were asked whether or not they had any intimate relationships with women responded directly and shortly, 'No' (sometimes I didn't find it appropriate to pose this question). In general, my focus here will be limited to the women's narrations of heterosexuality.

The majority of the women I interviewed had undergone divorce proceedings in Sweden. As a result, at interview time, some lived with other men while others lived on their own or with their children. The experience of separation had not only made the meeting and entry of other men into their lives feasible, it had also given the

---

1   To see more on women's narration of marriage and divorce see Farahani 2007.

women the opportunity to reflect upon the differences between dating, approaching men and being intimate under new circumstances and previous experience(s) in Iran. Besides that, the very lengthy process of seeking and being granted asylum, and then waiting for family reunification, had resulted in the interviewee women living apart from their husbands and other family members. The asylum period furnished new options for both partners who were apart from each other for the first time for an uncertain period. Overall, the interviewees described the asylum/ reunification period as very demanding and stressful, yet a thought-provoking time of self-reflection. Subsequent relationships that some of the women had initiated were partly accountable for these newly emerging thoughts and concerns.

Several studies on the adjustment process of immigrants have demonstrated that, particularly in the early period of residency in a new country, most individuals seek assistance from other members of their communities (Bauer 2000; Moghissi 1999). The establishment of strong new bonds with people who have undergone similar processes can offer newcomers immense support and act as a reliable source of information. However, the desire to create a homogenous collective around a shared political and social commitment and cultural project may result in extensive social control within the communities (Lindqvist 1991). Sometimes these heterogeneous, newly established, constantly shifting communities position their members (particularly women) in increasingly vulnerable ways. For instance, some women stressed repeatedly that they had become deeply self-conscious about their new position – 'a young woman apart from her husband' and with or without children in a new society. Some became more (self-)policing than ever before about their behaviour, with whom they socialized and how they socialized.

Despite enthusiastic support from the newly established Iranian community, as 'a woman without male protection in a foreign land,' some of the interviewees felt constantly subjected to the judgment of others as well as to other men's unwanted advances. However, as Michael Foucault (1990a, 1990b) has shown, the exercise of disciplinary power involves the very corporeality of individuals to which it adheres. The self-imposed discipline not only protected women from being at the centre of communities' circulated gossips, but also provided them a sense of self-gratification. Through self-disciplining, the women received not only communal appreciation and acceptance but, due to the repetition of previously influential gender norms, helped to emblemize a newly (re)configured (re)presentation of the chaste and uncorrupted woman in a diasporic context. For some of the women, like Simin, this self-imposed discipline went to the extent that at the time of the interview – more than a decade after separation from her husband – and despite her wish, she had not engaged in any other intimate sexual relationship. She convinced herself that she should avoid intimate relationships as a compromise for having custody of the children. Simin's husband had demanded that she never date or marry another man if she wished to keep their children in her custody, yet Simin informed me that her husband was living with another woman and had children from this new relationship. Another woman, Farideh, had lived mostly with her children as a result of her husband's occupation. Because of her husband's frequent absences, Farideh had similar approach in regard to her behaviour while her husband was away. While emphasizing that she has never abused her husband's trust towards her, Farideh believed that her precautions had protected her from jeopardizing her (and her husband's) good name.

By selectively rejecting the prevailing 'home culture' (a constant source of disparity and heated discussion inside as well as outside the community), some other women had behaved in a different way (compared with Simin and Farideh) in their new diasporic settings. For instance, Nooshin, who acknowledged that she had never loved her ex-husband, shared with me that even prior to her arrival in Sweden she had already felt that all emotional bonds with her husband had broken down. She divulged that during her early residency in Sweden, while her husband was still in Iran, she was occupied fully with tackling her sexual urges. As her 'husband's legal wife,' Nooshin tried to keep herself 'untouched' until he joined her. 'But my body desired something else, and I couldn't overcome it,' she said. When questioned how it was possible to be unfaithful to someone that she had never loved, Nooshin asserted that she never felt she was disloyal to her husband. However, she explained that she frequently hovered between conflicting feelings when she started to engage in 'illegitimate' sexual interactions. On one hand, she could hear her own voice, berating her for being a 'licentious woman' acting immorally. On the other hand, she felt pleased, too. With contradictory feelings, she stated clearly:

> I understood that I was experiencing some of the things that I always wanted to do but never had the chance. And I thought, why shouldn't I? /.../

> So, my first relationship here was what in our culture is called nā-mashroe′ (illegitimate).

> You see, we carry this whole set of baggage with us... rābete-ye nā-mashroe′ (illegitimate relationship), bachche-ye harām-zādeh (illegitimate child), what else... eshgh-e mamnue′ (forbidden love) and so on.

Nooshin's discontent with her marital life and precarious commitment to what she considered a '[sexual] culture back home' – seemingly long before she left Iran – encouraged and prepared her to welcome new (sexual) experiences. When the opportunity emerged, she decided to respond to her desires rather than holding them back or limiting them to prescribed rules set by norms of family life. Such new relationships offered her new insights into her body and sexual desires, she declares. She also talks about conflicted feelings. Women's contradictory experiences and continuous oscillation of valuation and devaluation between good/bad, right/wrong, appropriate/inappropriate, acceptable/unacceptable, and dignified/undignified as revealed through their life narratives implies a *fragmented subjectivity* (Bloom 1998) rather than an uncomplicated, unified, rational subjectivity. According to Leslie Bloom, the modernist masculine notion of the human being considers 'fragmentation, conflict, ambiguity, messiness, mobility, border-crossings, and changes in subjectivity' (1998: 6) to be signs of weakness, instability and lack of an enviable, unified (masculine) self. Disengaging from the notion of a unified subject and taking up instead the co-existence of contradictory elements within a space or a person corresponds with Foucault's notion of heterotopia. By contesting the homogenous space of the unreal utopia, Foucault (1986) advocates such a space. According to him, all cultures and human communities constitute heterotopias that contain contrary sites. The contradictory sites of discourse are concurrently presented, contested and upturned. Obviously, there is no one single and homogenous heterotopia; rather, heterotopias are constantly shifting. Diasporic space and heterotopic space contain each other. By expressing discrepancies and contradictory feelings, another woman, Mehri, also portrayed the heterotopic space within which she struggled. By explaining how every step that she has taken has been shadowed by doubt and hesitation, she described the dilemma she had been experiencing as a result of navigating multiple cultural contexts:

> I have gone through lot of changes /.../. I cannot claim that it has been easy. I really suffered very much for where I stand today and who I am. I sacrificed many close emotional relationships for it. I even sacrificed the person I loved for it. But I did it.

> You know, it's not easy to be alone, a woman and an immigrant, too. First when you get here you're not familiar with how everything works in the society. Then, as soon as you learn a little bit, you decide to jump for it. You decide to change things quickly. Yet, you're all alone in this mess. It is tough. I think I was not made for such a tough life. /.../ but I managed it.

> Let me tell you about my situation as an immigrant woman. Within our community, particularly within the Kurdish community, I am not acknowledged as a person, in particular, as a woman. Most likely I am accepted because of my political capabilities. I am one of a few Kurdish women who are politically active. I have a lot of ideas and this is not always popular. Then, when you enter Swedish society, it's not any easier because I think they sometimes look at you and think you're just an ignorant, immigrant woman. They [the Swedish people] don't see me [in the same way] as they see a Swedish woman seeking equality.

Mehri's persuasive account of her predicament illustrates that, despite the complexities manifested in diasporic space, she is expected to operate according to predetermined patterns that come from all sides – from Iranian/Kurdish communities as well as from Swedish ones. In this condition, the construction of (ideal) femininity and sexuality intermingles with the contrasting models to those ideals across a variety of borders in intersecting and contradictory ways. Women's articulations of conflicting feelings and their constant attempts to create self-defining spaces show how simplistic the Orientalist's utopian (mis)interpretation of the 'suppressed Middle Eastern/Muslim woman' gaining the chance to turn into a 'liberated free woman' due to the influence of Western liberal culture truly is. The entangled paradoxical feelings articulated by women reveal nuanced negotiations rather than unsophisticated, straightforward, black-and-white revolt against tradition, religion, or patriarchy.

Contradictory and Simultaneous Gender Discourses

In addition to continuous socio-cultural comparisons and frequent navigations between past and present, the interviewees narrated plenty of stories about bumping up against dominant cultural stereotypes of themselves as 'Iranians,' 'Muslims,' 'immigrants' and 'Middle Eastern' women. They also bluntly distinguished a relationship with a 'Swedish' man from a relationship with an 'Iranian' man. At the time of the interviews, two of the women lived with ethnic European men, one with a Swedish man and one with a man from a country in central Europe. Two more had very short-term relationships with Swedish men in the early periods of their residency in the country; they both talked pleasantly about those experiences. However, due to their lack of proficiency in Swedish at that time and thus their limited ability to communicate with these boyfriends, in hindsight each woman had concerns in regards to her judgment. One of the women, Nooshin, expressed curiosity about Swedish men yet had never dated one due to her highly female-dominated working place.

In addition to the highly gender-segregated labour market in Sweden (Emerek et al. 2003[2]), which prevented Nooshin from meeting (Swedish) men at work (since the workplace is in general the most common site for many immigrants to meet and socialize with Swedish people), she attributed the hurdles for dating Swedish men to two other reasons. To begin with, Nooshin could not see herself being intimate with a man with whom she had to negotiate whose turn it was to pay the bill every time they went out for a coffee together. Distaste for the economic concerns within a relationship, as Nooshin and some other women pointed out, reflects what is perceived as the underlying problem in romantic relationships with ethnic Swedes, namely, lack of courtship. In other words, the women equate the 'exaggerated emphasis' on an equal (economic) division to be an expression of the absence of chivalrous behaviour amongst 'Swedish men.' Some associate the reluctance of 'Swedish' men to offer to pay their share of a date as part of what they see as an individualistic Swedish mindset, in contrast to an Iranian mindset of collectivity. Some of the interviewee consider the lack of

---

2   In their report 'Indicators on Gender Segregation,' Ruth Emerek et al. (2003) show data from the European Union that indicates high levels of gender segregation in Scandinavian countries. According to the report, while the gender segregated labour market in countries such as Greece and Italy is combined with women's low employment rates, in Scandinavia it is combined with high female employment rates. Despite established anti-discrimination legislation in Nordic countries, gender segregation across the labour market has grown horizontally (between different professions and industries) as well as vertically (hierarchically).

'chivalrous' behaviour to be a consequence of women's financial independence. While the perceived absence of courteous acts in Sweden made some women 'to feel less as a woman', some others said that they would feel completely patronized if a man initiated paying for them. Parvin, for example, thought a man's invitation to pay would eventually put a woman in an economically dependent and subordinated position. Needless to say, the positions that men and women occupy in this 'polite and respectful' heterosexual encounter are highly gendered, class-based and hierarchical. In sum, varying opinions as to what constituted courteous manners differentiated the women. While some women were interested in an 'old-fashioned' display of courteous manners, others conceded that the qualities of 'so-called romantic' manners were no longer appropriate. Yet, they all yearned for some gestures of politeness and respect as integral features in a romantic relationship.

In Karin Söderholm Lindelöf's (2006) study among young, well-educated Polish women who consider courtliness as a particularly 'Polish phenomenon', similar kinds of concerns are raised. By connecting love and sexuality to courtliness, Söderholm Lindelöf studies how those practices are gender-creating. The desire for receiving men's admiring attention, according to her, disciplines women to not only fulfill specific beauty standards, but also urges them to operate according to predefined gender norms that put women on an unequal playing field. So, what are considered to be 'romantic manners' represent an exhibition among many manoeuvres that recognize and acknowledge norms that are discursively constituted by gender. Therefore, those behaviours (re)create gender and are shaped by a *heterosexual dramaturgy* (Laskar 2005). This dramaturgy constructs the heterosexual desire(s) within the heterosexual matrix (Butler 1999: 45–100). Despite the multiplicity across different factors, such as culture, class, ethnicity and age, the heterosexual matrix is an apparatus that identifies the intelligibility of sex, gender and sexual norms and sexual identity. In doing so, heterosexual privilege, according to Butler, 'operates in many ways, and two ways in which it operates include naturalizing itself and rendering itself as the original and norm' (1998: 384). Without the intelligibility and governed acceptability of the heterosexual matrix, any articulation of sex and gender would be incomprehensible, because the gender identities are embodied within the heterosexual matrix. So, the manly, courteous behaviours for which some women yearn along with (male) admiration, and the positions that each occupies in courtliness as a (hetero)sexual practice and encounter, are only attainable and intelligible within the discourse of the heterosexual matrix.

Further, Nooshin mentions language barriers as a hindrance to intimacy with Swedish men. The inadequate ability to express herself verbally puts her in an awkward position, carrying many unarticulated thoughts and emotions. In a study on immigrant women's transformations of sexuality in the US, Oliva M. Espín (1999) noticed two reactions among women in regard to being intimate in a language other than their mother tongue. Like Nooshin, who expressed difficulty in being intimate in Swedish, some of the women in Espín's study declared that they 'cannot make love in English' (1999: 76). Espin's study also points out that often cultural values are profoundly intertwined with one's mother tongue. As one of the women in Espín's study explains: 'Spanish carries a lot of feeling. But it also carries shame. Sex words in Spanish are dirty' (1999: 88). I also found my interviewees tossed in Swedish words and avoided using Persian words anytime there was any connotation to sex and sexuality. Words like *hångla* (making out), *orgasm, ha sex* (having sex) are some of the Swedish terms often used by the women in the interviews. Seemingly, the use of the second language allows a topic that might have been taboo in the native language to be entertained in sensitive conversations. So, by facilitating a sense of verbal distance, the new language assists in veiling the mother tongue as it offers a new space to talk about what was/is regarded as taboo. What's more, it may also assist in discovering a new aspect of one's (sexual) identity while the burden of some cultural values becomes lighter. As one of the women whom Espín interviewed states, she 'discovered "her lesbian self" in English' (1999: 78). So, while the second language might limit some women's sexual and emotional experiences, it might also assist others in becoming unshackled from unwanted boundaries and cultural values.

Stereotypes on Watch

As well as 'inadequate' language skills, Nooshin (like other women) offers additional explanations as to why she finds it difficult to get (emotionally) close to Swedish (men). With a sigh, she says; 'You know, you [have to] spend [a] long time to clarify that I am not this, I am not that. You have to constantly explain yourself. You [have to] answer lots of "why," "how," "what for" [questions], and this troubles me a lot.' By explaining how every single encounter with a Swedish man (or woman) involves a lengthy recitation of her background, which then requires her to confront stereotyping prejudices, Nooshin's account indicates that fluency in language is perhaps not the most important obstacle to intimacy with Swedish men. The Orientalist construction of 'women from the Middle East/ Muslim women/veiled women' serves a dual function of presenting them either as the oppressed woman or as the exotic and sexually mysterious woman (which are not necessarily exclusive). Almost all the interviewee women narrated different tales about their daily interactions that reduced them to emblematic symbols of either victimhood and passivity, or of the exotic and erotic. This illustrates how the gendering and sexualizing of women contributes to the growth of a racialized/ ethnicized self within specific diasporic spaces. Therefore, sexual and racial differentiation and marginalization cannot be understood in isolation (Eng 2001).[3]

---

3   Obviously, the sexualization of women's bodies is not exclusive to Orientalist discourses. The same phenomenon is evident in Occidentalist discourses. In his historical overview of how European women were imagined in the first encounters Iranians had with Europeans, Iranian historian Mohamad Tavakoli Targhi (2001) explains how misogyny and

Through an exhaustive analysis of what she calls 'everyday racism', Philomena Essed (1990, 1996) calls the subtle racist expressions based on gender stereotypes gendered racism, indicating how men and women are racialized differently.

These observations draw attention to not only how colonial discourses have historically employed sexuality as the most prominent signifier for (re)presenting otherness, but also how racial distinctions are fundamentally arranged in gender terms (Stoler 1998). So, women are degraded not only as Oriental/colonial subjects but also in gender-specific ways. Some women shared with me how their Swedish lovers and partners have called them nicknames such as 'my little dark doll', 'my Eastern little dark girl', 'my Shahrzad', 'my Eastern storyteller',[4] and my 'exotic bird'. This racialized gendering of exoticized sexual submissiveness exacerbates the contradictory gender discourses. For example, while pointing to her hair, Mehri says: 'You know Swedish men who approach immigrant women are looking for an obedient woman, I really mean it. It seems this black hair signals submissiveness to their [the Swedish men's] brains'. Later, Mehri also explains how disappointed some Swedish men who had approached her became when they failed to find the compliant, dignified, and family-oriented woman whom they expected. Nor was she a skilful cook and housewife. So 'they left me almost the very first night!' she adds, laughing out loud. Nooshin also explains how her co-workers usually offer her 'positive remarks'. When I ask her what she means by 'positive remarks', she looks at me wittily and says, 'They think I am modern. They say I have become 'Swedish'. And we share a good laugh over Nooshin's co-workers' familiar comment.

Nooshin's co-workers' 'positive remarks' about her transformation into 'becoming Swedish' indicates how any 'independent' or 'progressive' thinking or behaviour that Nooshin exhibits stems from this notion of 'Swedishness'. She is seen as a subject only because she is perceived to have become a Western subject. Since women's oppositional practices in diasporic communities and in the Middle East are invisible and the women are marked as docile, submissive, passive victims of their (backward) culture (and of men), the general image of 'the Third World woman', as Chandra T. Mohanty (1998) suggests, is in terms of her object status. This denies Third World women agency and thereby grants only Western women the agent and subject position. Women from the Third World who fail to conform to the framework of Western expectations are then seen as Westernized. They are not 'real' Third World women. This myopic thinking suggests that only

---

ethnocentrism were the shared characteristics of both European and Persian narration of the *Other*. According to Tavakoli-Targhi, both Persians and Europeans constituted the body of the 'other' woman as a site of sexual and political imagination (2001: 61).

4 Numerous studies have discussed and shown the ongoing impact on gender and race stereotypes of *The Thousand and One Nights* (1995) and its main figure, the storyteller Shahrzad, as well as paintings of the Orient, particularly 'Oriental' women. For further discussion, see: *Gendering Orientalism: Race, Femininity and Representation* (Lewis 1996), *Rethinking Orientalism: Women, Travel and the Ottoman Harem* (Lewis 2004) and *Scheherazade Goes West. Different Cultures, Different Harems* (Mernissi 2001).

by becoming 'Westernized' does a Third World woman gain a subject position. This view also dismisses the nuanced negotiations that women deal with on a daily basis, and thereby tends to construct a black-and-white picture of a subject who is either victim of her culture or liberated subject because she has become a Western subject.

Longing and Belonging

Preoccupation with how their lives would have unfolded had they not left Iran was a theme the women engaged in enthusiastically during the course of the interviews. The reflection 'what if I had stayed' was soon followed by whether or not they had changed due to the migration, how they had changed, what they had gained, what they had lost. The interviewees' accounts of change are frequently caught in the complicated traces of cultural instructions stemming from their upbringing, the options and borders that they now encountered, and how they felt as women in their forties and early fifties. Drawing on their past experiences, the women talked continuously about the impact of previous instructions and social compulsions on their current lives. Not only did the women fall back on their experiences in Iran, but they also utilized them enthusiastically to disaggregate the Swedish part of their identity. By emphasizing change (or the lack of it), the women's narrations indicate how their 'Swedishness' has gone through their 'Iranianness' as well as how their 'Iranianness' has now been filtered through their 'Swedishness'.[5] For instance, in the following passage, by talking about the difficulty in dealing with what she had learned in the past and her desire to undo (some of) that teaching, Mehri shows how contradictions are lived:

> I lived in Iran until I was 27 years old. I was raised within that cultural context. This is the way I see it: every year a brick was added. Some of these bricks were placed when I was a little girl. /.../ These kinds of bricks are placed on the bottom. If we take that all away, the other bricks, which are placed on top, will fall down.

> (Pause)

> It means you cannot change these things easily. I started to wear pants only four or five years ago without constantly being preoccupied to cover my buttocks. I

---

5   Pamela Sugiman documents the same phenomena among first- and second-generation Japanese female post-war immigrants in Canada. These women's understanding of Japan and the Japanese in the post-war years, Sugiman argues, 'helps them to disassociate themselves from the latter, and in the process, underlines their Canadianness. But it is equally important to note that this Canadianness has become, for some of the women, a Japanese-Canadianness' (2005: 66).

am not so comfortable yet, but one thing is clear to me – when I started to wear pants I believed in it.

While articulating eloquently the existence of contradictory feelings, Mehri, and some other women, expressed a need for an 'erasing stage' that would demolish the learned values that they disliked. They expressed a desire for reaching the desirable 'construction stage' where they would build up 'new' values. Apparently, the women consider the presence of conflicting feelings to be a sign of failure in accomplishing the most desirable 'cultural makeover'. This view stems from taking up the concept of a modern unified self, which does not tolerate the simultaneous presence of conflicting thoughts and emotions. It also considers the influence of one culture to be possible only when the traces of the former one are completely erased. In doing so, it produces a paradoxical positioning between assimilation, on the one hand, and alienation on the other. In the following passage, Shirin tries to explain her (dis)attachment to specific practices.

Shirin: I see myself somehow in between, but I feel closer to Swedish culture.

(Pause)

I mean Swedish society's values and standards are more acceptable to me. For example, in terms of casual human relationships, cultural, emotional and even sexual ways of being, I feel I am closer to this society.

Fataneh: Could you specify in what ways you feel closer to Swedish culture sexually? What do you mean by that?

Shirin: You see, while I am saying that I feel closer to this society, to me, I still somehow find one-night stands not acceptable. /.../

This might sound like double standards or double morality, but I absolutely don't want my daughters to do it. /.../

Fataneh: How about yourself?

Shirin: (She waves her head determinedly). No.

For me, it is very important to feel safe with a person /.../. I just cannot accept one-night-stands. /.../ I mean, somehow it feels wrong.

Shirin is not alone in her reluctance to engage in 'one-night stands.' By expressing their distaste for sexual interaction without 'being in love', most of the women articulate explicitly or implicitly a homogenizing assumption of 'Swedish' women's easy-going attitude towards casual, single-encounter sex with a stranger.

Assuming that 'Swedish' women get easily involved in 'one-night stands' originates from a generalizing Occidentalist discourse that, similar to Orientalist views, has historically employed women's bodies and sexuality as an obvious signifier to represent otherness in gender-specific ways (Tavakoli-Targhi 2001). At times I confronted the women regarding these homogenizing comments by asking them if they thought this was true for all Swedish women. In response they immediately played down their comments and offered nuances to what they had said. However, often, the majority of the women positioned themselves differently in relation to most Swedish women. They regarded themselves as 'sexually naïve', 'sexually self-conscious', 'ignorant about their bodies', and 'not quite equal', among other self-judgments. From the women's perspectives, Sweden and (female) Swedishness, as media researcher Ylva Brune (2005) discusses elsewhere, are allotted a utopian position where freedom and equality are attainable. In taking up such a self/other split, the interviewees self-orientalize (Tavakoli-Targhi 2001) themselves. They compare themselves to the 'equal' and 'sexually conscious' 'Swedish' women and view themselves as women who put the needs of men (and their children) ahead of their own.

By considering her distaste for 'one-night stands' as a 'double standard' and 'double morality', Shirin not only sees 'Swedish culture' as total and homogenized, but she also sees individuals as all-encompassing and non-contradictory. Because she feels 'closer to Swedish culture', she feels she should engage in 'one-night stands' easily (like all Swedish women). So, she believes that she is not honest with herself and views herself as applying a double standard. Her position stems from a stagnant definition of culture as well as from that of a unified modern subject. None of the definitions allow space for conflicting thoughts and feelings. Besides, the effect of simultaneously experiencing different cultures and values causes diasporic women to be, as James Clifford points out, 'caught between patriarchies, ambiguous pasts, and futures. They connect and disconnect, forget and remember, in complex, strategic ways' (1999: 259). Challenging fixed and cohesive ethnic and cultural origins, along with recognizing frequent border crossings, compels one to recognize the importance of what Gilroy (1993) calls cultural routes instead of cultural roots. Applying the concept of cultural routes, consequently, necessitates observation of identity formation as fluid, flexible and hybrid. The concept of hybridity and hybrid identity, however, should without doubt be regarded relationally in regards to context, class, race, gender, etc.

While mediating through different perplexities, most of the time the interviewees expressed a linear relation between their attachments to one culture *vis-à-vis* detachment from the other. In another words, by distancing themselves from 'Iranian culture', they articulate attachment to 'Swedish culture', and vice versa. However, what is unearthed according to women's narratives rarely shows a pattern of remoteness from Iranian communities leading to nearness to and acceptance of the host community. Despite their (sporadic) discomfort with their 'home' communities, most of the women socialize mainly with Iranians rather than ethnic Swedes. This has marginalized the women differently in different contexts. This situation puts women, to use Homi Bhabha's words, in a position of 'unhomeliness' (2001: 9). To be 'unhomed', Bahbha declares, is not to be homeless. Rather, 'the "unhomely" is a paradigmatic colonial and post-colonial condition; it has a resonance that can be heard distinctly, if erratically, in fictions that negotiate the powers of cultural difference in a range of transhistorical sites' (1994: 9). Therefore, the unhomed negotiator and transgressor subjects mediate in a fluid but discursively constructed space. This shows how, and in what ways, as the women's narratives demonstrate, '"home" can simultaneously be a place of safety and of terror' (Brah 2002: 180). In hindsight, the questions I posed to the interviewee women – 'Where do you feel home?' – should be replaced with the question, 'When does a location *become* home?' (Brah 2002: 193). To Brah's complication of the notion of home, I would like to add that a place/space can hardly once and for all be 'home'. Home can only be momentarily grasped; it is a fleeting concept, an unattainable fiction. The concept of home is inextricable from the search for roots, and the women's accounts reveal nostalgia for a sense of complete belonging that has hardly existed.

Recapitulation

With gender and sexuality as the main subjects of the analysis of Iranian women's narrations of diasporic life in Sweden, my attention mainly focused on issues involving sexuality, identity, subjectivity, sameness, difference, otherness, domination, agency, and marginality. By destabilizing essentialist approaches to identity, and by being alert to different (sometimes contradictory) realms, I examined the dominant monolithic, heteronormative notions of sexuality in the women's narratives. The moral values of the women regarding appropriate sexual behaviour underwent various and sometimes contradictory transformations. The changes occurred as a result of the women's constant negotiations and struggles. They took up parts of multiple (Iranian and Swedish) discourse and discarded others while striving to make spaces for themselves 'inside' these constraining norms; in so doing, they carved out 'counter spaces'. However, the heterotopic space of diaspora drew attention to the dilemmas the women experienced as a result of having to operate within expected cultural boundaries that might see them accused of having abandoned their cultural values, and hence threatening the community's social cohesion; at the same time, they had to balance cultural expectations and the existing racist-sexist stereotypes of the 'host' environments. Therefore, the women experienced a discrepancy as a result of being thwarted by two 'seemingly' different cultures – while both cultures constructed discourses filled with stereotypes of so-called natives and outsiders. However, living in Sweden, where such racist/sexist discourses come to life on a daily basis, it is not a thwarting by 'two cultures.' It is, in fact, a merger of Swedishness (with all its complexities) with Iranianness (with all its complexities), along with other characteristics. It is a complexity within the culture(s) in which the women live.

References

Ahmadi Lewin, F. (2001), 'Identity Crisis and Integration: The Divergent Attitudes of Iranian Immigrant Men and Women towards Integration into Swedish Society', *International Migration* 39(3): 121–35.

Alinia, M. (2004), *Spaces of Diasporas: Kurdish Identities, Experiences of Otherness and Politics of Belonging.* (Göteborg: Department of Sociology, Göteborg University).

Anthias, F. (1998), 'Evaluating "Diaspora". Beyond Ethnicity?', *Sociology* 32(3): 557–80.

Bauer, J. (1994), 'Conversations on Women's Rights among Iranian Political Exiles. Implications for the Community-Self Debate in Feminism', *Critique*, Spring, 1–12.

Bauer, J. (1998), 'The Right to Cultures. Cultural Communication, Media and Iranian Women Refugees in Germany and Canada', *Media Development* 3, 27–33.

Bauer, J. (2000), 'Desiring Place. Iranian "Refugee" Women and the Cultural Politics of Self and Community in the Diaspora', *Comparative Studies of South Asia, Africa and the Middle East* 20(1): 180–99.

Berg, M. (1998), *Hudud. En essä om populärorientalisms bruksvärde och världsbild* (Hudud. An Essay on the Use, Value and World View of Popular Orientalism). (Stockholm: Carlsson Bokförlag).

Bhabha, H.K. (2001), *The Location of Culture.* (London and New York: Routledge).

Bloom, L.R. (1998), *Under the Sign of Hope. Feminist Methodology and Narrative Interpretation.* (Albany and New York: State University of New York Press).

Brah, A. (2002), *Cartographies of Diaspora. Contesting Identities.* (London and New York: Routledge).

Brah, A. (2005), 'Difference, Diversity, Differentiation. Process of Racialisation and Gender', in L. Back and J. Solomos (eds), *Theories of Race and Racism. A Reader,* 431–47. (London and New York: Routledge).

Brune, Y. (2005), '"Invandrare" i mediearkivets typgalleri' ('Immigrants' in the Typography of Media Archies), in P. de los Reyes, I. Molina and D. Mulinari (eds) *Maktens (o)lika förklädnader. Kön, klass och etnicitet i det postkoloniala Sverige* (The (Un)equal Disguises. Gender, Class and Ethnicity in the Postcolonial Sweden), 150–181. (Stockholm: Atlas).

Butler, J. (1998), 'Gender Is Burning. Questions of Appropriation and Subversion', in A. McClintock, A. Mufti and E. Shohat (eds) *Dangerous Liaisons. Gender, Nation, and Postcolonial Perspectives*, 381–95. (Minneapolis and London: University of Minnesota Press).

Butler, J. (1999), *Gender Trouble. Feminism and the Subversion of Identity.* (New York and London: Routledge).

Clifford, J. (1999), *Routes. Travel and Translation in the Late Twentieth Century.* (Cambridge: Harvard University Press).

Darvishpour, M. (2003), *Invandrarkvinnor som bryter mönstret: Hur maktförskjutningen inom iranska familjer i Sverige påverkar relationer* (Immigrant Women Who Break Established Patterns. How Changing Power Relations within Iranian Families in Sweden Influence Relationships). (Stockholm: Almqvist & Wiksell International).

Eng, D.L. (2001), *Racial Castration. Managing Masculinity in Asian America.* (Durham and London: Duke University Press).

Enteshari, F. (1994), Iranska Flyktingars Identitetsproblem (The Identity Problem of Iranian Immigrants), *Kvinnor och Fundamentalism* (Women and Fundamentalism), 2, 14–34.

Espín, O.M. (1999), *Women Crossing Boundaries. A Psychology of Immigration and Transformations of Sexuality.* (New York: Routledge).

Essed, P. (1990), *Everyday Racism. Reports from Women in Two Cultures.* (Claremont: Hunter House).

Essed, P. (1991), *Understanding Everyday Racism. An Interdisciplinary Theory.* (Newbury Park: SAGE).

Essed, P. (1996), *Diversity, Gender, Color and Culture.* (Amherst: University of Massachusetts Press).

Farahani, F. (2007), *Diasporic Narratives of Sexuality: Identity Formation among Iranian-Swedish Women.* (Stockholm: Acta Universitatis Stockholmiensis).

Foucault, M. (1986), 'Of Other Spaces', *Diacritics* 16, 22–7.

Foucault, M. (1988), *Madness and Civilization. A History of Insanity in the Age of Reason.* (New York: Vintage Books).

Foucault, M. (1990a), *The History of Sexuality. An Introduction.* (New York: Vintage Books).

Foucault, M. (1990b), *The History of Sexuality. The Use of Pleasure.* (New York: Vintage Books).

Foucault, M. (1995), *Discipline & Punish. The Birth of the Prison.* (New York: Vintage Books).

Gilroy, P. (1993), *The Black Atlantic. Modernity and Double Consciousness.* (Cambridge, Massachusetts: Harvard University Press).

Gilroy, P. (1997), 'Diaspora and the Detours of Identity', in K. Woodward (ed.) *Identity and Difference*, 299–343. (London: SAGE Publications in association with Open University).

Hall, S. (1992), 'Questions of Cultural Identity', in D. Held, S. Hall and T. McGrew (eds) *Modernity and its Futures*, 273–325. (Cambridge: Polity Press/Open University).

Hall, S. (2000), 'Who needs "Identity"?', in S. Hall and P. du Gay (eds) *Questions of Cultural Identity*, 1–18. (London: SAGE).

Hall, S. (2005), 'Old and New Identities, Old and New Ethnicities', in L. Back and J. Solomos (eds) *Theories of Race and Racism: A Reader,* 144–53. (London and New York: Routledge).

Kamali, M. (2005), *Sverige inifrån. Röster om etnisk diskriminering* (Sweden from the Inside: Voices on Ethnic Discrimination). SOU 2005:69. (Stockholm: Fritzes).

Laskar, P. (2005), *Ett bidrag till heterosexualitetens historia. Kön, sexualitet och njutningsnormer i sexhandböcker 1800–1920* (On Contribution to the History of Heterosexuality. Gender, Sexuality and the Norms of Pleasure in Sexual Manuals During 1800–1920). (Stockholm: Modernista. PhD dissertation).

Lewis, R. (1996), *Gendering Orientalism. Race, Femininity and Representation.* (London and New York: Routledge).

Lewis, R. (2004), *Rethinking Orientalism. Women, Travel and the Ottoman Harem.* (London: I.B. Tauris).

Lindqvist, B. (1991), *Drömmar och vardag i exil. Om chilenska flyktingars kulturella strategier* (Dreams and Reality in Exile. Cultural Strategies of Chilean Refugees). (Stockholm: Carlssons Bokförlag).

Mahdi, A.A. (1999), Trading Places. 'Changes in Gender Roles within the Iranian Immigrant Family', *Critique* 15, 51–75.

Mahdi, A.A. (2001), 'Perceptions of Gender Roles among Female Iranian Immigrants in the United States', in S. Ansari and V. Martin (eds), *Women, Religion and Culture in Iran*, 185–210. (London: Curzon Press).

Mahdi, M. (ed.) (1995), *The Thousand and One Nights.* (Leiden: Brill).

Mernissi, F. (2001), *Scheherazade Goes West. Different Cultures, Different Harems.* (New York: Washington Square Press).

Moghissi, H. (1999), 'Away from Home. Iranian Women, Displacement Cultural Resistance and Change', *Journal of Comparative Family Studies* 30(2): 213–17.

Moghissi, H. (2005), 'The 'Muslim' Diaspora and Research on Gender. Promises and Perils', in V. Agnew (ed.) *Diaspora, Memory, and Identity. A Search for Home*, 254–67. (Toronto: University of Toronto Press).

Moghissi, H. (ed.) (2006), *Muslim Diaspora. Gender, Culture and Identity.* (London and New York: Routledge).

Molina, I. (2005), 'Kolonial kartografier av nation och förort' (The Colonial Cartography of Nation and Suburb), in P. de los Reyes and L. Martinsson (eds) *Olikheten Paradigm. Intersektionella perspektiv på o(jäm)likhetsskapande* (The Paradigm of Difference: Intersectional Perspective on creating (In)equality), 99–123. (Lund: Studentlitteratur).

Nassehi-Behnam, V. (1991), 'Iranian Immigrants in France', in A.A. Fathi (ed.) *Iranian Refugees and Exiles since Khomeini*, 102–18. (Costa Mesa, California: Mazda Publishers).

Öhlander, M. (ed.) (2005), *Bruket av kultur. Hur kultur används och görs socialt verksamt* (The Use of Culture. How Culture is Used and Made Socially Effective). (Stockholm: Studentlitteratur AB).

Ristilammi, P.M. (1994), *Rosengård och den svarta poesin. En studie av modern Annorlundahet* (Rosengård and the Black Poetry. A Study of Modern Alterity). (Stockholm and Stehag: Brutus Östlings Bokförlag Symposion).

Runfors, A. (2003), *Mångfald, motsägelser och marginaliseringar. En studie av hur invadrarskap formas i skolan* (Diversity, Contradictions and Marginalization. A Study of How the Immigrant Category is Formed in School). (Stockholm: Prisma).

Safran, W. (1991), 'Diasporas in Modern Societies. Myths of Homeland and Return', *Diaspora* 1(1): 83–99.

Shahidian, H. (1999), 'Gender and Sexuality among Iranian Immigrants in Canada', *Sexualities* 2(2): 189–223.

Söderholm Lindelöf, K. (2006), *Om vi nu ska bli som Europa. Könsskapande och normalitet bland unga kvinnor i transitionens Polen* (If We Are to Become Like Europe. Gender Construction and Normality among Young Women in Transitional Poland). (Göteborg and Stockholm: Makadam. PhD dissertation).

Stoler, A.L. (1998), 'Making Empire Respectable. The Politics of Race and Sexual Morality in Twentieth-century Colonial Cultures', in A. McClintock, A. Mufti and E. Shohat (eds) *Dangerous Liaisons. Gender, Nation, Postcolonial Perspective*. (Minneapolis and London: University of Minnesota Press), 344–74.

Sugiman, P. (2005), 'Memories of Internment: Narrating Japanese-Canadian Women's Life Stories', in V. Agnew (ed.), *Diaspora, Memory, and Identity. A Search for Home*, 48–80. (Toronto, Buffalo and London: University of Toronto Press).

Tavakoli-Targhi, M. (2001), *Refashioning Iran. Orientalism, Occidentalism and Historiography.* (New York: Palgrave).

Vertovec, S. (1997), 'Three Meanings of "Diaspora", Exemplified among South Asian Religions, *Diaspora* 6(3): 277–99.

PART III
Reflections on Islamic Positionings of Youth in Diaspora

Chapter 9
Styles of Religious Practice: Muslim Youth Cultures in Europe

Thijl Sunier

Introduction

The attacks on the Twin Towers on the 11th September 2001 and subsequent events have had tremendous effects on the general image of Islam and the position of Muslims in the world. Not only do intelligence services all over the world monitor Muslims more than ever before, but all kinds of statements by Muslims are evaluated in an ideological climate in which Islam is considered the prime source of a wide variety of political, social and cultural problems. Muslims in Europe are depicted as proverbial aliens, adherents of a 'border-defying global Islam' (Silverstein 2005), with irreconcilable cultural differences with the West. The long-term effects have yet to be seen, but some trends are becoming clear already. The events have not only resulted in the worldwide 'War on Terror' with its own dynamics and ideological logic, they have also invigorated a 'war on civilization' that had been launched towards Muslims in most countries of Europe with a large immigrant population. In all countries of Europe with sizable Muslims populations, we have witnessed a turn towards stricter assimilation policies and an overall trend to domesticate Islam (Sunier 2009).

In this highly politicized post-9/11 climate, young people of Muslim background across Europe, irrespective of their religiosity, are confronted with world views, on the side of both European societies and mainstream Muslim organizations, that divide the world into 'good people' and 'bad people'. Even young people of Muslim background who no longer practise Islam are almost forced to relate to it in one way or the other. This 'discursive closure' not only demands an almost absolute loyalty to either side, it precludes, and even delegitimizes, any hybridization and creativity of cultural production. In many Western European nation-states with sizable Muslim populations, the already existing sharp distinction between the secular and the religious as two irreconcilable discursive categories has been reinforced (see De Vries 2008).

The current widespread anxieties and tensions remind us of the nineteenth-century worries about radicalism arising among the European peasantry, or the 'dangers' of the spread of communism among either the impoverished masses in Europe or colonial subjects abroad. In those days the general answer to that challenge was also civilization. The explanations that accompanied the worries in those days bear a striking resemblance to present-day discourses on Muslim radicalization. The combination of a deracinated migrant youth and an unpredictable 'globalized Islam', as Olivier Roy (2002) puts it, forms a dangerous and easily inflammable mix. Be it the riots in the suburbs of Paris, the formation of radical political cells in many poor quarters of big cities, the development in those cities of no-go areas, or the simple hanging around of youngsters on public squares or sexual harassment of girls, all point to this clash and contribute to the urgency of a civilizing mission. The fact that Mohammed B., murderer of filmmaker Theo van Gogh in Amsterdam, and the perpetrators of the suicide bombings on the London underground were all 'blokes from the next bloc,' born and raised in the countries in which they committed their crimes, makes this civilizing mission of European nation-states all the more imminent, it has been claimed.

Radicalization and the Discourse of Integration

One of the main consequences of the strong discursive relation between radicalization and civilization is that integration discourses in western European nation-states have been imbued with implicit notions of religiousness. Radical Muslims are perceived as non-integrated Muslims. Radicalization, as it occurs among a small proportion of second-generation immigrants with an Islamic background, is the result of failed integration (Buijs et al. 2006; see also Lewis 2002).

Integration will eventually lead to more individualized forms of religiousness, in line with modern Western notions of religiousness and religious belonging, it is argued. In the majority of publications on Muslims in Europe, the mass immigration of people with Islamic backgrounds in the second half of the twentieth century is being explained as the beginning of a series of fundamental transformations in the makeup of Islam. Not only has this diaspora caused a change in the social structure of indigenous Islamic communities, but it has also led to a fragmentation of religious normative thinking. In the past years we have witnessed a sharp increase in studies that deal with the question of how Islam is transformed in the new European context. There are a considerable number of authors on Islam who argue that with the spread of modern mass media and the continuous process of globalization, normative religious frameworks have been critically undermined and there is a gradual retreat of religion from the public realm (see e.g. Cesari 2006). This process, it is argued, has been instrumental in the spread of individualized 'copy-paste Islam,' especially among young Muslims. By using all kinds of modern (re)sources, young Muslims create their own Islamic self-understanding, one that has no need for religious authority. This so-called 'individualization-thesis' thus also assumes the delegitimization of religious authority (Amir-Moazami and Salvatore 2003; Peter 2006; Volpi and Turner 2007). This often turns these young people into unpredictable and even dangerous subjects that are up to anything, it is argued (see Roy 2002).

But it is also often assumed that individualization is the first phase in a secularization process and the beginning of a complete loss of religious conviction. Some have argued that the migration process itself is instrumental in this transformation because it has unsettled the social texture from which Muslims migrated. This has led to a critical attitude among second-generation Muslims in Europe towards the 'Islam of the parents' and religious authority (see e.g. Mandaville 2001, 2003, 2007). They consequently break away from the 'Islamic culture' of their parents in search of a pure Islam.[1] Others have argued that it is the engagement, or should we say confrontation, of Islam with democracy and 'Western values' that has caused these transformations (Cesari 2004). Transformations are thus understood in the context of a more general process of modernization in which religion is retreating into the private sphere (see also Jacobson 1998). A considerable part of both qualitative as well as quantitative studies takes up the individualization thesis and assumes that young Muslims will increasingly neglect religious obligations and eventually lose their religious convictions altogether (see Phalet et al. 2002).

There are also a growing number of studies that arrive at opposite conclusions, namely that because of the unsettling of traditional Islamic authority, many young people opt for radical versions of Islamic thinking (see e.g. Kepel 2006). There is enormous interest in why and under what circumstances young people radicalize. This interest has of course to do with security, a prime political goal in Europe at the moment. When it became evident that a number of young Muslims were willing to use violence, the prevention of radicalism became a prime goal in integration policies.[2] In the twenty-first century, research on radicalization has become the dominant field in the study of Islam among young people.

But it is not just security that accounts for this focus on radicalization. The underlying assumption in most studies is that migration to Europe has caused a normative confrontation between traditional understandings of Islamic reasoning and traditional sources of authority on the one hand, and the modernized, privatized understanding of religion in a secular public realm in the West on the other. This confrontation has brought many Muslims into disarray. But where the first generation can rely on traditional networks, for young people it has brought chaos, existential uncertainty and, not least, identity crisis. They live in a no-man's-land between two irreconcilable cultural environments. Most young Muslims are able to reconcile the opposing requirements, but some cannot. This has led to feelings of resentment and envy that make them vulnerable to the influence of radical preachers and radical Islamist ideologies that foresee a better future (see Buijs et al. 2006; Eyerman 2008; Gielen 2008; Kepel 2006; Lewis 2002; Tibi 2009).

----

1   Thus Nederveen Pieterse (1997) has argued that it is not the manifold religious practices that travel, and that only the Quran is portable.

2   In many countries of Western Europe so-called 'deradicalization' programs are set up to meet that goal.

At this point we can observe a strange contradiction. The radicalization thesis rests on the assumption of a process of individualization, yet at the same time radicalization is depicted as the result of extreme ideological pressure 'from outside'. This contradiction is founded on a particular understanding of 'identity'. In most studies dealing with radicalization, culture and identity are key analytical concepts. The crucial question that implicitly and often explicitly underscores this kind of research is whether young people are able to cope with the 'cultural ambiguity that is brought about by migration. If not, then they fall in-between and develop behavioural problems. The assumption that lies behind this line of reasoning is that cultures are stable, identifiable and distinguishable categories (Brubaker and Cooper 2000). 'Culture', 'religion' and 'identity' are supposed to be basic features with explanatory power. Identity denotes a stable personal core that individuals must possess in a world that is in constant flux. When identity is not as stable as it should be, it may lead to an 'identity crisis.' It has been reintroduced in the study of youth from migrant backgrounds by linking it to cultural change (see e.g. Abdel-Samad 2006).

Acts of political violence are perceived to be the result of 'cultural pathology', and 'hybrid misfit'. Despite their thorough socialization in Western Europe, with its long-standing democratic traditions, radical Muslims totally reject modern society and are ready to fight that society with violent means out of sheer frustration. This psychological distress is brought about as the result of cultural clashes. Also, young people who do not resort to radical, violent or criminal behaviour are said to live 'between two cultures', which can easily lead to 'identity problems' and thus constitute a potential category of 'cultural dropouts'. The sensationalists who gaze at radical practices and styles in television programs and in popular academic writings and portray radicalization as a giant step into another universe, incomprehensible to ordinary people, are widespread.

The 'between two cultures' image not only assumes inbuilt cultural tensions in the trajectory towards modernity framed in an evolutionist discourse, but also shapes perceptions on processes of cultural change. A girl of Muslim background donning the veil and observing religious duties, while at the same time wearing jeans, attending university, and shaking hands with male co-eds, is perceived as a 'transitionary hybrid' (Ferguson 1999), combining 'traditional' and 'modern' cultural elements as two clearly separable fields.

One now understands why radicalization is often so easily conflated with other forms of 'deviant' behaviour. There is a sharp increase in the number of research projects about these issues. Criminal behaviour among 'culturally different' youngsters was already a popular research topic (see Werdmolder 2005; van Gemert 1998; Freilich 2006). This type of study has recently been extended among potentially radical Muslims. The common assumption of most of these studies is that all forms of deviant behaviour are the result of the psychological distress caused by cultural clashes between newcomers and established society. The sensationalists gaze at radical practices and styles in television programs and in popular academic writings, portray radicalization as a giant step into another universe, incomprehensible for ordinary people.

Styles of Religious Appropriation

One of the consequences of this simplified view of religious engagement is that there is hardly any interest among researchers in agency, let alone in new forms of religious appropriation, signification and performative practice that are to be found among young Muslims in Europe.

A way to overcome the omissions and fallacies in much of the present-day research on young Muslims is to elaborate on insights in the study of youth cultures and bring back into the analysis the agency of young Muslims. By approaching young Muslims as active agents of their own cultural environment and not as victims of a cultural clash and/or trapped in an identity crisis, we get a much brighter picture. Instead of treating Muslim cultural practices as transitory and dependent phenomena, they should be assessed as (youth) cultural traits in their own right (see Amit-Talai and Wulff 1995). Islamic fashion shows and *salafi* practices are not opposite tendencies, but should instead be treated as practices of self-making and quests for authenticity and truth.[3]

When exploring religious practices and engagements among young people, one is struck by their endless creativity. Since there is no single field that qualifies as purely religious, there is no practice that must a priori be singled out. In my view, the production of religiousness and the making of religious 'selves' among young people reside on the nexus between performance and aesthetics, politics, and popular culture. Meaningful and productive research on Islam among young people should go beyond discursive dimensions alone and include the following four conceptual clusters: (1) performance and self-styling, commoditization and popular culture, (2) discipline, embodiment and techniques of the self, (3) authenticity, truth and authority, (4) identity politics and the public sphere. I intend to set up research that brings together these clusters, and shall further elaborate them.

Performance and self-styling, commoditization of religion, and popular culture refer to the obvious fact that religious engagement and religious expression are by definition public acts. Even if we subscribe to the privatization thesis of religion, and assume that religiosity resides only in the mind, it would be senseless to depict religious engagement as an invisible act. Religion exists by virtue of its practice, its acting-out, and its performance. Only then does it render social meaning. If we take Meyer's definition of religion as a 'practice of mediation' (2006), it follows that style, performance and aesthetics are central concepts in the understanding

---

3   One of the few recent thorough studies on Muslim youth that does not consider the attractiveness of *salafist* ideologies the result of cultural pathology is Martijn de Koning's *Zoeken naar een zuivere Islam* (*The quest for a pure Islam*) (2008).

of the reproduction of Islam among young people in Europe. Popular culture and the commoditization of religious products are essential contemporary practices of religious mediation and we are only beginning to understand how they work. There are numerous practices and activities, performative and aesthetic articulations that fall outside established definitions of 'mainstream' and thus 'regular' religion. The interplay of Islam, mass media, popular culture and the commoditization of religious experience is instrumental in producing new forms of community (Eickelman and Anderson 2003; Schulz 2006). A quick glance at the numerous websites set up by young people of Muslim background – and not just those of radical Muslims – reveals an ever increasing diversity of forms in which Islam is imagined, mediated and performed.

An Islamic fashion show, a religious entertainment evening, a 'halal reception,' a public speech, a religious hip-hop concert, an Islamic stand-up comedian, media training sessions for Muslims, a training session for Muslim women to learn how to act publicly, an Islamic healing session aimed at strengthening self-confidence, the public appearance of women in *niqaab* or *chadori*, the production of video testimonies, all pertain to the religious realm. For the people involved in these kinds of activities, they are utterly relevant in the making of the religious self and the constitution of a religious community. In spite of this, these forms are still largely neglected in mainstream studies on Islam in Europe.

The concept of self-styling denotes the specific forms in which religious belonging and religious practices among young Muslims take shape. The spread of new media in the past decades has had a tremendous effect on religious articulation.[4] Not only does style fit better with the public and sensational forms of religion we encounter today, it also covers more adequately the wide range of practices that I wish to include. Style, loosely defined as a 'signifying practice,' has been coined as a central analytical tool by the CCCS of the University of Birmingham in the 1970s in their studies on youth culture. The 'Birmingham School' shifted the attention from culture and cultural change as a source of coercion, stress and conflict to the active role youths play in the creation of youth cultures, and to the visible and performative aspects of culture (Hall and Jefferson 1976). Style is continually reproduced. It is not the expressive outcome of a preconceived identity, but rather a practice that generates identity. Styling is an essential prerequisite of modern religious subjectivation, the making of the religious self.

Religious styling, denoting an integrated set of signifying practices, has several advantages over the much more widespread term religious identity. It shifts the emphasis to what is practised, performed and acted out, as well as and not least, the economy of discipline, whilst also embracing a somewhat wider variety of forms, acts and attributes. Styling brings in agency, without ignoring the relations of power. As Ferguson (1999) has reminded us, style is not simply 'having ideas'

---

4   As Meyer puts it: '[…] Not only do modern media such as print, photography, TV, film, or Internet shape sensational forms, the latter themselves are media that mediate, and thus produce the transcendental and make it sensible' (2006:13).

and expressing them. It is an embodied practice that is durable and assumes cultivation and discipline. It assumes an achieved competence in performing a certain style. Styles, including religious styles, develop in a situation of duress, and this resonates well with embodiment and discipline, the second conceptual cluster.

Saba Mahmood, in her study of a pious group of female Muslims in Cairo, elaborates on the aspect of training – the second conceptual cluster under consideration here – and argues that through the disciplinary training of the *salat* (ritual prayer), these women articulate conventional formal acts of the ritual with intentions and spontaneous emotions. In other words, they identify the act of prayer as a key practice for purposely molding their intentions, emotions and desires (Mahmood 2001: 828, 2005). As such, far from being a formal and externalized act of religious duty, the *salat*, through techniques of training and disciplining, becomes an embodied practice that shapes the self. Mahmood understands the body not just as a signifying medium but also as a tool for arriving at a certain kind of moral disposition. The body is thus trained to acquire moral capacities and sensitivities one does not have beforehand, even if one is a convinced believer. Mahmood rightly emphasizes that an analysis of embodiment of ritual should pay ample attention to the pedagogical process by which the embodiment is achieved.[5] This is a conscious training that social actors may or may not embark upon, and it should always be looked at within a particular, power-laden context. The great advantage of this approach is that we are able to overcome the paralyzing contradiction between a kind of free-floating individuality on the one hand ('the ideal individual religious subject') and a suppressive and normative understanding of religious doctrines that leave no room for reflection, interpretation and self-making.

Donning the headscarf, for example, is a stylistic and aesthetic device. In that respect it is appropriate to classify the headscarf as a form of headgear as is often done in public spaces such as schools.[6] But we cannot fully understand its religious implications when we ignore the symbolic significance of the veil, its normative underpinnings and, not least, the embodied moral disposition that comes with it. Style, it should again be emphasized, is not a kind of free-choice self-making activity. Particular styles are conventionally connected to particular communities (Maffesoli 1996: 16). Donning the veil is as much a 'body technique,' invested with passion and emotion, as a religious symbolic act that enacts a certain relation towards a discursive tradition. Many young Muslims I spoke with emphasized

---

5 '[…] the point is not simply that one acts virtuously but also *how* one enacts a virtue' (Mahmood 2001: 838).

6 In a secondary school in which I conducted research, the wearing of headscarves was allowed explicitly *not* as a religious symbol, but as one of the many headgears worn by pupils. This policy turned out to be beneficiary for Muslims in a number of situations, but it may also lead more easily to a total ban of any headgear should this be deemed important by the staff (for an elaborate discussion of the case see Schiffauer et al. 2004).

that bodily discipline, be it veiling in public or any other act that arouses public reaction, is an important means to distinguish oneself from mainstream 'fast' styling. It is a way to deepen one's convictions (see also Moors 2004, 2008).

The same can be said about religious music. If we depict the wide variety of religious musical styles as simply one more musical genre, we overlook the religious impact of particular modes of presentation During an interview I had with a couple of young Muslims, they explained to me how the music of Native Deen, an Islamic hip-hop group from the United States, brought about a certain religious experience that is reminiscent of the effect of a *zikr*.[7]

Authenticity, truth and authority, the third conceptual cluster, are crucial to understand religious engagement among young Muslims in Europe. One of the fallacies of the privatization and individualization thesis is that it assumes that religious authority becomes obsolete. However, young Muslims do not just construct their own Islam out of nothing; they relate to Islam as a discursive tradition and they relate to other Muslims in a variety of ways. Religious engagement is a process of community-building and of subjectivation in that the religious self develops in a context of regimes of truth (see e.g. Foucault 1983; Roeland 2009). The sources of authority and the process of authorization of religious knowledge among young Muslims is still a rather underdeveloped field of research.[8]

If we take performance, style and public appearance as inherent elements of modern religiosity and religious practice, it follows that religious engagement with the public sphere is almost by definition identity politics, the fourth conceptual cluster. When Muslims act publicly they comment on the characteristics of the public sphere and contribute to its transformation. The question of how, under what conditions and with what intentions Muslims engage with the public sphere is part of a much more general scholarly debate on the accessibility of that public sphere with its conceived secular and neutral character (see Asad 2003; Calhoun 1992; Meyer and Moors 2006). The numerous so-called headscarf affairs that regularly occur throughout Europe, and also the public reactions that both the public and political activities of Muslims arouse, are indications of the profoundly contentious character of the presence of Muslims in Europe. Young people who were born and raised in Europe argue that they do not want to be treated as guests

---

7   The *zikr* is one of the central meditative rituals in Islam. It can consist of repetitive exclamations of the name of Allah, but there is a wide variety of other practices aiming at bringing practitioners to a mental state that enhances the religious experience.

8   There are at present, however, some promising projects being carried out in this field. Anthropologist Annelies Moors of the University of Amsterdam is conducting research on Islam and fashion among Muslims in Europe. Anthropologist Loubna el-Morabet of the University of Leiden is also working on a research project that deals with these processes in several countries in Europe. These projects go beyond the sole emphasis on textual sources and take on board the multiplicity of settings, formats and circumstances in which religious knowledge is produced and conveyed.

who have to earn their place in society. They are already a part of that society whether some people like it or not.

Religious Performance

To illustrate my argument, let me discuss three examples that in my view capture the importance of the performative, aesthetic and, not least, the innovative and transgressive dimensions of religiosity.

The first example, which probably speaks for itself today, concerns the much discussed and overemphasized veil for Muslim women. Most of the writings on veiling in the context of the secular nation-state deal with the veil as a normative device, a symbol of religiosity. Most studies concentrate on the religious and cultural meanings attached to the headscarf or, rather, reduce the headscarf to the material bearer of immaterial religious meaning. These meanings not only seem to be fixed, but the women in question – those who wear the headscarf – seem to be neglected in the analysis. Most approaches show a general lack of attention to women's agency in headscarf issues. Fixed theological or cultural qualifications 'objectify' the meaning of the headscarf and leave no room for situational interpretations by actors themselves in specific circumstances. But even if women are asked about their motivations, the emphasis is on discursive dimensions. It is not only impossible to relate the enormous diversity in veiling styles to simple normative or cultural differences, but there is hardly any attention given to the performative, aesthetic or stylistic aspects of the veil and the crucial role of women themselves in styling practices. A thorough analysis of veiling and Islamic dress in general must take on board the role of modern media, mass consumption, youth culture and, not least, debates on religion and emancipation (Moors 2004, 2008). At school, Islamic stylistic devices constitute important prerequisites with which young people position themselves *vis-à-vis* their peers (Collet 2004). The still dominant approach, in which the increasing visibility of Islamic dress at school is only treated as an alarming sign of ethnic and religious concentration, must be seriously revised.

The second example concerns the shift in the production of religious authority that can be traced among Muslims in Europe. Modern media have fundamentally changed the modes by which religious messages are put across and disseminated (Meyer 2006). Believers today are addressed as audiences and not least as consumers. The role of modern media such as the Internet have been addressed in studies on radicalization, but mainly as a rival practice to the 'normal' traditional means of religious conveyance (see e.g. Eickelman and Anderson 1999). Modern media, however, are transforming religion itself. Religion and media are not separate spheres, but should be studied together. Religion, after all, is a practice of mediation. As Meyer and Moors argue: '[new forms of mediation not only create] new styles of self-representation, but also pinpoints new forms of religious experience that cast believers as spectators, spectacles as miracles, and God's blessing as prosperity' (2006: 9).

With this in mind, the increasing number of lecturers with an Islamic message, new religious experts, and cultural brokers that deliver speeches, appear on television, take part in debates and operate websites should be taken seriously as new forms of religious mediation that constitute new audiences. Cultural brokerage is an essential source of power typical for an urban environment with a multiplicity of cultural production and change. To understand the production of cultural and religious authority, we should analyse carefully how brokers utilize and instrumentalize cultural change and how cultural competence is produced precisely in these (perceived) cultural border areas. It is not just the exotic self-made radicals who seem to attract the attention of the media and intelligence services that are relevant here. This is but a very marginal part of a much larger process of transformation. And it is not just the content of the messages that are relevant. Preliminary findings in this field have revealed that it is crucial to take into consideration how messages are put across, how speakers relate to audiences and on what principles their popularity is based. Their styles of arguing, their rhetoric strategy, the specific settings in which they operate, and their image in the media are as important, and probably even more important, than mere content. The dissemination and the impact of a specific text may be influenced more by the popularity of the person who produces the text than by the content of the message. Phrases may be taken out as key statements of a particular discourse, much in the same way as the work and particular concepts of well-known scholars, such as Freud, Marx, Foucault or Bourdieu, have become popular beyond their reading audiences.

The last example concerns the turmoil following the arrest of some alleged Muslim radicals in the Netherlands. I will deal with this case in more detail since it nicely illustrates the biased approach with which radicalism is addressed. In September 2006 the Dutch secret service AIVD passed on to the police some video footage containing a so-called 'video-testimony' of Samir A., which 'for unknown reasons' turned up at the Dutch news board NOVA. A. is one of the protagonists of the Hofstad group, a network of alleged Muslim terrorists in the Netherlands that had been arrested by the police in late 2004. This round-up was part of the police investigations following the murder on filmmaker Theo van Gogh in November of that year. The video made by Samir A. was the first one of its kind to turn up in the Netherlands. The news program NOVA dedicated a special item to the case in September 2006, in which experts on Islam were asked about the religious meaning of such practices and about the religious convictions of the killer.

The video-testimony has become a well-known means by which Palestinian suicide bombers announce their intended attacks on Israeli targets publicly. In the short performance of generally some ten minutes, the bomber explains his/her planned attack, and motivations based on quotes from the Quran and other sources. He or she explains the political goal of the attack, and salutes his or her family, rejoicing in their reunion in Heaven. The practice was soon to be taken over by al-Qaeda bombers. The perpetrators of the bombings on the London underground in July 2005 issued a similar statement. Most of the video messages of this sort have an ominous, sometimes sinister look. The more professionally made videos have background music, images of previous attacks, well-thought-out camera directions and a well-prepared statement. The performer looks straight into the camera, addressing the spectator directly. We should keep in mind that these kinds of video messages have also become standard communicative devices for many radical Islamist organizations. For quite some years now al-Qaeda leader Osama Bin Laden has been sending out his messages through videos that are distributed and submitted to broadcasting companies. His facial expressions, his gestures, his well-chosen words, his phrasing and timing should be considered aspects of a particular communicative style that has been mimicked by many other radicals.

On the video being discussed here, we see Samir A. dressed in a white suit and a black waistcoat, a scarf around his head and an automatic gun leaning against the wall behind him. In perfect classical Arabic he first addresses his parents, warning them to obey God and to follow the Quran. He addresses his fellow members of the Hofstad group to encourage them in their struggle. He then gives a warning to the Dutch audience.

By mimicking the gestures of Bin Laden, Samir A. replicates meticulously the style of his great model. According to some of the experts in the news item, this is a means to invoke the respect of young fellow Muslims. More importantly in my view is the fact that he knows that his performance will have an impact on the Dutch public. I contend that his public platform is principally Dutch society and his message is designed for a primarily non-Islamic audience. Certainly since al-Qaeda applied and elaborated this strategic device, communication with the 'West' and with the 'enemy' has become much more important in determining and developing the particular format and language used. The careful composition of the video-testimony and the specific narrational buildup reveals a thorough understanding and application of particular elements of performative style and figures of speech that make sense in the 'West.' Instead of concentrating only on the religious content, as most experts on Islam and radicalization tend to do, one has to examine how these particular styles, which should be understood against the background of the aftermath of 9/11, are being applied. The video message is not an anomaly, a traditional message in a modern communicative guise, as some argue. It is a fundamentally modern phenomenon.

Conclusion

The rooting of Muslims in Europe starts from the actual fact that Muslims constitute an integral part of European society, but at the same time modern mass media and modern means of communication enable Muslims to build networks and communities across borders. This is very much in evidence. Religious practices and religious modes of expression reflect multiple attachments and multiple orientations. Instead of evaluating these practices as integration issues, as researchers we must develop new ways and new approaches that do justice to new realities. This is especially the case with young Muslims. It is not their position on an integration trajectory as such that accounts for their engagement with Islam. Their position in receiving societies is but one aspect of the complex process of religious identity formation.

The religious practices of young Muslims especially in Europe also point to another important development. They convincingly demonstrate that the dominant secularist perceptions of society need a thorough revision. Categories such as 'the religious' and 'the secular' have rendered far more complex meanings. The interplay between Islam, mass media, popular culture and the commoditization of religious experience is instrumental in producing new forms of community and religious experience. It shows an ever increasing diversity of forms in which Islam is imagined, mediated and performed. Simple dichotomies like radical/non-radical, democratic/non-democratic, but also religious/non-religious fail to capture the wide range of expressive, performative and sensational forms that we witness today. This should guide our future research agendas.

References

Abdel-Samad, H. (2006), 'Alienation and Radicalization: Young Muslims in Germany', in Jonker, G. and Amiraux, V. (eds) *Politics of Visibility. Young Muslims in European Public Spaces*. (London: Transcript Publishers), 191–213.

Amir-Moazami, S. and Salvatore, A. (2003), 'Gender, Generation, and the Reform of Tradition: from Muslim Majority societies to Western Europe', in Allievi, S. and Nielsen, J.S. (eds) *Muslim Networks and Transnational Communities in and across Europe.* (Leiden: Brill), 52–77.

Amit-Talai, V. and Wulff, H. (eds) (1995), *Youth Cultures: A Cross-Cultural Perspective*. (London: Routledge).

Asad, T. (1993), 'The Concept of Ritual', in Asad, T. *Genealogies of Religion*. (Baltimore: John Hopkins University Press).

Asad, T. (1999), *Formations of the Secular.* (Stanford: Stanford University Press).

Asad, T. (2003), *Formations of the Secular. Christianity, Islam, Modernity.* (Stanford: Stanford University Press).

Bauman, Z. (1991), *Modernity and Ambivalence*. (Cambridge: Polity Press).

Brubaker, R. and Cooper, F. (2000), 'Beyond "Identity"', *Theory and Society* 29(1): 1–47.

Bucholtz, M. (2002), 'Youth and Cultural Practice', *Annual Review of Anthropology* 31, 525–52.

Buijs, F., Demant, F. and Hamdy, A. (2006), *Strijders van eigen bodem*. (Amsterdam: Amsterdam University Press).

Butler, J. (1997), *Excitable Speech: A Politics of the Performative*. (New York: Routledge).

Calhoun, C. (ed.) (1992), *Habermas and the Public Sphere.* (Cambridge: MIT Press).

Cesari, J. (2004), *L'islam à l'e'preuve de l'occident.* (Paris: La De'couverte).

Cesari, J. (2006), *When Islam and Democracy Meet: Muslims in Europe and in the United States.* (New York: Palgrave Macmillan).

Collet, B. (2004), 'Muslim headscarves in four nation-states and schools', in Schiffauer, W., Baumann, G., Kastoryano, R. and Vertovec, S. (eds) *Civil Enculturation. Nation-state, School and Ethnic Difference in Four European Countries.* (Oxford: Berghahn Books), 119–47.

De Vries, H. (ed.) (2008), *Religion Beyond a Concept.* (New York: Fordham University Press).

Eickelman, D. and Anderson, J. (1999), *New Media and the Muslim World: The Emerging Public Sphere.* (Bloomington: Indiana University Press).

Eyerman, R. (2008), *The Assassination of Theo van Gogh.* (Durham: Duke University Press).

Ferguson, J. (1999), *Expectations of Modernity.* (Berkeley: University of California Press).

Foucault, M. (1983), 'Afterword: The Subject and Power' in: Dreyfus, H. and Rabinow, P. (eds) *Michel Foucault: Beyond Structuralism and Hermeneutics.* (Chicago: University of Chicago Press), 208–26.

Freilich, J. and R. Guerette (eds) (2006), *Migration, Culture, Conflict, Crime and Terrorism.* (Aldershot: Ashgate).

Gielen, A. (2008), *Radicalisering en Identiteit.* (Amsterdam: Aksant).

Hall, S. and Jefferson, T. (1976), *Resistance through Rituals.* (London: Routledge).

Hebdige, D. (1979), *Subculture. The Meaning of Style.* (London: Routledge).

Jacobson, J. (1998), *Islam in Transition: Religion and Identity among British Pakistani Youth.* (London: Routledge).

Kepel, G. (2006), *The War for Muslim Minds.* (Boston: Harvard University Press).

Lewis, B. (2002), *What Went Wrong? The Clash between Islam and Modernity in the Middle East.* (New York: Harper).

Maffesoli, M. (1996), *The Contemplation of the World. Figures of Community Style.* (Minneapolis: University of Minnesota Press).

Mahmood, S. (2001), 'Rehearsed Spontaneity and the Conventionality of Ritual: Disciplines of the Salat', *American Ethnologist* 28(4): 827–53.

Mahmood, S. (2005), *Politics of Piety.* (Princeton: Princeton University Press).

Mandaville, P. (2001), *Transnational Muslim Politics.* (London: Routledge).

Mandaville, P. (2003), 'Towards a critical Islam: European Muslims and the changing boundaries of transnational religious discourse' in: Allievi, S. and Nielsen, J. (eds) *Muslim Networks and Transnational Communities in and across Europe.* (Leiden: Brill), 127–45.

Mandaville, P. (2007), 'Globalization and the Politics of Religious Knowledge', *Theory, Culture and Society* 24(2): 101–5.

Meyer, B. (2006), *Religious Sensations* Oratie VU. (Amsterdam: VU University).

Meyer, B. and Moors, A. (eds) (2006), *Religion, Media and the Public Sphere.* (Bloomington: Indiana University Press).

Moors, A. (2004), 'Islam and Fashion on the Streets of San'a, Yemen', *Etnofoor* 16(2): 41–56.

Moors, A. (2008), 'De opkomst van "islamitische mode" als wereldwijd fenomeen', *Al Nisa: Islamitisch maandblad voor vrouwen en kinderen*, 27(10): 6–13.

Peter, F. (2006), 'Individualization and religious authority in Western European Islam', *Islam and Christian-Muslim Relations,* 17(1): 105–18.

Phalet, K., Lotringen, C. van and Entzinger, H. (2002), *Islam in de multiculturele samenleving: opvattingen van jongeren in Rotterdam* (Islam in the Multicultural Society: Views of Youths in Rotterdam). (Utrecht: European Research Centre on Migration and Ethnic Relations).

Phalet, K. (2004), *Moslims in Nederland.* (Den Haag: SCP).

Rappaport, R. (1999), *Ritual and Religion in the Making of Humanity.* (Cambridge: Cambridge University Press).

Roeland, J. (2009), *Selfation. Dutch Evangelical Youth between Subjectivation and Subjection.* (Amsterdam: Pallas Publications AUP).

Roy, O. (2002), *l'Islam mondialisé.* (Paris: Editions du Seuil).

Schulz, D. (2006), 'Promises of (im)mediate salvation: Islam, broadcast media, and the remaking of religious experience in Mali', *American Ethnologist,* 33(2): 210–29.

Silverstein, P.A. (2005), 'Immigrant Racialization and the New Savage Slot: Race, Migration, and Immigration in the New Europe', *Annual Review of Anthropology,* 34, 363–84.

Sunier, T. (2009), *Beyond the Domestication of Islam in Europe.* (Amsterdam: VU University).

Tibi, B. (2009), *Islam's Predicament with Modernity.* (London: Routledge).

Van Gemert, F. (1998), *Ieder voor zich. Kansen, cultuur en criminaliteit van Marokkaanse jongens.* (Amsterdam: Het Spinhuis).

Volpi, F. and Turner, B. (2007), 'Making Islamic Authority Matter', *Theory, Culture and Society* 24(2): 1–19.

Werdmölder, H. (2005), *Marokkaanse Lieverdjes: Crimineel en hinderlijk gedrag onder Marokkaanse jongeren.* (Amsterdam: Balans).

Chapter 10

The Struggle to Stay on the Middle Ground: The Radicalization of Muslims in Sweden

David Thurfjell

Introduction

The years following the events of 9/11 have shown two tendencies within Sweden's Muslim communities. On one hand there is the so-called radicalization of the political climate of many Muslim communities, which have become increasingly polemical towards the Swedish majority culture in recent years. Groups related to the Salafiyya and Ikhwani movements have gained in influence and some young leaders of Islamist orientation have appeared. On the other hand, there have also been quite a few dropouts from the Muslim community. Many prominent leaders, mostly converts, have either officially left Islam or significantly lessened their engagement as leaders or representatives of the Swedish Muslim community. Several female leaders have ceased wearing headscarves. There are no reliable statistics on this, but much still indicates that the general politicization and massively negative publicity that Islam and Muslims are getting in the media have had a great impact on decisions to leave Islam.

It hence seems reasonable to argue that there are mutual processes of radicalization and abandonment going on among Muslims in Sweden. The present situation seems to lead people away from the religious middle ground and into maximalist or minimalist extremes. For some reason Muslims are being pushed away from the semi-secular religious position that is so predominant among adherents of other religions in the country. This situation, one could argue, makes Europe's Muslim communities different from their Christian and Jewish counterparts who, to a larger extent, have developed a religious mainstream that is more or less in line with the values of the modern society surrounding them.

Muslims in Sweden

Before elaborating further on this observation, it is appropriate to present some basic facts about the Muslim communities in Sweden. According to Jørgen Nielsen, Sweden is the European country whose demographical situation has changed most dramatically as an effect of immigration since the 1960s (Nielsen 2004). There are no statistics on religious affiliation in Sweden, but it is estimated that there are some

400,000 cultural Muslims living in the country today. A vast majority of these are immigrants, or the children of immigrants, with backgrounds from many different countries, including Turkey, Iraq, Iran, Lebanon, Bosnia, Somalia and Pakistan. Due to the great diversity within their numbers, it would be faulty to speak of one Swedish Muslim community. Although there are several national umbrella organizations and some active attempts to create a Swedish Islam, denominational and ethnic differences still dominate the Muslim communities in the country.

There are also some converts, and it is interesting to note that these adherents have played an important role in the organization of the country's Muslim communities, along with the public relations efforts pertaining to them.[1]

The Post-Colonial Condition

If the above observation about mutual processes of radicalization and abandonment is correct, the next question is why this is so. What is it that forces or inspires Muslims to make a choice between extremes? In this chapter I will put forth one perspective that might contribute to answering this question. In order to understand the special situation of the Muslim communities in Europe, we need to take into consideration not only the post-9/11 world order, but also the general post-colonial situation of the Muslim *ummah*, or world community. The experience of and the narrative about Western suppression and colonization of Muslims have contributed, I believe, to the emergence in this context of two relevant attitudes towards European modernity, namely, suspicion and indignation. Let me linger for a little while on each of these.

Suspicion

First, then, some words about suspicion. It has to be remembered that European modernity as an ideological movement, although largely anti-religious, to a great extent sprang from the traditions of Judaism and Christianity insofar as its main thinkers were Christian or Jewish Europeans. For most Muslims, on the contrary, the ideas of modernity were largely introduced alongside the political oppression of colonialism in a time when the Muslim empires, step by step, lost their positions of political power. The ideals that in Europe came together with wealth and global political supremacy in the Muslim world came alongside political disintegration, poverty and marginalization. Among certain layers of the population in the Muslim world, the experience of colonial oppression left a lingering tinge of bitterness towards the ideals of the European Enlightenment.

---

1 Some examples of converts who have had an important role in representing Islam in Sweden are Helena Benouda, Abdalhaqq Kielan, Muhammad Muslim, Pernilla Ouis and Anne Sofie Roald.

Quite naturally, people have asked themselves whether these ideals can be seen as independent of the oppressors who delivered them, or if they are also in some way part of a greater scheme, the intent of which is to manipulate, control and exploit Muslim lands. Is modern empiricism not an assault upon the very core of the Islamic belief in divine revelation? And, hence, a way to disqualify Muslim demands for justice – demands that are based in the promises of this revelation? And, is the fragmentized world view of postmodernism not just another version of the old divide-and-rule-principle whereby Muslim claims to be united under certain principles can be neglected?

Maybe its association with colonial oppression and manipulation partly explains why the modern world view has failed to catch on in Islamic theology the way it has in its Christian and Jewish counterparts.

Indignation

Let me now move on to say something about the second significant Muslim attitude towards European modernity: indignation. As, for instance, the incidents in connection with the Danish caricatures of Mohammad in 2006 showed, many young Muslims in Europe and elsewhere are aggravated about the way Islam is treated in the majority culture. People are frustrated. Many feel that Islam and Muslims are under attack, that an assault with the purpose of forcing Muslims to adjust to Western hegemony is taking place on many levels. Of course, the so-called War on Terrorism, the invasions of Afghanistan and Iraq, the Israeli-Palestinian conflict, the prison camps of Guantanamo bay, and the incidents of Abu Ghraib prison serve as the foremost proofs of such an assault in Muslim homelands and other areas.

But, as the incident with the caricatures in Denmark showed, people are also under pressure in the diaspora. A recent report from the European Monitoring Centre on Racism and Xenophobia provides a frightening picture of the situation in Europe (Allen and Nielsen 2002). The report gives clear evidence that Islamophobia is widespread on the continent. Muslims have greater difficulties in the housing and labour markets; vandalism on Muslim property is common, and verbal or physical assaults on Muslims are frequent. At the same time as Muslims in these ways are systematically discriminated against in almost all societal spheres, the image of Islam as an ideology that constitutes a great threat increasingly gains hold.

Needless to say, the feelings of indignation and humiliation that this situation creates make people less inclined to adjust to the agendas of the majority culture.

Modernity has forced all three of the Abrahamic religions to reinterpret their traditions in order to adjust them to changes in society. But compared to Christians and Jews, Muslims have been less inclined to elect the theological middle ground of liberal interpretation. Feelings of suspicion and indignation caused by the colonial experience may partly explain this.

The Meaning-Making Perspective

Let me now approach from a slightly different perspective the question of why many Muslims seem to have difficulties remaining on the religious middle ground: namely, a cultural studies perspective that focuses on the mechanisms of social meaning-making. I will begin with a definition of Islam from such a point of view.

Islam, from a cultural studies perspective, is a name that is given to a rich, varied and often contradictory collection of ideas, stories, symbols and attributes. From this collection individuals inherit or choose the particular set of components that constitutes their own personal Islam. The meaning or function of Islam in an individual's life depends on the components that one chooses to include or exclude in one's own definition of the religion. This selection, in its turn, relies heavily on the personal background and situation of the particular individual.

However, the meaning of a particular Islamic component (for instance, the veil, the daily prayers, or the notion of *jihad al-nafs*, or inner struggle) is not only dependent on the choices or preferences of individual believers. The meaning of these components, like all other elements of culture, is also exposed to the meaning-making forces of external societal discourses. Hence, the cultural significance of, for instance, the 'Muslim beard' becomes the matter of a debate in which not only Muslims are involved. In culturally heterogeneous societies such as the ones of present-day Europe, it is especially difficult to escape this public examination of ideas. Hence, regardless of the will of Islamic authorities, we have a situation in which non-Muslims and even anti-Muslim opinion-makers have a say in the discussion of what Islam should be like for Muslims. This situation creates a tension between *the desired meaning* of a particular attribute, on one hand, and the *ascribed meanings* of it on the other.

This tension, of course, exists for all individuals and groups in a culturally heterogeneous society. Everyone has to deal with the divergent and critical opinions of one's surroundings. However, in today's Europe there exists a particularly strong non-Muslim discourse on Islam and what Islam should be like. Governments make efforts to control what imams preach in the mosques, and the teaching of Islam in Muslim schools is especially scrutinized. Newspapers and weeklies are full of articles on the problems of Islam written *by* non-Muslims *for* non-Muslims. In Sweden and elsewhere there have even been attempts at correcting Islamic scholars in matters of Koran-exegesis. In all of these public discussions, Muslims are strikingly absent.

Arguably, the vivid engagement in Islamic matters that these discussions seem to be proof of makes the tension between desired and approved meaning, which all humans deal with, especially strong for Muslims living in the diaspora.

It is important to emphasize that the influence that this non-Muslim discourse on Islam has on Muslims does not merely or even predominantly occur on an intellectual level. Of course, Muslims relate to what is said with arguments and reason, but the influence of the non-Muslim majority culture is also discursive and tacit insofar as it defines normality. Muslims, like all others, live in society. They go to school, watch television, listen to music and follow most trends like everyone else. Islam might be an important part of one's identity, but it is rarely more than just one piece of it.

To live in a secular society means to internalize the ways of living and believing that are dominant there. And – and this is important – to live in an Islamophobic society means to internalize the Islamophobia that is also predominant there. To certain extent, this is also true for Muslims, who are largely dependent on media to get information about what is going on in the world, and on the opinions of their neighbours when forming their views of themselves.

In the wake of the 'War on Terrorism' and the increasing polarization of world politics, Islamic symbols are furthermore caught up in a process of heavy politicization. Because of Islamists, who have made Islam the foundation of a modern political ideology, and the already mentioned strong non-Muslim discourse on Islam, Islamic attributes of dress have become markers of a particular political position, even if the individual who wears them thinks and speaks of them as something else.

To be Muslim in an Islamophobic society, hence, is difficult not just because Muslims are discriminated against, but also because one can internalize the negative and politicized image of Muslims that is found in society at large, and so risk being caught in a paradox of self-contempt. It is difficult to know that one is a Muslim and to simultaneously learn that Muslims are 'the bad guys'.

Conclusion

For Muslims in Sweden, staying on the middle ground means participating fully in society while still maintaining a solid Muslim identity. It entails finding a way to believe and practise Islam that is not in conflict with the people and environments one meets in everyday life.

In today's Europe it is very difficult to maintain this middle ground. It takes a lot of strength and self-confidence to swim against the tide. And, since few Muslims have the societal backing or platform to even be heard in public, the meaning and significance of one's choice will always be interpreted by others. In such a position one constantly has to withstand or struggle against the meanings that others ascribe to one's beliefs and practices. It is socially strenuous and in the long run difficult to endure.

What, then, should one do? Many Muslims find themselves in a situation where they feel socially forced to choose between two extremes: either to abandon Islam altogether and thereby silently consent to the majority's condemnation of it, or to leave the majority culture and try to build a life within one of the more or less secluded Muslim groups that the majority has labelled radical or extremist. And, by doing so, accept that in the eyes of the majority one becomes a representative for an Islam that has come to be associated with radical and anti-secularist political viewpoints.

Choosing this second option manifests what is often called the radicalization of young Muslims in Europe. I have tried to show that it may be unintentionally encouraged by the majority culture.

References

Allen, C. and Nielsen, J.S. (2002), *Summary Report on Islamophobia in the EU after 11 September 2001*. (Vienna: European Monitoring Centre on Racism and Xenophobia).

Nielsen, J.S. (2004), *Muslims in Western Europe*. (Edinburgh: Edinburgh University Press).

Chapter 11

Young French Women of Muslim Descent: Discriminatory Social Context and Politicization

Sepideh Farkhondeh

Introduction

Methodological Issues Raised by the Choice of Religious Denomination

Any study focusing on religious criteria is difficult in France. The official French statistical institution (INSEE[1]) is the only organization accredited to make population censuses. As the French Republic characterizes itself as secular and universalist, it considers that the ethnic and religious characteristics of its citizens are not its concern, since the constitution stipulates that 'no distinction of race, age or religion shall ever be made among French citizens.' None of the seven censuses made during the last 50 years included any question about ethnic and religious considerations.[2]

One of the reasons for this is that the common perception of the principle of secularism, or 'laïcité', deems any question about religion intrusive. This principle is highly respected in France since beliefs are considered as belonging only to the private sphere. Freedom of religion is ensured by the sacredness of the private sphere. But when this notion leads to the reduction of a whole religious community to those who bear the external signs and symbols attributed to a particular sect, then the refusal to consider religion as part of the public sphere becomes equivalent to a refusal to know and understand. Indeed, the pernicious effect of this discretion is that in public opinion, but also in the media and in political speeches, Muslims are often seen only as those who can be visibly detected as such: they necessarily wear headscarves, have beards and, according to some very widespread confusions, practise polygamy and even excision. The lack of reliable statistics, far from ensuring the impartiality of the public debate on religion and an equitable image of citizens regardless of their faith, contributes to the political exploitation of the image of Islam more or less linked to terrorism.

---

1   Institut national de la statistique et des études économiques (National Institute of Economic and Statistical Information).

2   The last census in which the religion of people was mentioned was made in 1872.

Public institutions and media give the impression of knowing such information. However, broad consensus has gradually emerged that is based on popular but inaccurate figures and imagined statistics. Governmental organs have not been encouraged to spend money to get data they think they already have, or that are not the subject of vocal dispute. Moreover, collecting information is costly.

The question of reliable statistics is interesting and important from a methodological point of view. Michèle Tribalat was one of the first sociologists to formulate the problem clearly.[3] She showed that the number of Muslims in France, commonly cited as five or six million by journalists, politicians and even scientists, was an overestimation without any scientific base. She also demonstrated that the polls concerning the Muslim population, made by private polling organizations in the absence of reliable national statistics, were biased. She then proposed to use the results of a census about familial histories to assess the number of the population likely to be Muslim by affiliation. This type of assessment was not easy to make but it was based, for the first time, on real data. According to this census, made in 1999, at maximum about 3.7 million people, potentially Muslim because of their affiliation, lived in France.

According to the projections of Michèle Tribalat, among potentially Muslim residents, only 2.35 million had come of age. Tribalat and Kateb[4] showed that among adults of Muslim descent living in France, half were of foreign origin. As the migratory influx is relatively new, the population likely to be Muslim is rather young, and French society will have to take this population into account more and more. Only 1.2 million of potential Muslims are actually French citizens. In 2005, the number of French adults of Muslim culture or denomination was roughly 1.1 million. The real statistics are thus probably lower than what is usually quoted.

What's more, researchers or journalists who try to focus on the Muslim population often choose as their subjects individuals who bear some visible religious signs. They often encounter people who have specific claims or exhibit militant behaviour. The accounts of people who do not wear distinctive signs are underestimated. By ignoring these people, any investigation of the Muslim population potentially neglects the silent and invisible majority of French Muslims, so rarely heard in the French public scene. Moreover, statistical assessments do not take into account the real and intimate beliefs, but only the potential faith, of the people examined.

In 2004, after years of silence, hundreds of girls wearing headscarves became a public problem for the nation. In public debates, most of the questions and intense discussions about immigrants are related to Muslim women. Considering the statistics and the typically French difficulty in questioning people on religion, I was led to choose my sample not among explicitly Muslim people but among

---

3   'The number of Muslims in France, what do we know? / A peculiar secret: How many Muslims in France?', in *Cités, Hors-Série*, 2004.

4   'De l'étranger à l'immigré et de l'ethnique au religieux: les chiffres en question?', in *Cités, Hors Série*, 2004, K. Kateb.

those of Muslim descent.[5] Given the demographic projections, it seemed to me that a study, even limited, of the young generation would be more significant. Finally, as a female researcher, interviewing young women was much more feasible to me and also more interesting given the specific issues encountered by women of Muslim affiliation.

French women of Muslim descent were the focal point of the political debate when the issue of secularism at school and the Islamic headscarf were the headlines of newspapers. Their existence has been linked to the inextricable issues of the suburbs where Islamic fundamentalism has become visible since the beginning of the 1990s. Legislation banning any external mark of religiosity was adopted in France, but insufficient attention has been paid to the aspirations and needs of young Frenchwomen of Muslim descent. And yet, the deterioration of living standards in deprived suburban projects (cités) affects them especially. Social and economic discrimination against the country's immigrant-origin population, massive unemployment undermining paternal authority and consequently strengthening that of the eldest sons, as well as the phenomenon of an underground Islam, have contributed to the vulnerability of young women of Muslim origin.[6] A quantitative survey would necessitate a scientific team; thus the sample of the interviewees is not a classic sociological sample: my analysis is also based on the last published scientific studies and statistics about French people of Arab, African and Turkish origin.

Double Identity, Discriminatory Context and Civil Claims

Frenchwomen of Muslim descent are facing a new set of challenges different from those faced by their mothers and grandmothers. They are often the first or second generation of women born and educated in France. They speak French fluently and are often culturally distant from their Arab country of origin. They don't feel the same longing or nostalgia for a remote motherland as their mothers or grandmothers did. They are the first generation to attain a high level of education.

Our 16 interviewees live in Paris and its suburbs. They are between 18 and 30 years old. Some are students, finishing their first year at university (Malika in computers, Farida in medicine, Leila in law, Chafia in chemistry). Kahina is an electronic engineer and Yasmina is a teacher. Lila, Mariam and Sofia are shop assistants, while Fenda and Kande go to high school. Ahlem is a medical secretary, Karima and Djamila are looking for jobs, and Nora is a legal secretary; Nadia

---

5   However, I didn't include Iranian women in this study because they are a very small minority. They are often political refugees or belong to families with a political past. Furthermore, they often reject religion. As such, they are not representative of the immigrant population in France.

6   Amara, Fadela and Zappi, Sylvia, *Ni Putes Ni soumises*, La découverte/Poche, Paris, 2003.

is a trainee baker. Seven are of Algerian origin, five of Moroccan origin, two of Tunisian origin and two of Senegalese origin.

The Islam these women practise is usually very personalized. Half of my interviewees pray every day; five say they pray occasionally and the other three, while not denying being Muslim, say they pray when they need to. Twelve claim to respect all the religious dietary restrictions, while four say they don't always eat *hallal*; two say they sometimes drink alcohol. They all fast during Ramadan, for at least half of the month. Only two go to mosque at least once a month.

If rites and religious ceremonies seem important in the life of these young women, mosque attendance is low. Their relationships to Islam are thus very different from each other and are indeed individualized.

But all of them complain about the prejudices existing against Islam in French society, and all say that being of Muslim descent is a handicap to social advancement. They challenge the very notion of integration, which is perceived as an insult to their Frenchness. They feel offended by those who see a contradiction between their religion and origin, on the one hand, and their French identity, on the other hand, but say it still happens quite often.

> I don't see why I would have to integrate into a society I was born in. It is the society who should learn to see me as a part of it (Malika, student in computers, 24).

> I feel I am French, Algerian, Muslim and respectful of secularism. I don't see any contradiction. Those who want to oppose everything are narrow-minded (Sofia, shop assistant, 22).

The lack of places of worship for Muslims in France is felt as an injustice.

> There is a chaplaincy in my high school and everybody finds it normal, but a mosque in the city shocks people. I don't say I'll attend the prayers but I believe my parents have the right to have a place of worship (Kande, high school student, 18).

After having succeeded in postponing the construction of the great mosque of Marseille in April 2007, some far-right elected representatives belonging to the Front National (FN), the Mouvement National Républicain (MNR) and the Mouvement Pour la France (MPF)[7] plan to delay the construction of a mosque in Montreuil, a suburb of Paris, by instituting legal proceedings against the town council. The prosecutors accuse the council of putting ground at the disposal of Muslim organizations. They claim that leasing out a piece of land for a nominal rent is a disguised subsidy. One could retort that among the 1,800 places of worship constructed since 1905 (date of the official separation of church and state in

---

7   These three parties all put forward xenophobic slogans.

France), 450 churches and places of worship have been built thanks to these leases. But according to a member of the far-right movement MNR, these proceedings are ways to fight against 'the Islamization of France': 'We do not consider that the Christian religion, which shaped history, is equal to Islam, established in France for 20 years against the will of the French people.' In the same city of Montreuil, a similar lease has been granted for the construction of synagogue, but the MNR has not contested this case.

The construction of Muslim schools hasn't yet been hindered by far-right parties, but France has only four such high schools, one of which is on the Island of Réunion, in the Indian Ocean. Each has less than two hundred pupils. Two other Muslim schools will probably open soon, if they obtain the necessary administrative permits. After the endless debates over veiled pupils at school, one can measure the marginal aspect of this phenomenon, which concerns a few hundred girls. In any case, a majority of Muslims in France want their children to go to state schools.[8]

Claim of Equal Citizenship

The absence of visible Muslim places and institutions hasn't caused any specific mobilization of people of immigrant origin. For a long time, people of African descent had been doubtful about politics, and their level of participation in the elections was lower than the rest of the French population. However, all the interviewees declared that they were registered on the electoral lists and determined to vote in the presidential elections.

Actually, French people of African and North African descent represent around 3 per cent of the electorate. Since the 1990s, politicians have renewed attempts to court the Muslim population. But, according to Sylvain Brouard and Vincent Tiberj, the majority of people of Muslim decent are left-wing, with 75 per cent coming out in favour of a party of the left and almost half declaring themselves close to the socialist party. No religious factor explains these stances. The creation of a French Council for Muslims (Conseil Français du Culte Musulman) or the appointment of a Muslim prefect by Nicolas Sarkozy when he was Minister of the Interior didn't allow the right-wing party to capture the electorate of North African and African descent. This proves that trying to address this section of the population by highlighting the religious criterion doesn't pay off. For this population, religion isn't what matters most in their conception of the nation and their identity as French citizens.

The first senses of belonging adhere to generation, gender, and social background, then to the French nation and, finally, to more specific characteristics. There is no contradiction in having several levels of identity: the closer one feels

---

8 Brouard, Sylvain and Tiberj, Vincent, *Français comme les autres?* (*French like the others?*) Presses de la Fondation Nationale des Sciences Politiques, Paris, 2005.

to one's country of origin and family, the more one feels a sense of belonging to the French nation.

Although young Frenchwomen of Muslim descent are determined to assert their French citizenship, it is not certain that the majority of the population is ready to admit them as fully-fledged French citizens. Actually, a poll taken by the research organization TNS-Sofres shows that 30 per cent of voters are unwilling to support a candidate of Muslim culture or denomination out of hand. As a point of comparison, 4 per cent are not prepared to vote for a woman and 5 per cent are unwilling to vote for a black candidate.

This poll contributes to understanding the extreme reluctance of most political parties in France to present candidates of North African origin in the elections. The Socialist Party, which is traditionally composed of members coming from diverse origins and includes many militants of the 'Beur' movement of 1980s,[9] has always appeared hesitant to act on discrimination, did not publicly criticized the governing political parties on this issue and created frustrations and disappointments. However, the last presidential elections confirm a new trend. The presence of Najat Belkacem, a young Frenchwoman of Moroccan origin with a modest background but highly educated, in the campaign team of the Socialist candidate Ségolène Royal, and the appointment of Rachida Dati as Minister of Justice, can be interpreted as the beginning of a new era. Is the tightly closed arena of French politics starting to open up to French citizens of Muslim descent? Yet, discriminations are still experienced every day. People don't change their behaviour just because new political speeches condemn discrimination, especially when, at the same time, they demonize Islam.[10] The interviewees are mistrustful.

The appointment of Rachida Dati as Minister of Justice was generally seen by our respondents as positive but fear that the promotion of a few figures overshadows daily discrimination was often expressed.

---

9   'Beur' is a distorted inversion of the word 'Arabe' and designated the young French generation of Arab descent in the 1980s. 'Beur' started to fight against racism and for their rights in the beginning of the decade when the Socialist Party won the presidential and legislative elections. The movement was then denied the opportunity to really invest in the French political scene by the conservatism and nepotism of the Socialist Party.

10   In a political television program during the presidential campaign, the former Minister of Interior and now President of Republic, Nicolas Sarkozy, questioned by citizens about Islam, reminded the audience in a professorial tone that 'one should not kill sheep in one's bath at home; one should not practise polygamy; one should not practise excision,' citing all the negative characteristics attributed to Muslims. In the audience, a young woman wearing an elegant suit replied: 'I am of Algerian origin, I am a Muslim, and I am shocked!'

Fundamentalism, Ghettoization and Civil Mobilization

Life in the suburban projects has deteriorated since the 1990s, and attacks against young women have increased. The French association '*Ni Putes Ni Soumises*' (Neither Whores Nor Doormats) fights against the outcomes of ghettoization and social and economic discrimination. Fadela Amara, the founder of this association and Secretary of State for Urban Policy since June 2007, worked for years in a local project in the city of Clermont-Ferrand. She noticed an alarming increase of violence in suburban areas (*quartiers*), especially against women. Girls and young women were subjected more and more to their parents' fear of gossip; they were more and more often kept under close watch and less often received permission to go out.

'The name of the association is aimed at two types of audiences,' Amara has said of her effort to change the situation. "Neither Whore" is intended for the inhabitants of the deprived estates; "Nor Doormats" is aimed at the right-thinking people who imagine that the submission is total' (Amara, 2003). *Ni Putes Ni Soumises* tries to make both the public living in the suburbs and the well-off classes of the cities aware of the situation of women.

Along with other activists, Amara also organized seminars on the history of the feminist movement. Several associations joined together and worked in partnership with sociologists, and a book was written about the women living in deprived estates. In November 2002, a terrible event occurred that revealed the seriousness of the violence the girls of the suburbs were confronting. Sohane Benziane, 17 years old, was burned alive in the cellar of a building in Vitry-sur-Seine, a suburb of Paris. She was known as an independent character, a girl who didn't let others dictate her behaviour. Public opinion was hit by a sudden realization: the malaise of the suburbs made women especially vulnerable.

Job Discrimination

One of the causes of the increasing violence against women in France was the social and economic situation. In the beginning of the 1990s, the industrial sector was going through a major restructuring and many factories closed down; in families of immigrant origin, the fathers were the main victims of these mass layoffs. Many became jobless, losing their social status. Their authority at home was then undermined. The suburbs, some entirely inhabited by people of immigrant origin, sank into poverty, and those who could manage to hastened to leave those areas. The ghettoization worsened. At the same time, governments reduced the number of tutors and youth workers, reduced public utilities in the deprived areas, and basically withdrew from these districts.

Discrimination and mass unemployment favour an unofficial and underground economy. Drug trafficking and trading in stolen goods became the only ways for many young men to earn money easily and exist socially. Young Frenchmen of immigrant origin living in these ghettos were often confronted with racism as soon as they left their neighbourhoods to look for jobs or simply to go out to nightclubs. Some turned their frustration against their own family, or their own neighbourhood, the only spaces they could control and over which they sometimes ruled. They started to live split lives: they reigned over the family unit but didn't take part in it. Some became the new, self-proclaimed guardians of their area. They started to keep watch over their sisters' appearance, attack unmarried couples and insult girls wearing tight-fitting jeans. Being violent and male-chauvinistic is their way of being recognized outside and inside the cité.

Surge of a New Fundamentalism

It is in this context of violence and worsened ghettoization that underground Islam appears in the 1990s. Self-proclaimed preachers, usually promoting a reactionary reading of the sacred texts as far as the status of women is concerned, start their sermons in the ghettos. They are called 'les imams des caves' or the imams of the cellars since, in the absence of any place of worship, practising Muslims often pray in the cellars of their buildings. In some areas, they become role models. Yet, these imams don't profess the quiet and tolerant Islam of elder generations.[11] They sometimes even generate conflicts between generations. Radicalized young people start to criticize their parents for their lack of rigour and their faulty knowledge of the Quran. Some young women also appropriate the views expressed by fundamentalists and see themselves as victims of global injustice. They identify with the victims of Middle-East conflicts.

But one of the main damages of the new fundamentalism in the deprived French suburbs is the deterioration of the relationship between girls and boys, which is more and more dominated by male chauvinism and reaffirmation of reactionary dogma such as virginity before marriage.

The myth of sacred virginity before marriage is a key of the code of honour. The girls guarding their virginity are considered responsible for the honour not only of their family but also of their district in the town. The boys who watch over the girls are then perceived as the protectors of the neighbourhood. If a girl makes a mistake, her mother will be first physically affected – often through battering by the father – and then morally subjected to the court of public opinion.

> I noticed a growing attachment to religious references. In the period of Ramadan,
> more and more pupils want to fast, even when they don't belong to Islam.

---

11   France regularly expels radical imams from its suburbs. In January 2010, Ali Ibrahim el-Soudany, an Egyptian citizen born in 1973, was expelled for praising Jihad in Seine-Saint-Denis. In July 2005, Abdelhamid Aissouai was the first imam to be expelled. This 41-year-old Algerian was well-known by the security and anti-terrorist services. He had previously been sentenced to four years' imprisonment for belonging to the network of Khaled Kelkal, suspected of a terrorist attempt against a TGV train in 1995. This occasional imam was suspected of secretly preaching in various mosques near Lyon.

Usually the teenagers don't understand the meaning of this fast: for them it is like affirming their identity. The language also has changed. Before they swore on their mother's life, nowadays they swear on Mecca. When you ask them if they understand what they say, they reply they are used to this way of speaking – it's the language of the neighbourhood. One of my pupils once said that women should not work, meaning that religion didn't allow it (Yasmina, teacher, 30).

The problem is that they have been educated as if they were kings. How many times my mother told me 'Go and make your brother's bed'? They had all the rights since they were kids… So they can't bear any annoyance. Vexations make them furious… (Djamila, 25).

Once, I thought I should wear a headscarf, so that they would stop pestering me. Then I thought it would be ridiculous. I wouldn't dare to walk in Paris like that and I would have to take it off in the subway before reaching Paris. I had to be at ease with myself. Now I ignore them but I don't wear exactly what I want. In front of them, I try to be neutral (Ahlem, medical secretary, 26).

A judicial decision made public in the French press in May 2008 is symptomatic of the pressure many young French women of Muslim descent go through. In Lille, in the north of France, a judge annulled a marriage with reference to Article 180 of the civil code. According to this article, a marriage can be annulled if 'an error' is noticed in the 'essential qualities' of the spouses. The day after his wedding, a French engineer of Moroccan origin, in his thirties, used this article to annul his marriage under the pretext that his wife, a 22-year-old nurse, had lied about her virginity. The judge considered that there was indeed an 'error in the essential qualities' of the young woman, since she had lied and deceived the confidence of her husband. This case was made public by a newspaper months after the court's decision and provoked a scandal. Women's rights advocates expressed their fears that virginity would become an 'essential quality' of future wives and this annulment would set the precedent.

The young woman and her husband had both grown up in France, and had met at a wedding. She was completing her studies to become a nurse and he had already been an engineer for a few years. They saw each several times platonically before he asked for her hand and insisted on organizing a Moroccan wedding ceremony to honour traditions. The marriage took place in July 2006. But on the wedding night, when the young woman, wanting to share a secret with her husband, told him that she had experienced a serious relationship that lasted four years, and that at the end of this relationship her lover had taken her virginity before abandoning her, the husband blew up at her. The day after the wedding, the young woman was brought back to her father's place as damaged merchandise and her husband decided not to sue for divorce but to annul this marriage he was ashamed of. He found a lawyer clever enough to use Article 180 of the civil code to obtain his annulment.

After this painful personal experience and the annulment of the marriage (in April 2008), the young woman started to recover her freedom and serenity. But when the judgement was mentioned in the press, it gave rise to a scandal and was put into question again. She confided anonymously to a journalist how difficult it was to hear everyone talk about her. 'I am not the leader of a movement; I don't demand anything.' This young woman also felt deceived: while he thought she was a virgin, she thought he was kind and intelligent.[12] Rachida Dati, the Minister of Justice, at first played down the judgement in this case, describing it as a release from the marriage for the young woman as well as the man. But the controversy increased in scale and jurists reminded the public that, since the French Revolution, marriage had been considered not only a private agreement but also a civil and public institution. Therefore, the 'essential qualities' of the spouses must be in accordance with Republican values, and a lie about virginity couldn't be ruled on. What if a woman claims she loves football when in fact she never watches a match? And can a woman obtain an annulment when she discovers that her husband who claimed to be gentle proved to be violent?

According to feminists, but also many jurists and politicians, the public prosecutor should have appealed this annulment so that the decision wouldn't set a precedent; the husband would then have had to sue for divorce. This simple annulment was considered an infringement on the equality of men and women in France. Finally, the Minister Dati turned around and accepted an appeal against the judgement.

Meanwhile, the young woman whose hymen became a national affair desperately wants to remain anonymous and rebuild a new life.

This case has provoked many other controversies. Does the Koran require virginity before marriage? To what extent can justice be adapted to the traditions or religious beliefs of different communities? Can respect for religious beliefs justify the recurrence of patriarchal practices? To what extent can lawyers exploit law in order to validate traditions and customs? How can respect for the law and for equality be asserted without putting into motion bureaucratic machinery that can crush individuals? Young French women of Muslim descent are willy-nilly at the crossroads of these challenges.

Multiple Sites of Exclusion

Excluded as Women by Men and as Daughters by Parents

Women's rights activists often consider the regression in Muslim women's rights as serious, after a small improvement thanks to the 'Beur movement' in the eighties. Although the feminist associations active in some suburban areas are

---

12   *Nouvel Observateur*, 5 June 2008, Isabelle Monin, Agathe Logeart, Marie Lemonnier.

totally secular, many young people ask the local militants to interpret the sacred text for them. So feminists are sometimes reluctantly led to interpret the Quran, thinking they have the duty to destroy the feeling of guilt that the fundamentalist reading wants to impose on women.[13]

> Once I was walking in the middle of Paris. A guy came to me and asked insistently, "Are you a Muslim, are you a Muslim?" I automatically answered yes. He then started to tell me that I shall wear a headscarf; otherwise I would not be a good Muslim. I got upset. Later, I thought it was a stupid attempt to chat me up. He was just a disoriented guy from a deprived area. They would like to think that we belong to them in a way. I am happy to live in Paris in a well-educated family but I can imagine what the girls living in deprived areas [*les quartiers*] can feel (Leila, law student, 24).

> My brother is a fundamentalist. He is wearing a long dress and a beard and is buried in his readings. Fortunately, he is not obsessive with girls but is going through a crisis of identity, I guess. My parents can't do anything about it; they only encourage him to pursue his studies in economics... (Mariam, shop assistant, 24).

> I had a boyfriend who was very tender with me when we were together, but as soon as his friends approached, he became aggressive and insulting, as if he had to conform to a male-chauvinist model. When he told me that anyhow he would marry a virgin, I stopped seeing him. The neighbourhood was rotten and I had to give the impression of being a serious girl, despising boys. From then on, I had only one idea in the mind: being successful at school and escaping from this neighbourhood. I had sad teenage years. It's as if tenderness was forbidden to us because of our origin... (Farida, medical student, 25).

Some Muslim associations, such as UOIF,[14] would like to represent Muslims in the public sphere of debate about their identity. But my interviewees don't know them and mistrust any official forum suspected of promoting the point of view and the discourse of their leaders. To them, these organizations seem far from being representative.

Excluded as Migrants by the State

Even though politicians showed public interest in the mobilization of Muslim women willing to change their conditions and fight against the effects of ghettoization, tensions have increased since the crises in the suburbs of November

---

13   Amara Fadela, Abdi Mohammad, *La racaille de la république*, Seuil, Paris, 2006.

14   In French, l'Union des Organisations Islamiques de France or Union of the Islamic Organizations of France.

2005. French people not of immigrant descent, following the official statements,[15] associated the events with young migrant people of African and North African origin vaguely manipulated or inspired by fanatics, before any investigation took place. This interpretation of the riots is not shared by the inhabitants of the problem areas, and created a state of tension between suburbanites of French origin and those of immigrant descent. The French inhabitants of immigrant descent blame the discriminatory and violent behaviour of the police acting against them as one the main reasons for the starting of the riots.

The creation of a Ministry of National Identity and Immigration was commonly perceived by many French citizens of foreign descent as a will to oppose two notions of citizenship, putting into question the authenticity of nationals of immigrant origin. Since the end of the 1990s and after the violent riots in the French suburbs in 2005, several harsh realities, which had long been lost sight of, became undeniable to youths of immigrant origin. Almost all the interviewees say they have been victims of racism.

> Several times in job interviews, I was asked to show my resident permit. As if I were a foreigner. The guy didn't ask for the French ID but for the resident permit. Yet, I don't have an accent when I speak French. Curly hair is often sufficient to categorize you as Arab… (Djamila, 25).

> When you are of French extraction, you are favoured, even if you are less educated. We live in a country that is supposed to give a lot of importance to diplomas but if your name is Karima, you don't have the same chances as if you were called Catherine or Anne-Marie, especially when you live in the slums [*la zone*] (Karima, 27).

The academic success of a child of French origin is similar to that of a child of immigrant origin.[16] The main handicap to academic success is social background and not origins. But despite a similar level of success at school, the unemployment rate varies considerably according to one's origins. Jean-Luc Richard notices that this unemployment rate reaches 29 per cent among those who have a parent of Algerian origin and 15 per cent among those whose parents have been settled

---

15   The Minister of the Interior declared that the riots were mainly organized by small groups of young foreigners linked to Islamist groups, denying the spontaneous nature of the rioting that took place after the accidental death of two young men pursued by the police who, panic-stricken and without having anything to reproach themselves with, took refuge in a deadly electric transformer.

16   Jean-Luc Richard, 'Une approche de la discrimination sur le marché du travail' (An introduction to discrimination in the job market), in *Revue Européenne des Migrations Internationale*, 2000, Vol.16, No. 3, 53–83.

in France for at least two generations. French people of immigrant origin are definitely hit by discriminatory practices.[17]

I am twenty years old and I live in Clichy-Sous-Bois. I took part in the riots that broke out and I regret that we girls were not more numerous because the country thinks that boys are the only victims of a society that takes care of us and addresses us every four years only [for the legislative elections]. In the neighbourhoods, you also have girls who live in badly maintained, low-rent buildings with elevators working two months a year, girls witnessing the provocations of the policemen (*gardiens de la paix*)[18] towards the boys and the latter's replies, sometimes violent. Society ignores the daughters of immigrants who see how difficult it is to get hired when you live in Seine-Saint-Denis, daughters of Muslim immigrants, victims of a society full of prejudices toward us, leading to all kind of discriminations. After twelve months and 28,000 cars burnt, I have the impression of having dreamt all the speeches and the promises that politicians made, saying they were ready to accept us as young French citizens, because nothing has changed (Fenda).

Once, I went to the 17th District of Paris, which is posh. I wanted to visit one of my classmates. As soon as I went into the entrance of the building, the caretaker said, 'There are no black people living here…' She didn't want me to go in the building. She was so racist that she simply couldn't believe I had a friend living there (Kande, high school student, 18).

When I went to secondary school, one of my classmates called me a dirty Arab *(sale arabe)*. I was shocked and afraid of going to school for a while. Fortunately, my mathematics teacher liked me. I decided to tell her. She took me aside and told me that I was much more gifted than this girl and should ignore her. If I hadn't this special relationship with my teacher, I don't know how I would have followed my school career. Fortunately, in France, you have people who compensate for the commonly shared stupidity… (Kahina, engineer, 30).

Where have you seen an Arab newscaster on the main French TV channels? One day, maybe they'll end up hiring an Algerian French, at last. But me, Djamila, I'll never be hired if a Caroline or a Marie applies for the same job as me. And nobody could ever prove it (Djamila, 25).

---

17   Jean-Luc Richard, *Partir ou rester? Les destinées des jeunes issus de l'immigration étrangère en France* (*To leave or to stay? Fates of youths of immigrant origin in France*), Paris, PUF, 2004.

18   Another way of designating policemen in French is to say les gardiens de la paix; it is the expression used by Fenda in an ironic and bitter tone.

Actually, the use of anonymous curriculum vitae was voted for by the French parliament in 2006, but the decree specifying how this law should be enforced never came out and the anonymous CV was never put into practice.

Conclusion

The invisible young French of Muslim descent, those who 'do adapt without problems' (Roy 2005) are a majority. They do not necessarily commit themselves in expected associative structures. Their social demands against discrimination are more vocal than their claim to be publicly recognized as Muslims. French nationals of Muslim descent hardly represent 3 per cent of the electorate and can influence the results of the presidential elections only if the candidates are in a very close race and running neck and neck. However, new registrations on electoral lists in order to vote confirm a general trend of politicization of French people of African and North African affiliation. Until 2005, the rate of non-registration among this population was twice higher than among other voters. But even more than the presence of Jean-Marie Le Pen, the overtly xenophobic candidate, in the second round of the presidential elections in 2002, the riots of 2005 seem to be the determining factor in the political realization of French people of Muslim descent.[19] Nicolas Sarkozy promised to fight against discrimination by establishing 'positive discrimination' (*discriminations positives*), somehow equivalent to the American idea of affirmative action. One wonders how such a policy could be implemented when the question of whether or not the origins of people can be asked is not yet resolved by the French public administration and when the use of the anonymous CV has been abandoned before being put into practice.

No unique voice speaking in the name of all Muslims in the country could epitomize the claims of an imaginary and non-existent French Muslim community. But all young women of Muslim descent, even those who are veiled, share the same claim to be recognized as fully-fledged Frenchwomen. Many of them go through pressures imposed on them by traditions and by family, and some rebel against this situation. Many try hard to reconcile their own modern way of life with the requirements of familial customs. But their main claim is not to be discriminated against because of their origin, their name, the colour of their skin, or their neighbourhood. They would like their faith not to be synonymous with violence in the media and in political debates. The principle of 'laïcité,' or secularism, is a deep commitment for them.

International studies show that France is one of the countries in the world where the level of religious practice is the lowest. This is also true for the country's population of Muslim origin, whose practices are largely personal and private.

---

19   Most of the interviewees felt hurt and personally insulted when Nicolas Sarkozy said he would clean the neighbourhoods with a high-pressure water cleaner ('Karcher') and would rid the deprived areas of the riffraff ('racaille').

References

Amara, F. (2003), with the collaboration of Sylvia Zappi. *Ni Putes Ni Soumises (Neither Whores Nor Doormats)*. (Paris: La Découverte).

Amiraux, V. (2006), 'Speaking as a Muslim: Avoiding Religion in French Public Space', in Amiraux and G. Jonker (eds) *Politics of Visibility: Young Muslims in European Public Spaces*. (Bielefeld: Transcript), 21–52.

Brouard, S. and Tiberj, V. (2005), *Français comme les autres? (French like the others?)* (Paris: Presses de la Fondation Nationale des Sciences Politiques).

Césari, J. (2004), *L'islam à l'épreuve de l'Occident (Islam and the Test of the West)*. (Paris: La Découverte).

Commission Islam et Laïcité (2005), *1905–2005: Les enjeux de la laïcité, (1905–2005: The Issues of Secularism)*. (Paris: l'Harmattan).

Etienne, B. (2003), *Islam, les questions qui fâchent (Islam, the Questions that Anger)*. (Paris: Bayard).

Etienne, B. (2005), *Heureux comme Dieu en France? La République face aux religions*. (Paris: Bayard).

Fetzer, J.S. and Soper, J.C. (2005), *Muslims and the State in Britain, France and Germany*. (Cambridge: Cambridge University Press).

Kepel, G. (1991), *Les banlieues de l'Islam: naissance d'une religion en France (The Suburbs of Islam: Birth of a Religion in France)*. (Paris: Seuil), 425.

Leveau, R. and Kepel, G. (1988), *Les musulmans dans la société française (Muslims in French Society)*. (Paris: Presses de Sciences Po).

Monin, I., Logeart, A. and Lemonnier, M. (2008), 'Une justice communautariste? Scandale pour un hymen' (Communitarian justice? Scandal over a hymen), in *Nouvel Observateur*, 5 June.

Richard, J.-L. (2004), *Partir ou rester? Les destinées des jeunes issus de l'immigration étrangère en France (To Leave or to Stay? Fates of Youth of Immigrant Origin in France)*. (Paris: PUF).

Roy, O. (2005), La *laïcité face à l'islam (Secularism Faced with Islam)*. (Paris: Stock).

Tawan, C. (2005), 'Les immigrés en France: une situation qui évolue' (*Immigrants in France: An Evolving Situation*), in *Insee Première*.

Tribalat, M. (1995), *Faire France: une grande enquête sur les immigrés et leurs enfants (To make France: A Survey of Immigrants and their Children)*. (Paris: La Découverte).

Tribalat, M. (1996), *De l'immigration à l'assimilation (From Immigration to Assimilation)*. (Paris: La Découverte).

Tribalat, M. (2004), 'Le nombre de musulmans en France, qu'en sait-on?' (The number of Muslims in France, what do we know?), in *Cités, hors-série*.

Venel, N. (2004), *Musulmans et citoyens (Muslims and Citizens)*. (Paris: PUF).

Venner, F. (2005), *OPA sur l'islam de France: les ambitions de l'UOIF (The Takeover of Islam in France: The Ambitions of the Union of Islamic Organizations of France)*. (Paris: Calmann-Lévy), 247.

Withol de Wenden, C. (1998), 'Young Muslim Women in France: cultural and psychological adjustments', *Political Psychology* 19(1): 198–210.

Withol de Wenden, C. (1998), 'How can one be Muslim? The French debate on allegiance, intrusion and transnationalism', *Revue internationale de sociologie*, 1998(07): 275–288.

Withol de Wenden, C. (2003), 'Le bilan du mouvement beur: l'embourgeoisement?' (The result of the Beur movement: the adoption of middle class attitudes?), *Cahiers de l'Orient*, 07/09(71): 117–124.

PART IV
Diasporic Space and Locating Space

Making Homes in Turbulent Times: Moroccan-Dutch Muslims Contesting Dominant Discourses of Belonging

Marjo Buitelaar and Femke Stock

Introduction

Summing up her experiences as a young adult, Farida, a Moroccan-Dutch woman stated that as a result of the dominant image of Muslim women in Dutch society:

> You get the feeling that you belong neither here in the Netherlands, nor elsewhere.
> I don't belong in Morocco either, I couldn't live there, I'm used to living here.
> This is my home, but I feel as though I do not belong here.

This chapter analyses narrations of home and belonging in the life stories of descendants of Moroccan migrants to the Netherlands, who, like Farida, participated in a life story research project carried out by the two authors of this chapter.[1] Creating homes that incorporate various sites of belonging, especially when one does not find one's home culture represented in mainstream host culture, is an ongoing process of negotiation. This is particularly the case for citizens of Muslim descent in present day Dutch society, which is going through turbulent years.

As elsewhere in Europe, over the last decade Islam has become the primary marker of identity attributed to citizens of Muslim descent. Besides the events of 9/11 and the subsequent 'war on terror', several local incidents have influenced the Dutch discourse on Islam. In 2002, it shook the nation when the liberal-rightist politician Pim Fortuyn, who spoke in very negative terms about Muslims, was killed. Even though the murderer was an environmentalist of Dutch background, Fortuyn's death is often associated with the perceived danger posed by the presence of fundamentalist Muslims in the Netherlands. Then, in 2004, the Dutch filmmaker

---

1   The life story project started in 1998 with a focus on the legacy of migration in life stories. Twenty-five higher educated women participated, 15 of whom were interviewed again in 2008. In 2007 a new subproject focusing on 'home and belonging' was launched. 16 higher and lower educated men and women have been interviewed so far. In this chapter, we draw from life stories from both subprojects.

Theo van Gogh was killed by a young man of Moroccan descent who motivated his act in religious terms.[2] Most recently, Geert Wilders, a populist member of Dutch parliament whose flagrantly anti-Islam statements receive much media attention, enjoys a quickly growing constituency (15.5 per cent of all votes in the 2010 national elections).

All collected life stories included references to these societal developments which indicate that making homes in the context of this growing Islamophobic climate is hard work to say the least. In general, our interlocutors report an increased preoccupation by others with their connectedness to Islam and their Moroccan roots and a pressure to relinquish these connections and assimilate into Dutch society.

Particularly the comparison of self-narratives related by the women who participated in both the 1998 and 2008 interviews allows a unique insight in how societal and personal issues intertwine in feelings of home and belonging. Since life stories take us on an imaginary journey across temporally and spatially situated experiences back to people's roots, they are particularly well suited to study developments in various notions of home and belonging. Indeed, the self-narratives of our interlocutors abound with narrations about different places, routines and people that are meaningful to them. Since many of them invited us to their homes for the interviews, often stories about objects that they surround themselves with to construct personal symbolic home spaces in their dwellings also entered the narratives.

In order to study the ways in which past and present homes are interrelated, we find Brah's distinction between 'a desire for home' and a 'homing desire' helpful (Brah 1996: 180). Brah distinguishes a 'homing desire,' a more general wish to belong, from a 'desire for home.' The latter concerns a specific conception of home that is situated in one's roots and refers to a place somewhere else. She argues that whether migrants locate home primarily 'here' or in a temporally and spatially faraway place is not simply a matter of personal choice, but is intrinsically linked with how processes of inclusion and exclusion operate to allow them to satisfy a 'homing desire.' The question of home, then, is about positioning oneself and being positioned in relations to others and concerns both political and personal struggles over the social regulation of 'belonging' (Brah 1996: 192).

For the purpose of this chapter, we adopt Rapport and Dawson's approach, taking home to refer to a cognitive environment where one is at ease and through which one finds one's identity best mediated (Rapport, N. and Dawson, A. 1998: 10). Our focus is on how our interlocutors relate to their Moroccan and Muslim 'roots' in their endeavours to satisfy their 'homing desire' in a social context where their right to belong is increasingly being denied. We will trace the ways in which individuals position themselves towards such external voices in their

---

2   Van Gogh was the producer of the film *Submission*, which contains shots of Quranic texts written on a naked female body. The film-script was written by Ayaan Hirsi Ali, a former Dutch member of parliament of Somalian descent. *Submission* was part of what she called her '*jihad*' against Islam's oppression of women.

home-making. We see talking about home as an identity-constructing activity (Blunt and Dowling 2006: 24; Kraus 2006) that involves exploring one's 'roots and routes' (Gilroy 1993) and locating oneself in the present by joining references to one's past experiences with hopes for the future (Ghorashi 2003). Focusing on narrations on home in life stories allows us to document the relational and fluid nature of identity and its embeddedness in (social) time and space.

The analysis of the stories of individual persons, allows us to trace how processes of home-making are both highly personal and deeply embedded in larger society. Even if one would maintain the highly debatable binary divide between 'private' and 'public' domains, the home could not be restricted to the private realm. The notion of home can refer to levels that can hardly be deemed private: one's community, city, nation, or, in the case of our interlocutors, the global *umma* or Community of Muslims. Also, on more intimate scales, processes of home-making take place through dialogues with multiple collective and personal voices representing one's various positions in society. Narrations about home and belonging in the life stories direct our attention to the relevance of the voices of others in personal home-making.

In what follows, we will demonstrate how our interlocutors relate to such external voices in claims about belonging or not-belonging. Since the concept of home can refer to many different things (Mallett 2004), we will begin with a more general reflection on the multiple meanings of the concept 'home' in a diasporic context. We will then trace how descendants of Moroccan migrants in the Netherlands negotiate belonging through an analysis of our interlocutors' expressions about living in one country while relating to, and being associated with, another. As our opening quote suggests, it is often through being othered as Muslims that Moroccan-Dutch citizens find their sense of home in the Netherlands contested. The role of religion in the politics of belonging comes to the fore most explicitly in our final section. There we will look at the stories of two women whom we interviewed in 1998 and again in 2008. The focus will be on narrations about their efforts to carve their own spaces at the intersection of various discourses of belonging and not-belonging in a quickly changing Dutch society.

Diasporic Meanings of Home-Making

In more emic or insiders' ideal understandings of the term, 'home' refers to a place that is stable, exclusive and profoundly familiar. Yet, in the reality of diasporic settings even more than elsewhere, social and cultural belongings can no longer be seen as based within bounded and 'fixed' places (Gupta and Ferguson 1992). Especially for migrants and their descendants 'home' is far from self-evident, while at the same time carrying strong connotations of exactly such a self-evidence.

Starting from one's own house as a first territorial base, 'home' may refer to different scales and multiple locations in various ways, or it may be not be conceived of in territorial terms at all (Al-Ali, N. and Koser, K. 2002: 8). Feelings of belonging are directed both towards physical places and remembered, imagined, or symbolic spaces (Rushdie 1991: 70; Salih 2003). For example Malika, one of our informants, mentioned cherishing good memories of her natal Moroccan village. Yet she refuses to go back there, preferring her idealized image over the changed reality she might encounter.

While specific places often function as diasporic sites of belonging, a sense of home can also be evoked by or expressed through many other means (Rapport, N. and Dawson, A. 1998). Feelings of home can be triggered by familiar habits and smells, or anchored in certain objects, the presence of close family, friends, or a certain category of people (Hoskins 1998; Miller 2008). Ouarda told us, for instance, that she frequently uses a certain combination of spices in her cooking, because the smell recreates the homey feelings of her grandmother's kitchen in Morocco. The 'gustatory nostalgia' (Holtzman 2006) thus experienced concentrates on the person of her grandmother, who was a second mother to her. She has never felt attached to the Moroccan family house, which rather figures as a locus of not-home to her. In Ouarda's case, the 'home' evoked through taste and smell has more to do with social relations than with place.

Particularly in a diasporic context, different home-settings may compete, collide or complement each other. Yet, they are hardly ever exclusive: one belongs in more than one locality or community. How one relates to these different home-settings can vary greatly. For Yasin, both travelling to and from Morocco feels like coming home:

> I don't really miss anything when I am over there. But I am always happy to have certain things again. Really, being in Morocco feels like I'm home again. It feels good: I'm back! But I feel exactly the same when I'm back in the Netherlands. It's just about different things.

Yasin presents his relationship to Morocco and the Netherlands as unproblematic. Each in their own way, both countries are home to him, or as he phrases it, they are 'about different things.' Yasin volunteered that many of his peers are more ambivalent about their multiple belongings. Indeed, several of our interlocutors emphasized that they carry with them a sense of longing for their 'other homes' wherever they are.

Nabil, for example, told us how he had felt one summer when people around him started leaving for a holiday in Morocco while he had decided to stay home that year:

> You see all those cars on the road, and you are stuck here in the Netherlands. Then it feels like they're all going that way and leaving you behind. So it hurts to stay here.

Many interviewees reported similar feelings. Also, their stories often illustrate that while one may long for a remembered far-away home, one may feel highly ambivalent about one's belonging there upon return (Salih 2003). At first it generally brings great joy to be reunited with family and friends whom one was looking forward to come home to in Morocco. After a while, however, boredom and irritations about constraints to one's freedom of movement also enter the scene.[3] Most informants stated that at some stage, they inevitably start longing for the personal privacy and freedom they enjoy at home in the Netherlands, as well as for their friends and the 'taste' and habits associated with their Dutch homes. Moreover, virtually all Dutch Moroccans we spoke to complained about being treated as foreigners by 'local' Moroccans.

These examples arc illustrative of the ambivalence and layeredness in the ways diasporic persons may conceive of home. They also call attention to the fact that the gaze of others greatly influences the extent to which one may perceive oneself to be at home. One can feel at home in relation to certain people, specific social settings or imagined communities. In the narratives we analysed this social dimension appeared to be a factor of importance. Often it did so in a positive sense, but even more prominently it featured in a negative manner: virtually all interviewees mentioned experiences of exclusion as a reason for not feeling at home somewhere. Malika, the woman that does not want to go back to her beloved natal village, mainly seemed to fear that the people she remembered would no longer recognize her. About the Netherlands she stated:

> This [country] is a part of me, that's the only way I can describe it. But through what they say, people can make you feel like you're not at home.

Malika's statement illustrates that feelings of home and belonging are not only a matter of personal choice; they are also shaped through the (mis)recognition by others. In many instances, Moroccan-Dutch citizens find that they are perceived or treated as 'locals' neither in the Netherlands nor in Morocco. Despite their attachments to certain places or social settings, this can obstruct experiencing them as truly home. This illustrates that others have a voice in where and with whom we feel at home.

The freedom to claim a place as home is probably the greatest in one's own house. However, the narrations on home-making indicate that even self-positioning through home-decoration is informed by the ways we are embedded in certain constellations of power. The following story of a squabble over a water jar illustrates how external voices from the 'public' realm may enter the living room.

---

3   The complaint about mobility constraints in Morocco is mainly uttered by female informants. This reminds us that home-making is always gendered. In many Moroccan families (as well as in stories about home by Europeans (Richards 1990)) the house is considered predominantly a female space. Accordingly, men may offer more instrumental meanings of home, whereas women may express feelings of confinement to the home. Unfortunately, our subproject on home and belonging has not yet advanced to a stage where we can systematically compare the stories of our male and female interlocutors.

Boushra told us about a disagreement with her mother about an enormous earthenware water jar that she had brought home from a trip to Morocco and put on display in her living room. For Boushra, the jar symbolizes the simplicity and authenticity of the culture of her grandparents, which she contrasts with her own hectic life in the Netherlands. Displaying it in her living room allows her to express a symbolic proximity to her rural Moroccan 'roots.' To her mother, however, the water jar is an old fashioned utensil which reminds her of a harsh existence she gladly left behind. She told Boushra that she would die of shame if other Moroccans were to find out that Boushra keeps it in her otherwise elegantly decorated living room.

The story about a squabble over a water jar points to intergenerational differences in the experience of migration. Although Boushra and her mother refer to the same locality when thinking about their place of origin, as a result of differences between the social positions and life trajectories of the two women, the Moroccan home that each of them remembers is shaped differently. Also, while both women may long for the Moroccan home that they left behind, the moments when and reasons why they do so vary. The different connotations of the Moroccan water jar to Boushra and her mother illustrate that we construct our past in ways that reflect our present needs (Ghorashi 2003: 131). Particularly for people with a migration background this means that the cultural context of 'where you're at' always informs and articulates the meaning of 'where you're from' (Ang 1994: 35).

Contesting and Accommodating Dominant Discourses on Home

The story about a disputed water jar illustrates once again that individuals are not in full control of their ties of belonging. In the production of homes and belongings, collective voices partake in our internal dialogues as parts of the self, but we may also be forced to position ourselves in relation to the external voices of collective and individual others (Hermans 2001). Both Boushra and her mother are engaged in dialogues with the collective voice of (first generation) Moroccan migrants. While Boushra situates herself in opposition to the expectations expressed by this external voice, her mother experiences them as her own.

Particularly in the case of migrants, others have a say in where or to whom they belong, and on what terms (Salih 2003). Diasporic home-making takes place in specific power-laden historical contexts. It is bound up in a set of political positions and is based on negotiation, dislocation and conflict (Bhatia and Ram 2009). Certain homes are ascribed to our interlocutors through public opinions and by significant others in both the Netherlands and Morocco. Dominant discourses on home and otherness inform and restrict their options for developing notions of (non)home. Individual migrants may contest and/or accommodate elements from such discourses in their home-making. Shortly after 9/11, for example, when claims about 'us-them' distinctions between the West and Islam peaked, the then

15-year-old daughter of one of our interlocutors replaced the Michael Jackson posters in her bedroom by a Palestinian flag.

Presently, Moroccan-Dutch citizens find their public and private personae under intense scrutiny and evaluation from both within Moroccan circles and the wider Dutch society. They are increasingly labelled and addressed 'as' Muslims and pressed to state their undivided loyalty in 'either-or' terms. Yasin, for example, told us:

> After September 11th I really felt cornered and different in a certain way. Apparently I did not fit in. Considering my childhood, and my Dutch friends, and I speak the language – I never thought about it before, but from that moment you start to think differently. Because in the end you do not belong there. You're a stranger, anyway. (…) Or you would have to leave your own religion behind.

In this interview excerpt, Yasin reflects on how a historical event changed the way others perceive him, thus forcing him to reposition himself. He considers the 9/11 attacks as a key event in his life. Its impact transformed his perception of Dutch society as 'home' and he began to identify himself first and foremost as a Muslim.

While Yasin states explicitly that not being accepted as a Muslim has made him realize that he does not belong in the Netherlands, on other occasions in our two interview sessions with him, he expressed strong attachment to the country and situated his future in it. At one point, for instance, he said that 'secretly' he felt quite proud of the Netherlands, despite the fact that he feels betrayed. Throughout his life story we found statements in which Yasin expresses, either implicitly or explicitly, ambivalence towards his contested sense of belonging in the Netherlands.

This comes to the fore, for example, in the way he described his apartment. The main room in his flat is divided in two by sliding doors. In the front living room Moroccan couches and many Moroccan souvenirs left no doubt about Yasin's background. Starting our tour around the house, Yasin pointed out a poster in browns and oranges, depicting Moroccan mud houses which had been the starting point for his decoration of the apartment:

> I said, that's what it should look like. Arid, but warm. Because that is what southern Morocco, where we originally came from, is like.

Yasin has only visited southern Morocco once. He usually spends summer in Fes, where his grandparents moved to when his father was a child. Nevertheless, Yasin connects to his ancestral 'roots' by attempting to recreate its atmosphere in his Dutch home.

Walking through the room, Yasin pointed out the lamps, pottery, and other souvenirs that his mother and sisters had supplied him with to add to the 'Moroccan' atmosphere he tried to create. For each object, he mentioned the family member who had given it, which may indicate that he appreciates these souvenirs as much for their references to family bonds as for their Moroccanness. In the back room that he uses as a study, Yasin pointed out objects that are related to his hobbies, his passion for reading, his job and other achievements, often adding 'that is another part of me.'

In a sense, then, Yasin gave us a tour of the various aspects of his self-image and his daily life, which together constitute his identity and make him feel at home. In telling us about his apartment he expressed his attachments to his family and to the Morocco of his holiday memories as well as to the 'original' Morocco of his southern roots, thereby fulfilling a 'homing desire' by developing habitual routines and inscribing new objects and places with meanings through storytelling. Meanwhile these 'biographical objects' also express a specific 'desire for home', incorporating into his daily environment references to Morocco as a faraway home he longs for.

As Yasin himself observed, the Moroccan presents from his family are all situated in the front room. Jokingly, he volunteered that some might say that he is a schizophrenic: while the front room represents his Moroccan side, the back room expresses his Dutch side:

> A psychologist might say that those two are only just kept in balance by the overall colour scheme. Because I haven't mixed them. Some people claim that you should do that.

In this last quote, Yasin disputes the stance of 'some people' who apparently claim that one can only 'balance' one's belonging in two countries by 'mixing' them. Yasin himself takes a more fluid stance towards his Dutch and Moroccan 'sides.' At this point in the interview he talked about having two 'backpacks' from which he could pick what suited him best in a specific context. Yet, in other instances he talked about the merging of his Dutch and Moroccan identifications. Even more frequently, he maintained that there is 'no real difference' between the two. The latter also comes to the fore in the earlier quotation where he states that visiting Morocco feels just as much like coming home as returning to the Netherlands. In the context of his other remarks, however, this can also be interpreted as a refusal to give in to external pressures to take sides.

The spatial metaphor 'to take sides' occurs frequently in the narrations of our interlocutors. Leyla, for instance, like many others noted that it is no longer possible to deal with her Muslim background in a flexible way, but that different groups in Dutch society force her 'to take sides.' She finds it disturbing to be caught between a Muslim and a non-Muslim 'camp' that both claim definitional power over her. Talking about what happened directly after events like 9/11 and the murder of the politician Fortuyn, she stated:

> As a person of Muslim background, you were not allowed time reflect on your personal view. Before you realized what was happening, waves of insults were

poured over Muslims. You never got a chance in the Netherlands to be moderate. Time and again I feel cornered. So I pulled out.

Leyla also feels cornered by people who feel that Muslims should act as one body:

Take all those girls who wear headscarves nowadays. I'm sure that the majority of them have no religious reasons for doing so. It just gives them a sense of belonging and appreciation. The headscarf has come to distinguish 'righteous women' from 'bad women'. And guess who the bad woman is?! Me again. It really pisses me off.

Feeling 'cornered' and excluded from two sides, Leyla 'pulled out' of the public debate to the privacy of her home and other places where she is among close family and friends. Her negative experiences in the Dutch public domain has also affected her stance towards her natal country. Previously, she dismissed Morocco as a patriarchal society and hardly ever visited the country. Of late, however, she has discovered an intellectual and artistic 'scene' there that she can identify with. She describes her recent visits to Morocco as welcome 'time-outs' from the tense societal climate in the Netherlands. She has even bought a small apartment in her natal town.

Leyla's shift in orientation is reflected in subtle changes in the home decorations in her Dutch home. Until recently, Leyla's spacious apartment showed hardly any references to her Moroccan background. Presently, however, her otherwise bare walls are decorated with two highly stylized screen prints of Moroccan mud castles. These pieces of modern Moroccan art point to Leyla's new orientation to Morocco as a place of belonging. From an etic point of view, they can be interpreted to symbolize Leyla's recourse to a stronger sense of belonging to her Moroccan homeland. To a considerable extent, the attractiveness of this homeland is informed by her negative experiences related to her 'Moroccanness' in the Netherlands, thus illustrating Ang's contention that 'where you are at' produces a specific cultivation of 'where you are from.'

Leyla's new 'home-making' illustrates how the forced selfing and othering that she and many other interviewees experience may influence their feelings of home and belonging and result in a reshuffling or renegotiating of various self-identifications. Ironically, they seem to be confronted with a call to integrate if not assimilate, to become 'one of us.' Yet they are often addressed solely in terms of their otherness. As we noted before, this is not only expressed in terms of national belonging but also in religious terms. By being summoned to privatize and relativize their religious attachments on the one hand and being addressed first and foremost as a Muslim on the other hand, Dutch-Moroccans are caught in a 'double bind' (Watzlawick et al. 1967): it is impossible for them to comply simultaneously with the conflicting demands they are confronted with.

How do they respond to this double bind? In what follows, we will give an impression by tracing narrations of notions of home and belonging in the trajectories of two women who were first interviewed in 1998, and then again in January 2008. Here the importance of being Muslim comes to the fore both in self-narratives of exclusion from contemporary Dutch society, and as a source of motivation to actively engage with this society and carve out one's own personal spaces of belonging in a Dutch context. This micro level discussion will allow us to trace in more detail the interface between societal and life course developments in our interlocutors' endeavours to fulfil their homing desires over time.

Narrations on Home and Belonging by Two Dutch Women of Moroccan Descent

Tahara

Tahara is relatively well-known politician, born in Amsterdam. At the time of the first interview, she was 25 years old. Tahara describes her teenage years as a time for experimenting with lifestyles and finding her own place in society. During a summer visit to Morocco, it strikes 16-year-old Tahara that while she lives in a country which has so much to offer, she feels much closer to God in her ancestral village. Wishing to preserve this feeling and bring it home with her, she decides to begin wearing a headscarf. She also takes it upon her as a 'mission' to testify to others about the beauty of Islam and its guidelines for good citizenship.

In the narrations about her mission, Tahara anchors her religion in several locations. It is in rural Morocco that she feels closest to God. She inscribes this new dimension of her faith on her body through the symbol of the headscarf, thus making it mobile. Back in the Netherlands however, she does not merely relate to Islam as something 'imported,' but anchors her religion in her Dutch context by connecting her political stances to her religious values. She interweaves an Islamic discourse with a social democratic discourse by stating that she is a social democratic by (Islamic) origin:

> I am here with a message, because why has God bestowed all those blessings on me? I was raised in a European country. I've had all the chances that one could wish for: good parents, a good upbringing and a good education. I can't just keep it to myself. Because, as you can tell, I am a social democrat by origin: share and share alike!

Tahara describes how her appearance as a headscarved girl was met with negative reactions. She experienced this as a 'wake-up call' which gave the impetus to a political career aimed at demanding respect and 'a place of their own' for Muslims in Dutch society.

A recurrent theme in Tahara's 1998 life story is the importance to be seen and heard. She seeks public recognition as a Muslim citizen. She wishes to participate as a Dutch citizen not *despite* the fact that she is a Muslim woman, but *as* a headscarf wearing Muslim woman. In the first few years after the 1998 interview, Tahara appeared frequently in the media. Such appearances, however, later diminished. During the 2008 interview, Tahara explains what has become of her seemingly indefatigable identity politics as a Muslim citizen:

> The world has changed tremendously, and that has affected me a lot personally. I grew up believing that I was an Amsterdam girl. But after 9/11 I became a Muslim. I remember well receiving the first call after the attacks from a journalist who wanted to know how I, as a Muslim, felt about what had happened. I was being reduced to a single label: I was no longer simply a town councillor, but 'the Muslim' town councillor. That hurt a lot.

For Tahara, the city where she grew up lost its self-evident character as home when others started to address her solely as 'a Muslim,' thus contesting her identification as an 'Amsterdam girl.' Against her will, others recast both her personal sense of belonging and her professional identity as town councillor in religious terms.

After the filmmaker Van Gogh was murdered, like several other politicians, Tahara received serious threat mails and phone calls. The Dutch state provided her with two body guards who accompanied her wherever she went for several months:

> I felt unsafe. No longer at home. I had always been so proud of being Dutch, but now my country was changing. People were not talking about me, Tahara, as a person, but as a representative of a group that was singled out to pile shit on. For the first time in my life I felt that in the eyes of others I did not belong. I got scared and lost my trust in people.

Referring to the Netherlands as 'my country' shows that Tahara not only considers herself an 'Amsterdam girl' but also identifies with the Netherlands as a nation. The remark that she used to be 'so proud' bespeaks a considerable emotional investment in her Dutch homeland. Therefore, the realization that she was being excluded from the national imagined community destabilized her profoundly.

That public and private domains cannot be neatly separated in home-making, is illustrated by the fact that needing protection literally brought the message home to Tahara that there were people in her own city in whose eyes she did not belong:

> It was the last day of Ramadan when I got those body guards. I remember being accompanied by them when I went to visit my parents. That was a disaster. Can you imagine: your daughter showing up with two body guards!

By the time of the 2008 interview, Tahara has learned that she has less power to define herself than she previously thought she did. Rather than being recognized as a full Dutch citizen of Muslim background, she feels reduced to being a spokeswoman for 'her kind.' Having found out that the same public presentation as a Muslim Dutch citizen that brought her fame during her first years in local politics has now turned against her, Tahara has decided to keep her religious inspiration to herself and no longer present herself as a Muslim citizen in the public domain:

> I gave up. There are many young smart people out there who can take over. Professionally, it's back to core business: my work aş a town councillor. If you want my view on projects to improve this town district, fine, but if you want an opinion on Muslims or Islam: go find someone else.

Tahara's accounts on her professional career show how the trajectory of her public identity was shaped by the growing preoccupation with Islam in the Netherlands.

During the first interview, much of her story focused on her indefatigable identity politics in the public domain as a female Muslim citizen. By the time of the second interview, not only have her youthful energy and drive been tempered, but due to incidents with great societal impact, she has also concluded that despite all her efforts, in the eyes of others, as a Muslim she cannot fully belong in Dutch society. Consequently, she chose to privatize her religious identity and restrict her political statements to 'secular' local issues. For the time being, then, Tahara's coming out as a Muslim has ended in a retreat.

The sentence 'there are many young smart people out there who can take over' indicates that not only societal changes have induced Tahara to reposition herself: life course related personal changes play a role as well. Homing desires and wishes for specific ties of belonging are not only spatially, but also temporally embedded. Tahara is now 35 years old, has recently gotten engaged and hopes to start a family soon.

Religion plays a pivotal role in Tahara's politics of belonging. Her then novel presentation in the 1990s as a committed Muslim social democrat was initially successful. This changed when the debate on Islam polarized. Increasingly experiencing being othered because of her 'Muslimness,' her sense of being at home in the Netherlands as 'an Amsterdam girl' ceased to be self-evident. In order to fulfil her homing desire she changed her strategy and privatized her religious commitment.

While societal and personal factors have led Tahara to shift her focus from religiously expressed engagement in the public arena to more 'private' settings, prioritising of family life can also result in the opposite, as the following story shows. We will trace how Farida, who initially kept her Muslim identity a private affair for which she sought no public recognition by non-Muslims, over time developed a sense of belonging in Dutch society through personal relations with Muslim friends and through becoming an active local community member.

Farida

When we first interviewed Farida in 1998, this married mother of one daughter worked in a local migrant community centre. Farida was seven years old when her father, who had migrated to the Netherlands before she was born, moved his wife and six children to the Netherlands in 1974. Her father plays an important role in Farida's life story. She depicts him as a 'tyrant' who 'terrorized' his children and warned them that they should stay clear of Dutch culture:

> Whenever my father had something important to tell, he'd line up all six children. And then he'd say: 'My name is not Piet, my name is not Jan, my name is Ahmed.' Meaning: you shouldn't think that you can do the same things as Dutch children, who were too free and rude in his view. Stating his name was Ahmed was really saying 'This is me: I am strict and these are my rules.'

Through his 'identity talk,' Farida's father pointed out that his children should not mistake living in the Netherlands for belonging there. Unlike Tahara, who grew up believing she was an Amsterdam girl, Farida was raised with constant reminders of her otherness. Her recollections of childhood indicate that her father's pedagogical regime failed to allow her to develop feelings of basic trust and self-esteem. Like Farida and her siblings, her mother was also ill-treated by her father, and therefore only partially capable of creating a safe home for her children. The lack of basic trust that Farida suffered as a child may account for the fact that she remembers discrimination from an early age. Her narrations about adulthood in the first interview indicate that she still felt excluded:

> There is a certain representation in Dutch society of Moroccan women, much of which concerns Islam. All kinds of tiny details convey the message that you are not accepted as a fellow citizen. That's how you get the feeling that you belong neither here in the Netherlands, nor elsewhere. I don't belong in Morocco either, I couldn't live there, I'm used to living here. This is my home, but I feel as though I do not belong here.

In this excerpt, Farida expresses the ambivalence about the question where she belongs. Being Dutch is problematic because others give her the feeling that she does not belong in the Netherlands, even though she sees the country as her home. In Morocco she feels even less at home. Being Moroccan has negative connotations to her; it is related to the restrictions and threats she experienced at home, and the insults and exclusion she experienced outside it. She therefore rejects national classification. Instead, she emphasizes her religious identification:

> To me, being Moroccan means being attached to Morocco. Which I am not. Nor am I Dutch. I am profoundly aware of the fact that I am different. I'm being

labelled non-Dutch every day. If I were free to give myself an identity, I'd prefer my Islamic identity.

Farida's words show an awareness of the fact that she is not entirely free to choose her belongings. At the same time, they illustrate that people can creatively deal with the opportunities and constraints provided by their different social identities to construct home-spaces. In Farida's case, this means foregrounding her religious identity, which she formulates in terms of *niya*, pious intentions, in contrast to her father's restrictive understanding of Islam. Another reason why being a Muslim appeals to her, is that in her view it precludes parochialism and discrimination. According to Farida, contrary to Dutch society, the Muslim community is open to everybody. This provides her with a sense of belonging which she lacked as a child:

> Being a Muslim is universal, anyone can be a Muslim; this religion relates you to everybody. Despite the feeling that one doesn't feel at home in this or that country, one's Muslim identity tells one that there is a home somehow. To me, that is a sense of security and protection. Islam is a kind of haven for me.

While in the first interview Farida stated that Islam provided her with a home and 'sense of security' that was absent in other dimensions of her identity, in later years the specific configuration of this space of belonging changed. The 2008 interview concentrates on two developments in her personal life. The first concerns the death of her father shortly after the first interview. On his deathbed, he asked Farida forgiveness for his harsh upbringing and told her how proud he was of her. This belated expression of recognition has helped Farida enormously to find peace with herself and her place in the world. The second event concerns what she called 'the experience of her life': performing the *hajj*, or pilgrimage to Mekka in the company of a multi-ethnic group of Dutch Muslim women. The women still meet, and some have become close friends. Ten years after the first interview, then, for Farida the Muslim community is no longer predominantly a mental space or an imagined community, but has taken the shape of a concrete network of friends located in the Netherlands.

Thanks to this network, she has been able to inscribe her personal history more concretely in a Dutch space. This was further enhanced by getting involved in projects to fight the polarization between Muslims and non-Muslims. She mentioned two reasons for taking this step. The first grew out of concern for her daughter, who she did not want to grow up in a hostile environment. Secondly, she considered community work as her responsibility as a Muslim citizen. Farida currently works for a secular organization that promotes social cohesion. She explained this job choice as follows:

> If you want to practise Islam, you should wish for social cohesion. In the Quran it says: 'We have made you peoples and tribes that you might know one another'

(S49:13, mb). So I joined a Muslim organization that cooperates with churches to combine our efforts as a shared Abrahamic tradition to do community work. But after some years I got the feeling that I was living in a cocoon too much. It's okay to work in a strictly Muslim organization, but I myself wanted to move on.

Interestingly, the hardening of the dominant Dutch discourse on Muslims appears to have been less unsettling for Farida than for Tahara. Expecting little acceptance as a Muslim in the first place, the increasing Islamophobia in Dutch society has not taken her by surprise. Also, the positive developments in her personal life over the last decade carried more weight than societal changes and she strives not to be affected by them. Comparing herself to her husband, who had been shocked when fellow train passengers were reluctant to sit down next to him shortly after the murder of Van Gogh, she pointed jokingly to the positive experience of having more space at her disposal. More seriously, she argued that Muslims should take the Islamophobic statements of people like Wilders as a challenge to strengthen their faith and engage in pious behaviour:

> In the Quran it is said that there will always be people who try to take Islam away from you. [...] It would only put Islam in a negative light if you were to make a fuss about them, so it is better to show others what your religion is really about.

In 2008, then, Farida finally feels more at home in Dutch society than ever. Inspired by her faith and a concern about her daughter's future, she has extended her network beyond Muslims and inscribed her personal history in the local community. From a 'safe haven' where she could retreat from what she experienced as a hostile Dutch environment, she has transformed the Muslim community into a springboard for active Dutch citizenship. To accomodate narrations about concrete, local ties of belonging, stories about being othered as a Muslim are relegated to the periphery of her life story.

Each in their own way, Tahara and Farida have accommodated the double bind of simultaneously being summoned to privatize their religious attachments and being addressed predominantly as Muslims. In the end, what they share is a religiously inspired motivation to act as accountable Dutch citizens involved in community building across ethnic and religious divides. The narrations on home and belonging in their life stories illustrate that the interplay of societal changes and developments over the life course compels us to reassess the meaning of home, and where and to whom we belong. Different stages of life and different dimensions of the self may correspond with varying notions of home and belonging. In efforts to make ourselves at home we draw on elements from various past and present contexts. As our positions in political and personal struggles over the social regulation of 'belonging' shift, the meanings and implications of ethnic and religious identifications may also change.

Concluding Remarks

In a globalized world, where people occupy and move between numerous positions and relate to different localities at the same time, the question of home and belonging is far from self-evident. Particularly for migrants and their descendants, making homes is an issue of locating oneself in, between and beyond different national, ethnic and religious sites of belonging. The central argument in this chapter is that in a diasporic context, creating a home takes place at the interface of societal and personal developments. It consists of ongoing process of positioning oneself and being positioned in relations to others, who have a voice in where and to whom we are allowed or expected to belong. In this context, the meaning of 'where you're from' is articulated in response to the specific situation 'where you're at.'

The question of belonging is often more pressing to those who 'inherited' migration than to those who experienced it first hand. Tracing narrations of home and belonging in the life stories of Moroccan-Dutch citizens, we have shed light on how a particular group of descendants of migrants may live and express the dynamics, nostalgia and ambivalences concerning feelings of being home and not at home, and of belonging and not belonging to varying places, people and discourses.

The 'home-making' stories of our interlocutors point to the interplay of multiple ties of belonging. For different reasons and in different ways they feel at home or specifically not at home in varying Dutch and Moroccan places and social settings. In their story-telling about objects, places, people and all kinds of sensations that represent 'home' they integrate references to their past and future plans in their present homes.

Their self-narratives also illustrate that they are not in full control of the spaces where they locate their sense of home and belonging. The increased forced selfing and othering they describe often influence their feelings of home and belonging and result in a reshuffling of the meaning of various self-identifications. Ironically, in demands from 'old' Dutch citizens to become 'one of us', Dutch-Moroccans are addressed predominantly in terms of otherness. In line with current international developments, this othering mainly takes place through the construction of a binary divide between the non-Muslim (Dutch) self and the Muslim other.

Reflecting this discourse of exclusion, the narrations of our interlocutors about home not only point to ways to accommodate a sense of belonging in two different countries, but also to their struggle to combine religious identification with a sense of belonging in the Netherlands and a refusal to take sides.

References

Al-Ali, N. and Koser, K. (eds) (2002), *New Approaches to Migration? Transnational Communities and the Transformation of Home.* (London: Routledge).

Ang, I. (1994), 'On Not Speaking Chinese: Postmodern Ethnicity and the Politics of Diaspora', *New Formations* 24, 1–18.

Bhatia, S. and Ram, A. (2009), 'Theorizing Identity in Transnational and Diaspora Cultures: A critical approach to acculturation', *International Journal of Intercultural Relations* 33(2): 140–9.

Blunt, A. and Dowling, R. (2006), *Home* (London: Routledge).

Brah, A. (1996), *Cartographies of Diaspora: Contesting Identities*. (London: Routledge).

Ghorashi, H. (2003), *Ways to Survive, Battles to Win: Iranian Women Exiles in the Netherlands and United States*. (New York: Nova Science Publishers).

Gilroy, P. (1993), *The Black Atlantic: Modernity and Double Consciousness*. (Cambridge, Massachusetts: Harvard University Press).

Gupta, A. and Ferguson, J. (1992), 'Beyond "Culture": Space, Identity and the Politics of Difference', *Cultural Anthropology* 7(1): 6–23.

Hermans, H.J.M. (2001), 'Conceptions of Self and Identity: Toward a Dialogical View', *International Journal of Education and Religion* 2(1): 43–62.

Holtzman, J.D. (2006), 'Food and Memory', *Annual Review of Anthropology* 35, 361–78.

Hoskins, J. (1998), *Biographical Objects: How Things Tell the Stories of People's Lives*. (New York: Routledge).

Kraus, W. (2006), 'The Narrative Negotiation of Identity and Belonging', *Narrative Inquiry* 16(1): 103–11.

Mallett, S. (2004), 'Understanding Home: a critical review of the literature', *The Sociological Review* 52(1): 62–89.

Miller, D. (2008), *The Comfort of Things*. (Cambridge: Polity).

Rapport, N. and Dawson, A. (eds) (1998), *Migrants of Identity: Perceptions of Home in a World of Movement*. (Oxford: Berg Publishers).

Richards, L. (1990), *Nobody's Home: Dreams and Realities in a New Suburb*. (Melbourne: Oxford University Press).

Rushdie, S. (1991), *Imaginary Homelands: Essays and Criticism 1981–1991*. (London: Granta Books).

Salih, R. (2003), *Gender in Transnationalism: Home, Longing and Belonging Among Moroccan Migrant Women*. (London: Routledge).

Watzlawick, P., Beavin Bavelas, J.H. and Jackson, D.D. (1967), *Pragmatics of Human Communication: A Study of Interactional Patterns, Pathologies, and Paradoxes*. (New York: Norton).

Chapter 13

Understanding Dutch Islam: Exploring the Relationship of Muslims with the State and the Public Sphere in the Netherlands

Martijn de Koning

Introduction[1]

Since 9/11 and the murder of Dutch film director Theo Van Gogh in 2004 by a young Muslim, radicalism among Muslim youth has been perceived as a threat to the security of a society based upon liberal, democratic and secular values (AIVD 2006). Such a dichotomy between secular society and (radical) Islam typically leaves the secular order uninvestigated and unquestioned. In order to understand the position of Islam and Muslims in the Netherlands, it is necessary to look at the historical answer the Dutch state has sought to accomplish in its project of building a 'homogenous' nation-state without compromising people's right to practise their religion. The solution the Dutch state has come up with is to transform Christianity in such a way that is compatible with a secular, liberal, and democratic political culture. This model, I will argue, still leading in current political thinking and shaped by the contemporary context of a secularized, pluralistic society, produces several contradictions that provide the basis for both the inclusion and the exclusion of Islam. This chapter explores how in the Netherlands the dominant political praxis of secularism leads to a tendency of stimulating and integrating a particular version of Islam while excluding a more assertive (and at times aggressive) version of Islam that is labelled as 'radical.'

---

1   This chapter is based upon my PhD research among young Moroccan Muslims: The quest for a 'pure' Islam and the new research 'Rise of Salafism among Muslim youth in the Netherlands,' which is part of the 'Transnational Salafism Movements' program of ISIM Leiden and Radboud University Nijmegen. An earlier version has been presented at International Workshop Muslim Diasporas: religious and national identity, gender, cultural resistance June 1–3 2007 at York University in Toronto, Canada. I would like to thank the participants of the workshop and Edien Bartels of the Vrije Universiteit Amsterdam for their valuable comments. In particular I would like to thank Frank Buijs, author of one of the first extensive books on radicalism among Muslim youth in the Netherlands (Buijs et al. 2006). Many thoughts in this chapter emerged during the discussions with him during our flight to Toronto and back. Unfortunately, Frank Buijs died suddenly in 2007. It is to him I dedicate this chapter.

In order to understand the current position of Islam in Dutch society, we should not only look at how contemporary politicians and opinion-leaders deal with it, but also at the historical trajectory of the management of religion and the changes in the political culture that have taken place over the years in the country.

The Dutch Moral Community

Since the nineteenth century most of the Protestant groups in the Netherlands (with the exception of a few orthodox Calvinist dissenters between 1830 and 1860 who rejected state interference with church matters) acknowledged the Dutch nation-state as their moral community, linking nation, religion and virtue. The secular regimes of that time promoted the idea of virtuous citizens realizing their moral selves by conforming to prevailing ideas of what constituted a good life and doing good acts on behalf of the welfare of the nation-state. After the secession of Belgium in 1830, the Dutch nation-state became a Protestant nation-state. The threat to the unity of this religious-nationalist community was perceived to come from the Catholics in the south, who were assumed to be more loyal to the Pope in Rome than to the Dutch nation-state (Van Rooden 1996). A new relationship between the nation-state and virtue came about after the Pacification of 1917. This appeasement of the 'education struggle' came with the passage of Article 23 of the Dutch Constitution, establishing complete state funding for schools with a religious (Christian) identity while safeguarding the freedom of these schools to determine their educational content. This laid the foundation for what is known as Dutch 'pillarization,' a system in which society was deeply divided into distinct and mutually antagonistic religious and ideological groups. Through overarching cooperation at the elite level, and by allowing each group as much autonomy as possible, a stable democracy was made possible (Lijphart 1968). The pillar system divided Dutch society into separate groups but also united them in one moral community, effectively replacing the notion of the Netherlands as a 'Protestant nation' with the concept of four groups (Catholics, Protestants, Socialists and Liberal-humanists) constituting one moral community (Van Rooden 1996: 29–31).

At the end of the 1960s the system collapsed as a result of secularization and individualization rendering the power of churches to mobilize people ineffective and obsolete (Kennedy and Valenta 2006). De-pillarization and ongoing secularization did not mean the establishment of a complete separation of church and state or separation of politics and religion and the disappearance of religion from the public sphere. It meant, for example, that the Catholic political party formed an alliance with two Protestant political parties to create the Christian-Democratic party (CDA). Several institutions, such as Christian broadcasting companies, toned down their religious outlook in order to survive and remain acceptable for a wider constituency. The pillarized organizations finally lost their dominant position with the changing of the Dutch constitution in 1983 when (in particular, financial) relations between the state and churches were severed. We should therefore not speak of a Dutch approach towards Muslims in terms of a pillarized model; there is no Islamic pillar in the same all-encompassing manner as in the past. More on that below.

The consequence of the collapse of the pillarized model in the 1960s was the changing of the basis of moral community: the Netherlands was no longer a moral community based upon religious and ideological nationalism. Ties between state and civil-society organizations on the one hand and churches on the other hand were loosened. At the same time debates about particular religious practices and beliefs emerged. The membership of orthodox groups in the Dutch moral community was never challenged, neither by themselves nor by others. The way these issues were resolved did not question the secular outlook of society. On the contrary, it was seen as an affirmation of Dutch tolerance and of a society committed to religious freedom.

The situation was different for Muslims. Although the Netherlands did have experience with Muslims during the time of the colonization of the Dutch East Indies and Surinam (cf. Kennedy and Valenta 2006: 344), from the time of their arrival, Turkish and Moroccan migrants were categorized as outsiders and as a 'problem' for Dutch society. In the 1980s and 1990s they were already seen as not willing to integrate, not treating women equally, being influenced by foreign powers, having a loyalty towards their country of birth instead of the Netherlands, a preference for non-democratic political rule, and not recognizing and respecting the separation of church and state (Rath, Sunier and Meyer 1997). Initially they were labelled as minorities or migrants, but later on these groups became defined by other labels, such as 'allochtonous' (meaning being from another place).This included first- and second-generation immigrants. Also, the label 'Muslim' carried the implicit meaning of being a migrant and from the outside. While in the time of pillarization (and before), nationalism was in part based upon belonging to a religious or ideological community (and vice versa), belonging to the Dutch moral community now seems to be more and more based upon the idea of a 'shared culture' in which sexual freedoms, emancipation of women and freedom of expression are believed to be the hallmarks. In light of this, it is in particular Muslims who are feared because of their alleged opposition to these freedoms and their religiosity, which remind native Dutch people of the (religious) constraints of the past with regard to these freedoms (Van der Veer 2006).

The focus on 'Dutch' values is part of a trend that emerged in the Netherlands and throughout Europe during the 1990s. Stolcke (1995: 7–12), focusing on the new rhetoric of exclusion and inclusion based upon cultural essentialism (a rhetoric she calls 'cultural fundamentalism') shows how in the process of building nation-states, national belonging and identity are interpreted as a cultural singularity. Internal differences are homogenized and cultural identity and sameness become the prerequisites to accessing citizenship rights. With this interpretation of citizenship, the need for migrants to accept 'Dutch norms and values' through education and assimilation became central. Migrants, it was felt, should abide by the same ideas of virtuous citizenship and good life that native Dutch citizens are believed to hold in high regard (see Tonkens, Hurenkamp, and Duyvendak 2008). The rhetoric of culture produces a homogenized and idealized vision of the national moral community and the exclusion of migrants (Butler 2008). The ongoing emphasis on Muslims as outsiders who need to be adjusted to this unquestioned idea of a shared Dutch culture has been maintained over the years and has produced what Schinkel (2007) describes as 'the paradox of integration.' This paradox means that migrants are inevitably part of society but are at the same time outsiders who have to be transformed in order to fit into the moral community. And they remain outsiders, since even the second and third generations are categorized as such.

State Regulation and Autonomy

Some researchers and policy-makers viewed the Dutch approach to migrants as a revised form of pillarization: the multicultural model (Statham et al. 2005; Sniderman and Hagendoorn 2007). In particular, the principle of retention of cultural identity is seen as an important feature of minority policy in the 1980s based upon the idea of religious freedom and autonomy. In theory this means that the state should not interfere with the identity expressions of these groups. This idea of Dutch multiculturalism based upon pillarization is not that strange. Kennedy and Valenta (2006: 340) make clear that the pillarized model enabled the state to closely monitor and regulate what religious groups were doing. This model sets the parameters for the continuing participation of religious groups in public life. Nevertheless, perceiving the Dutch integration model as a form of pillarization can be questioned. Vink (2007) argues that there is no such thing as a pillarized Dutch integration policy, or a multicultural model. He indeed makes some relevant and valid observations to sustain his claim. Dutch integration policy recognized the importance of cultural identity, but the emphasis always was on integration. Dutch policy reports on integration explicitly denied an unequivocal right for migrants to express their identity and outright rejected a relativist notion of identity. Stimulating activities contributing to the retention of cultural identity were seen as a matter for the organizations themselves and not part of government policy (Vink 2007: 355). Another factor is the degree of institutionalization of Islam in the Netherlands which might not be comparable to that of the pillarized system.

The collapse of the pillarization system on the one hand meant an important disadvantage for Muslims in building up an Islamic infrastructure; they could not receive the same funding as churches had in the past. On the other hand, it meant that the Dutch state had to reorganize and redefine its relationship with the churches concerning religious pastoral services to the army, Christian schools, ringing of church bells in public, and so on. Muslims as well as Humanists, Hindus and Jews were recognized as participants and stakeholders in the debates about these matters (Rath et al. 1999: 62). Because of their position as outsiders to the Dutch moral community, the presence of Muslims merged Dutch secularism with minority policies to promote the integration of migrants. It has been in particular Dutch minority policies (set up after the violent actions of young Moluccans in the 1970s) and, later on, integration policies that have served to recognize Islam and provide for its institutionalization in Dutch society. The aim was to 'alter' the development of a Muslim community towards a more liberal 'Dutch' direction, that is, against orthodoxism. As Rath et al. (1999: 61) stated, 'Officials and politicians wanted Muslims organized in the fashion that was viewed as *acceptable and efficient* in the Netherlands, i.e., with representative organizations or in coordinating bodies with approachable spokesmen, as if the Muslims in the Netherlands constitute a coherent community' (my italics). The key issue is, of course, the notion of 'acceptable and efficient' according to the standards of the Dutch state. The state funded several 'minority organizations' and established consultative bodies through which the government would discuss policy issues with representatives of minority groups. Although the formation of a single representative body of Muslims proved problematic over the years, the state managed to co-opt ethnic elites in policy-making structure (Scholten and Holzhacker 2009; Rath, Sunier and Meyer 1997). Religious freedom and autonomy for religious groups were turned into the principles of integration, with 'retention of cultural identity' according to the logic of the integration. Minority groups had the same rights as other 'identity groups' as far as public subsidies for broadcasting, education and welfare activities were concerned.

Muslims perfectly adjusted to this system. Statham et al. (2005) show that most claims and demands made by Muslims were acculturative rather than dissociative and controversial. Muslims established Islamic schools, two Islamic broadcasting companies, legal arrangements for *halal* slaughtering of animals, and special Islamic cemeteries, usually based upon the same principle that guided the pillar system. If Jews and Christians had the right to set up schools, make arrangements for slaughtering, and so on, Muslims had the same rights, too. Denying such rights, it was believed, could possibly lead to politicization and was seen as reprehensible (Rath, Sunier and Meyer 1997; Sunier 2005). Foreign influence (through funding) was hindered, although, for example, the Turkish Diyanet met sympathy because, as Rath et al. make clear, it was assumed that their Islam was a 'liberal' one compared to others.

Much of the institutionalization of Islam in the Netherlands took place in the 1990s. For example, constructing and building new mosques was often supported in a variety of ways (Maussen 2009). However, these perhaps somewhat idealistic ideas, taken for granted in the 1990s, became discarded after 2001. From 9/11 onwards the newly built mosques were increasingly seen as symbols of Muslim nostalgia and as examples of Dutch culture giving way to Islamization (cf. Cesari 2005; Landman and Wessels 2005).

Politicization of Culture and Religion

Sunier (2006: 248) makes it clear how a nation's political culture is embodied in the language people use to articulate grievances and demands. Political actors in a particular country are shaped within this political culture and have to engage with specific formative national narratives developed for the accommodation of claims. The Dutch pillarization system was chararactized by a consensual style of politics; conflicts were negotiated in a cautious way in order to avoid politicization and escalation (Lijphart 1968). During the 1980s this consensual style was maintained with regard to Muslims. The presence of Islam and the claims of Islamic groups did not challenge the political culture or the existing status quo. Although this changed after 9/11, we can trace the transformation prior to that time. During the 1990s, with the culturalization of citizenship, migration and integration became increasingly politicized, resulting in a gradual awakening of a public that had been silent or felt unable to speak out on these topics (Scholten and Holzhacker 2009). Throughout the 1990s a paradoxical development occurred in the Netherlands. On the one hand, ethnicity and religion became increasingly seen as private matters rather than issues for the state to deal with. On the other hand, the limits of religious and cultural difference related to the conditions for social cohesion and integration were questioned in a broad political spectrum ranging from ultra-left to ultra-right, socialist and liberal parties, and religious parties (Fermin 1997: 233–47). The private matter became the centre of the public debate.

Politicization of the debate took a new turn in 2001 and 2002 with Pim Fortuyn, effectively manipulating the already existing frustrations of native citizens on issues concerning migration and integration. He was in particular adamant in defending freedom of speech and sexual freedoms for homosexuals against Islamic traditions (Buruma 2006; Van der Veer 2006). His appearance, and after him that of outspoken activist and parliamentarian Ayaan Hirsi Ali and right-wing politician Geert Wilders, led to a stronger confrontational style in the public debate. This was fuelled by dramatic events such as the attacks of 9/11, the murder of Fortuyn in 2002 and two years later that of Theo van Gogh (a columnist and filmmaker who often expressed harsh and even foul criticism of Islam) by a Moroccan-Dutch Muslim. Also, the transgressions of Muslim youths (such as threatening outspoken critics of Islam) and Salafi imams (publicly exposed on television) contributed to further politicization. Vliegenthart (1997) shows how, after 9/11, the focus in the media and in politics on integration shifted almost entirely to Islam and Muslims and their alleged threat to Dutch society. Instead of pacifying Islam, several opinion leaders, such as Van Gogh and Hirsi Ali, argued for a more confrontational style in the public Islam debate, for example by claiming the right to insult the religious convictions and feelings of Muslims.[2]

---

2 Hirsi Ali was a member of the VVD, a conservative-liberal party and one of the most vocal critics of Islam and (radical) Muslims, stating that Islam is incompatible with democracy and renowned for her accusation that the prophet Muhammad is a 'paedophile'

This so-called 'new realist' (Prins 2000) discourse, emphasizing the inevitability of problems resulting from cultural differences, became widespread and, in line with the culturalization of citizenship, focused in particular on sexual freedoms and freedom of speech as typical of Dutch culture. The 'new realist' discourse, with its compellingly rude and harsh comments on multiculturalism, Islam and migrants, is part of mainstream political discourse, forcing other politicians to engage with it. This has led to a growing 'Islamization' of the public debate about migrants; people of Moroccan or Turkish descent are increasingly categorized primarily as Muslims, and the degree of maintaining Islamic beliefs and practices has become the standard to measure integration. Islam is not only perceived as the 'ultimate cultural other,' but also as a cultural system, and Muslims, as believers, are constructed as an immutable category (Bartels 2008).

Radicalization of Secularism: Liberal Islam vs. Radical Islam

As Asad (2003: 25) argues, the secular and the religious are not fixed categories. In secular societies particular modes of reasoning and argumentation, behaviours, knowledge and sensibilities are seen as the embodiment of a universal reason with which religious people have to comply, while only modestly expressing their religiosity (cf. Asad 2006: 515). This brings us to the notion of secularism as a political doctrine. Secularism is thought to create a neutral and objective arena in which people with different religious viewpoints can meet on the basis of subscribing to the same political principles (cf. Taylor 1998). Secularism is also the product of a specific history and embedded in a complex of influences that reflect and influence national political and religious culture (Amiraux and Jonker 2006: 16). Different nation-state conceptions, different historical experiences with immigration and different models of church-state relations lead to different trajectories of secularism and related differences in people in self-positioning and claiming recognition, and different modalities within the public sphere (Amir-Moazami 2005: 211). Secularism, then, is more than just a political stand about the place of religion in society, or a label for the alleged decline of religion. Secularism can be seen as a particular kind of cultural repertoire with its own beliefs, practices and experiences that can be organized, activated and mobilized by social actors to defend their interests and give meaning to the social world (especially the state) surrounding them (Gorski and Altınordu 2008). Research into the cultural repertoires of secularism and its uses by social actors is therefore important in appreciating the challenges to the nation-state and its citizenship

---

according to 'contemporary Western standards.' Together with film director Van Gogh she made the movie *Submission*. Hirsi Ali was threatened numerous times with an attack on her life and lived in hiding for several weeks after the murder of Van Gogh. Currently she works in the US for the conservative think tank American Enterprise Institute (De Leeuw and Van Wichelen, 2005).

politics posed by migrants and the second generation on one side, and the debates about multiculturalism and the management of religion on the other.

Central in those debates is the question as to what extent migrants should be given (individual or collective) religious rights and how these rights are related to their position within a particular nation-state (Bloemraad, Korteweg and Yurdakul 2008). At the heart of the idea of Dutch nation-state was the notion that every member of society, irrespective of background and religious affiliation, should subscribe to an imagined moral community – an imagined community based upon shared ideas about what constitutes a good and virtuous life. Rather than a strong sense of national pride, this idea of the moral community seems to be central in opting into the Dutch national project (cf. Sunier 2000). The Dutch public sphere, particularly since 2001, has partly been dominated by controversies about competing perspectives on moral citizenship and moral order, and about the need for educating and assimilating migrants to comply with an idealized vision of the Dutch moral community consisting of citizens who find virtue in secular freedoms and tolerance (cf. Mepschen 2009).

After 9/11 the debate shifted to key themes of violence, fundamentalism, intolerance, hidden agendas, religious tensions, and an orientation towards the Islamic world rather than the European world. This has led to a dual-track approach in Dutch policies. On the one hand the emphasis on integration remains, albeit with an almost exclusive focus on Islam and Muslims. What is new since 9/11 and especially since the murder of Van Gogh is a radicalization of secularist discourses. In these discourses we see a changing focus: particular trends in Islam are not incorporated, changed and adjusted, but are deterred and fought against.

I will examine the first track briefly because it is 'only' an adjustment of an already existing development of politicization and confrontation. Islamic schools as well as new mosques and other 'Islamic' institutions were usually supported by the state and/or local authorities with a clear and sometimes outspoken preference for a so-called liberal Islam. The same discussions played a role in the establishment of two Islamic universities (without official recognition), in particular the establishment of academic Islamic theology centres (for training academically educated imams) and the establishment of two (instead of one) representational bodies for Muslims (Boender 2007). A similar type of discussion emerged in 2006 after the announcement of plans for Marhaba, a centre for dialogue in Amsterdam. The plan failed, but the debate about it remains exemplary. Marhaba, backed by the municipality and the state, was supposed to support the construction of a 'European Muslim identity.' In the discussions that ensued, Islam was not treated as a religion, but as a 'social-cultural phenomenon and a topic of public debate.'[3] This does not necessarily go against the idea of separation of church and state, as some secularist opponents of the Marhaba centre, imam education, Islamic schools, and so on, argued (e.g. Cliteur 2002). On the contrary, it was an attempt to include

---

3   Tweede Kamer, vergaderjaar 2005–2006, 30 304, No. 8 (accessed 7.6.2009).

and produce a certain type of Islam and a related Muslim identity compatible to secular liberal politics.

Besides a more compelling integration policy, a second track has emerged after 9/11 and the murder of Theo van Gogh: counter-radicalization policy, which is an attempt to exclude those religious practices and beliefs (labelled 'radical Islam') that are deemed to be incompatible with liberal political rule (cf. Mahmood 2006). Both the debate and policy primarily target the Salafi movement. This movement aims to revitalize Islam based upon the lives of the first Muslims, and its adherents strive to live according to that idealized vision, which they find more just and satisfying than the present (De Koning 2010). During the 1980s and 1990s the Salafi movement emerged in the Netherlands via transnational networks, mosques and Islamic schools. Although this movement initially remained quietist, after 2002 it became more visible after incidents with youths trying to go abroad to fight jihad, the murder of van Gogh, and Friday prayer sermons in which imams attacked the Dutch government and politicians and stated that it is allowable to 'correct' women with force (De Koning 2010). For the Salafi movement and its participants, religion is not and should not be private, and particular modalities of going public as Muslim by Salafi participants – such as refusing to shake hands and women wearing the niqab – are controversial (Fadil 2009; Moors 2009).

A few remarks concerning secularism and liberal Islam are called for. As Haddad and Balz (2008) explain, the overall tendency in Europe with regard to integration, security and secularism is a convergence towards the French model, with a more rigid separation of church and state and a stricter approach to Islamic authorities. We should not forget, however, that the overall secularist outlook is shaped by compromise because, at least in the Dutch case, there is no agreement over the management of (public) religion by the state. Orthodox Christian parties try to defend the status quo while the Christian Democrats try to defend the status of religion in public by making the laws more apt to a pluralistic society. GroenLinks (GreenLeft) Party, along with progressive and conservative liberals, tries to further limit the public appearance of religion. The conservative and progressive liberals seem to opt for a stricter separation of church and state, while the right-wing Freedom Party (PVV) seems to be mainly interested in banning Islam. The ideas about the correct secular outlook for Dutch society therefore vary and do not only pertain to Islam, although it is the centre of all debates. There is also no agreement on what liberal Islam is. With the exception of the PVV (for which a moderate or liberal Islam does not exist) generally speaking we can argue that 'liberal Islam' is perceived by most political parties as a social-cultural and religious phenomenon (much in the same way as Christianity is perceived as a Dutch cultural tradition) with no political aspirations, kept private or only modestly displayed in public.

The background of this debate about radical or liberal Islam involves the ethics within religious groups of going public. As Casanova (1994) has convincingly shown, secularization of a society does not necessarily lead to a decrease in religiosity, nor does it necessarily lead to a privatization of religion. The emergence of groups that are unwilling to comply with the framework of liberal Islam and with the secular political culture has been labelled as radicalization (for example: AIVD 2007). An important characteristic of this labelling is categorizing and lumping together all (Islamic) ideologies that threaten the democratic order of Dutch society. The distinction between liberal Islam and radical Islam is reflected in the term 'good Islam vs. bad Islam,' a distinction made by Mamdani (2004). 'Good Islam' can be relegated to specific areas in the public sphere, but when Islam is experienced as entering into the public sphere in an assertive or even aggressive way, it can be typified as 'bad Islam.' 'Radical' Islam divides the Muslim community and separates its members from their identity as integrated, tolerant and liberal citizens (cf. Birt 2006: 294). As such, the Salafi imams in particular are denounced. A well-known incident is that of Salafi imam Ahmad Salam's refusing to shake hands with the then Minister of Integration, Rita Verdonk. After his refusal she asked the imam, 'Are we not equal?' and continued, 'Well, we have a lot to discuss then.' Later on the ministry explained that Minister Verdonk wanted to make it clear that shaking hands was a conventional Dutch habit. In her view it is important for imams to be aware of this and adjust to it (cf. Fadil 2009). Refusing to shake hands and also, for example, wearing the niqab, are seen by the Dutch government as symbols of a form of Islam that does not fit Dutch society (Moors 2009: 401). What is taking place here is not only the rejection of a public display of religion or an Islam that is expressed in ways that people experience as strange and different. It is also a denunciation of what is felt as an assertive and intrusive expression of Islamic religiosity and as an ostentatious, provocative rejection of the Dutch moral community. While for the right-wing PVV there is no such thing as a moderate Islam, other parties (including the secular ones) tend to support the establishment of a 'moderate' or 'liberal' Islam, although this support is contested within their own ranks. With regard to radical Muslims, however, all parties oppose their practices out of a firm support for liberal principles or in order to neutralize the PVV and co-opt its constituency (cf. Moors 2009).

It may appear to be self-evident that a democratic country should fight against intolerant ideas or that a secular country should try to contain religion, but it is not. Many of the ideas among Salafists, for example pertaining to homosexuality and the rights of women, do not differ very much from orthodox Protestants and members of churches such as the Pentecostal. Even 'conservative' Catholics in the Netherlands agree on this matter. Moreover, the visibility of religion in society and the public sphere is not seen in the same way for Muslims as for Christians. Among orthodox Protestants there are also groups becoming more visible in the public sphere and refuting the secular contract (cf. Roeland 2009). But their protests are not labelled as radicalism, nor is there any other policy trying to contain, for example, the Pentecostal movement or active migrant churches. Left-wing, right-wing and animal-rights radicalization is recognized but there is no policy countering radicalization from these sides, albeit that there are some efforts to counter right-wing radicalization among native Dutch youth. Schools and other institutions report more incidents involving right-wing radicalization than radicalization among Muslims.[4] The operationalization of radicalization policy is clearly aimed at Muslim youth, given the inclusion of imams, 'moderate' Islamic organizations and activities aimed at integration. In plans combating radicalization the dichotomy between 'Western' and '(radical) Islam' is central.[5] The dual-track policy with regard to Muslims, combining integration policy and counter-radicalization policy, shows that the main difference between orthodox Christians and right-wing youth on the one hand and (radicalized) Muslim youth on the other hand is that the first is seen as part of the Dutch moral community while the latter is not.

Conclusion

The Netherlands has witnessed an increasing Islamization of the public debate in which Islam becomes a standard for integration. This is combined with policies trying to make Muslims abide by 'typical Dutch' values. In particular, secular freedoms pertaining to sexuality, women and freedom of speech are instrumentalized into a cultural program of inclusion and citizenship producing a demarcation between a free secular society and Muslim immigrants. These freedoms work as a modality of the secular governance of Islam, and the need to protect them is more compelling since 9/11 and incidents such as the murder of Theo van Gogh by Muslims who adhere to a 'bad Islam'. The distinction between 'good Islam,' which still needs to be adjusted, and 'bad Islam,' which must be excluded, reveals a paradox within Dutch secularism and integration policy. While Islam is regarded as coming from outside and therefore needing to be changed, it is also acknowledged as a religion that is already institutionalized in the Netherlands (and therefore also 'inside'). Furthermore, radical Islam or 'bad Islam,' it is believed, has to be banned. These representations of Islam *vis-à-vis* Dutch society reproduce and nurture the image of the Netherlands as a homogenous secular country, based upon a Christian tradition, threatened by radicals, as has been noted by several scholars. It does more than that, however as the distinction between liberal and radical Islam produces unity among different political factions in society and therefore unity within the moral community. The Dutch moral community is consolidated by excluding radical Islam. All parties share the same idea of Muslims and Islam as being outside the moral

---

4   Trend-analysis Polarization and Radicalization 2008. http://www.tweedekamer.nl/ images/297540141bijlage03_118-182861.pdf (accessed 17.6.2009).

5   See for example: Action plan Radicalization and Polarization. http://www.mogroep. nl/scrivo/asset.php?id=65396 (accessed 7.6.2009).

Monitor counter-radicalization activities 2008. http://www.tweedekamer.nl/images/ 297540141bijlage02_118-182860.pdf.

Operations Radicalization and Polarization 2009. http://www.tweedekamer.nl/images/ 297540141bijlage01_118-182859.pdf (accessed 17.6.2009).

community and agree upon the need to fight against 'radical' Islam. The main difference between the right-wing PVV and others is that the first is convinced that a moderate Islam doesn't exist, while the others regard Islam as something that can be accommodated to Dutch political culture and its management of religion. Regarding Islam as something from outside and making the distinction between 'good' and 'bad' Islam allows political parties to criticize and focus on problems with Islam and Muslims, without the need to take up as extreme a position as that of the PVV, which is regarded as unethical and counterproductive (cf. Schinkel 2008).

References

AIVD (2006), *Violent Jihad in the Netherlands. Current Trends in the Islamist Terrorist Threat.* (Den Haag: Ministerie van Binnenlandse Zaken en Koninkrijksrelaties).

—— (2007), *Radicale dawa in verandering, de opkomst van islamitisch neoradicalisme in Nederland.* (Den Haag: Ministerie van Binnenlandse Zaken en Koninkrijksrelaties).

Amiraux, V. and Jonker, G. (2006), 'Introduction: Talking about visibility, actors, politics, forms of engagement', in V. Amiraux and G. Jonker (eds) *Politics of Visibility. Young Muslims in European Public Spaces.* (Bielefeld: Transcript).

Amir-Moazami, S. (2005), 'Reaffirming and Shifting Boundaries: Muslim Perspectives on Gender and Citizenship in France and Germany', in *Islam and the New Europe. Continuities, Changes, Confrontations*, Yearbook of the Sociology of Islam 6. (New Brunswick and Bielefeld: Transcript), 209–33.

Asad, T. (2003), *Formations of the Secular: Christianity, Islam, Modernity (Cultural Memory in the Present).* (New York: Cambridge University Press).

—— (2006), 'Trying to understand French secularism', in H. De Vries and L.E. Sullivan (eds), *Public Religions in a Post-Secular World.* (New York: Fordham University Press), 494–526.

Bartels, E. (2007), *Antropologische dilemma's en onderzoek naar islam, Talma Lezing.* (Amsterdam: VU Uitgeverij). http://www.fsw.vu.nl/nl/Images/Talmal ezing%202008%20Bartels_tcm30-56361.pdf. (accessed 20.11.2009).

Bloemraad, I., Korteweg, A.C. and Yurdakul, G. (2008), 'Citizenship and Immigration: Multiculturalism, Assimilation, and Challenges to the Nation-State', *Annual Review of Sociology* 34, 153–79.

Boender, W. (2007), *Imam in Nederland.* (Amsterdam: Bert Bakker).

Buruma, I. (2006), *Murder in Amsterdam: The Death of Theo van Gogh and the Limits of Tolerance.* (London: Penguin Press HC).

Butler, J. (2008), 'Sexual politics, torture, and secular time', *British Journal of Sociology* 59(1): 1–23.

Casanova, J. (1994), *Public Religion in the Modern World.* (Chicago: University of Chicago Press).

Cesari, J. (2005), 'Mosque Conflicts in European Cities: Introduction', *Journal of Ethnic and Migration Studies* 31(6): 1015–24.

Cliteur, Paul (2002), *Moderne Papoea's, 'Dilemma's van een multiculturele samenleving*. (Amsterdam and Antwerpen: De Arbeiderspers).

Entzinger, H. and Dourleijn, E. (2008), *De lat steeds hoger. De leefwereld van jongeren in een multi-etnische stad.* (Assen: Van Gorcum).

Fadil, N. (2009), 'Managing affects and sensibilities: The case of not-handshaking and not-fasting', *Social Anthropology* 17 (November), 439–54.

Fermin, A. (1997), *Nederlandse politieke partijen over minderhedenbeleid 1977–1995.* (Amsterdam: Thesis Publishers).

Gorski, P.S. and Altınordu, A. (2008), 'After Secularization?', *Annual Review of Sociology* 34, 55–85.

Haddad, Y.Y. and Balz, M. (2008), 'Taming the Imams: European Governments and Islamic Preachers since 9/11', *Islam and Christian-Muslim Relations* 19 (April), 215–35.

Kennedy, J.C. and Valenta, M. (2006), 'Religious Pluralism and the Dutch state: Reflections on the Future of Article 23', in W.B.H.J. van de Donk, A.P. Jonkers, G.J. Kronjee and R.J.J.M. Plum (eds), *Geloven in het publieke domein. Verkenningen van een dubbele transformatie.* (Amsterdam: Amsterdam University Press), 337–53.

Koning, M. de (2008), *Zoeken naar een 'zuivere' islam. Geloofsbeleving en identiteitsvorming van jonge Marokkaans-Nederlandse moslims.* (Amsterdam: Bert Bakker).

—— (2010), 'Understanding the "Others": Salafi politics in the Netherlands', In A. Boubekeur and O. Roy (eds), *Whatever happened to the Islamists? Salafis, Heavy Metal Muslims and the Lure of Consumerist Islam.* (London: Hurst).

Landman, N. and Wessels, W. (2005), 'The Visibility of Mosques in Dutch Towns', *Journal of Ethnic and Migration Studies* 31(6): 1125–40.

Leeuw, M. de and Van Wichelen, S. (2005), '"Please, Go Wake Up!" Submission, Hirsi Ali, and the "War on Terror" in the Netherlands', *Feminist Media Studies* 5(3): 325–40.

Lijphart, A. (1968), *The Politics of Accommodation: Pluralism and Democracy in the Netherlands.* (Berkeley: University of California Press).

Mahmood, S. (2006), 'Secularism, Hermeneutics, and Empire: The Politics of Islamic Reformation', *Public Culture* 18(2): 323–47.

Mamdani, M. (2004), *Good Muslim, Bad Muslim: America, the Cold War and the Roots of Terror.* (New York: Pantheon).

Maussen, M. (2007), 'The governance of Islam in Western Europe: A state of the art'. http://www.eukn.org/eukn/themes/Urban_Policy/Social_inclusion_and_integration/Integration_of_social_groups/Ethnic_minorities/Governance-of-Islam-in-Western-Europe_1436.html (accessed 20.11.2009).

—— (2009), *Constructing Mosques. The Governance of Islam in France and the Netherlands.* (Amsterdam: Amsterdam School for Social Science Research, ASSR – PhD thesis).

Mepschen, P. (2009), *Erotics of Persuasion. Sexuality and the Politics of Alterity and Autochthony*. (Amsterdam: Amsterdam School for Social Science Research, ASSR). http://www.assr.nl/conferences/documents/Burgerschap-EroticsofPersuasionbyPaulMepschen.pdf (accessed 20.11.2009).

Moors, A. (2009), 'The Dutch and the face-veil: The politics of discomfort', *Social Anthropology* 17(4): 393–408.

Prins, B. (2000), *Voorbij de onschuld. Het debat over de multiculturele samenleving*. (Amsterdam: Van Gennep).

Rath, J., Penninx, R., Groenendijk, K. and Meyer, A. (1999), 'The Politics of Recognition of Religious Diversity in Europe. Social Reactions to the Institutionalizaton of Islam in the Netherlands, Belgium and Britain', *The Netherlands' Journal of Social Sciences* 35(1): 53–68.

Rath, J., Sunier, T. and Meyer, A. (1997), 'Islam in the Netherlands: The establishment of Islamic institutions in a De-pillarizing society', *Journal of Economic and Social Geography* 88(4): 389–95.

Roeland, J. (2009), *Selfation. Dutch Evangelical Youth Between Subjectivization and Subjection*. (Amsterdam: Amsterdam University Press).

Rooden, P. van (1996), *Religieuze regimes: over godsdienst en maatschappij in Nederland 1570–1990*. (Amsterdam: Bert Bakker).

Schinkel, W. (2007), *Denken in een tijd van sociale hypochondrie. Aanzet tot een theorie voorbij de maatschappij*. (Kampen: Uitgeverij Klement).

—— (2008), *De gedroomde samenleving*. (Kampen: Uitgeverij Klement).

Scholten, P. and Holzhacker, R. (2009), 'Bonding, bridging and ethnic minorities in the Netherlands: changing discourses in a changing nation', *Nations and Nationalism* 15(1): 81–100.

Sniderman, P.M. and Hagendoorn, L. (2007), *When Ways of Life Collide. Multiculturalism and its Discontents in the Netherlands*. (Princeton: Princeton University Press).

Statham, P., Koopmans, R., Giugni, M. and Passy, F. (2005), 'Resilient or Adaptable Islam? Multiculturalism, Religion and Migrants' Claims-Making for Group Demands in Britain, the Netherlands and France', *Ethnicities* 5(4): 427–59.

Stolcke, V. (1995), 'Talking Culture: New Boundaries, New Rhetorics of Exclusion in Europe', *Current Anthropology* 36(1): 1–24.

Sunier, T. (2000), 'Civil enculturation: Nation-state, School, and Ethnic Difference in Four European countries', *Journal of International Migration and Integration* 1(3): 305–29.

—— (2005), 'Interests, Identities, and the Public Sphere: Representing Islam in the Netherlands since the 1980s', in J. Cesari and S. McLoughlin (eds) *European Muslims and the Secular State*. (Aldershot and Burlington: Ashgate), 85–98.

—— (2006), 'Religious newcomers and the nation-state', in L. Lucassen, D. Feldman, and J. Oltmer (eds), *Paths of Integration: Migrants in Western Europe 1880–2004*. (Amsterdam: Amsterdam University Press), 239–61.

Taylor, C. (1998), 'Modes of Secularism', in Rajeev Bhargava (ed.) *Secularism and its Critics*. (New Delhi: Oxford University Press US), 31–53.

Tonkens, E., Hurenkamp, M. and Duyvendak, J.W. (2008), *Culturalization of Citizenship in the Netherlands*. (Amsterdam: Amsterdam School for Social Science Research, ASSR). http://www.assr.nl/conferences/documents/StaffsempaperTonkens41108. pdf.

Van der Veer, P. (2006), 'Pim Fortuyn, Theo van Gogh, and the Politics of Tolerance in the Netherlands', *Public Culture* 18(1): 111–24.

Vink, M.P. (2007), 'Dutch "Multiculturalism" Beyond the Pillarisation Myth', *Political Studies Review* 5, 337–50.

Vliegenthart, R. (2007), *Framing Immigration and Integration. Facts, Parliament, Media and Anti-Immigrant Party Support in the Netherlands*. (Amsterdam: VU University Amsterdam).

Chapter 14

Between Iraq and a Hard Place: Iraqis in Diaspora[1]

Jacqueline Ismael and Shereen Ismael

Introduction

The term diaspora refers to the dispersal of people from their homeland and their scattering into many lands. Rooted in the notion of dispersion, the classic image of a diaspora comes from the uprooting of the Jewish people by Roman occupiers in 70 AD and their subsequent scattering around the globe; from this event also comes the corollary archetype of a diasporic population as one that has been displaced and alienated from a homeland, marginalized and racialized in other lands, and bound by a yearning to return to the homeland – in the case of the Jews, to Zion (Cohen 1997; Moghissi 2008). While this imagery has been challenged in the emerging field of diaspora studies (Butler 2001; Moghissi 2008), it remains the core around which the field has emerged. Butler (2001) similarly identified three basic features of diaspora that are generally accepted in diaspora studies: dispersal is the first feature and implies scattering to more than one country; the second feature is 'some relationship to an actual or imagined homeland'; and the third is self-awareness of a group identity.

This chapter will examine Butler's three dimensions of diaspora as they relate to Iraq. Specifically, we will examine the objective dimension of dispersal in terms of the forces that uprooted and scattered Iraqis, and the subjective dimension in terms of the intersubjective themes that emerged in the interviews we conducted; the objective and subjective dimensions of the interviewees' relationship with Iraq; and the objective and subjective dimensions of their perception of identity as a member of an Iraqi diaspora.

Re-examination of Interview Data

Mass displacement of Iraq's population followed the US-UK invasion of Iraq in 2003. According to UNHCR statistics, as of January 2009, over 2 million

1   We would like to acknowledge and thank the research support of the Social Sciences and Humanities Research Council of Canada, as the grant they awarded us allowed this research to take place.

Iraqis had fled the country, while another 2,650,000 had been internally displaced (UNHCR 2009). Our data on Iraqis in diaspora is based on secondary analysis of interviews conducted between 2005 and 2007 with Iraqi women (41) and their male relatives (23) living outside Iraq. The primary purpose of the interviews conducted face to face, unstructured and open-ended, was to explore the impact of political turbulence on Iraqi households (Ismael 2008). Although the interviews did not focus on diaspora, but on the changing political economy of Iraqi households over the last quarter of the 20th century, they allowed for information on diaspora to be extracted through recoding and secondary analysis.

A snowball sampling technique was used to recruit participants whereby each subject identified others that might be recruited. Sample selection was purposive and targeted women in the 40-plus age bracket. Iraqi men were recruited from the households of female subjects. The total sample included interviews conducted of Iraqis residing in Iraq as well as those residing outside the country. Only the interviews of Iraqis living outside Iraq were included in the re-examination. This constituted 64 in total, composed of 41 women and 23 men. Interviews were conducted in Canada, the United States, the United Kingdom, France and Jordan.

Largely an artifact of the recruitment technique, the sample was relatively homogeneous in terms of educational level for it drew from a pool of urban-based professionals – academics, artists, research scientists, and medical doctors. However, targeting was used to ensure variability in the dimensions of religion and ethnicity. Table 14.1 reflects the ethno-cultural characteristics of the sample.

Fleeing Iraq

While the mass population movement from Iraq occurred after the invasion and occupation of the country in 2003, all of the 64 participants in this sample had fled Iraq prior to that time. The absence of post-2003 émigrés from the sample likely resulted from a combination of sample selection (purposive and targeted) and

Table 14.1   Ethno-cultural Characteristics of Sample

	ARAB	KURD	ASSYRIAN
MUSLIM	-	-	-
Sunni	21	6	-
Shi'a	19	-	-
CHRISTIAN	8	-	6
MANDAEANS	4	-	-
TOTAL	52	6	6

sample technique (snowballing). Nevertheless, we will argue that the decades of pre-invasion flight from Iraq reflected in our sample were in fact the initial waves of a displacement tsunami that culminated in the 2003 mass population surge from the country – a wave triggered by political shocks. Table 14.2 juxtaposes the period of immigration of the sample with the political context.

The image of fleeing from oppression was common in the interviews we conducted. As one member of the sample noted, 'Iraqis don't emigrate from Iraq. We flee – from the Ba'th, from the war, from the sanctions.' Each of the interviews suggested a longer, untold story of emigration as a flight from oppression. One member of the sample described his departure from Iraq as an adaptation of the 'fight or flight response,' and another as an act of 'resistance to oppression.'

The nature of the political shocks is suggested in Table 14.2. In the 1960s and 1970s, the political context in the country was framed by the terror of Ba'thist oppression. As an oil-rich state located in a geopolitically strategic region, Iraq was caught in the currents of Cold War politics and, like many developing countries in Africa and Asia, became a proxy state in the ideological conflict between superpowers. Presaging the US-sponsored counter-revolution against the progressive Allende government in Chile by a decade (Klein 2007: 116–27), the ideologically left-leaning regime of General Abdul Karim Qasim was overthrown in 1963, with US backing, by a vehemently anti-communist nationalist party, the Ba'th, who initiated a nine-month-long reign of terror against social activists in general and communists in particular, with over 10,000 people killed. As described by a political historian of contemporary Iraq:

> Bands of the National Guard roamed the streets and carried out summary executions, arbitrary arrests and savage torture. Sport grounds, military camps and schools were turned into concentration camps and interrogation centres for tens of thousands of people from all walks of life. At the top of the list were leaders, cadres, and activists of the trade unions and the mass democratic organizations, including the Iraqi Women's League and the General Union of Students of the Iraqi Republic (Zaher 1986: 31).

Table 14.2   Period of Emigration

Period	Number	Political Context	Emigration in period
1960s	16	Ba'th terror	Social activists fleeing Ba'th terror
1970s	10	Ba'th oppression	Social activists fleeing Ba'th terror
1980s	22	Iraq-Iran war	Nationalists disillusioned with Ba'th policies; leftists, religious activists and ethno-cultural groups (i.e. Iraqis with Iranian heritage and Kurds) fleeing Ba'th oppression
1990s	16	Sanctions	Political/economic oppression

A military coup removed the Ba'th Party from power in November 1963, and for the next four years Iraq was governed by a pragmatic regime that attempted to pander to both nationalist and parochial affinities. However, another coup d'état returned the Ba'th Party to power in 1968, and it ruled Iraq for the next 35 years, largely under the dictatorship of Saddam Hussein.

The political shocks of the 1980s were propelled by the Iraq-Iran war. Unchecked by financial constraints, and inflamed by a toxic combination of geopolitics internationally, heady nationalism regionally and dictatorial power nationally, the Ba'th Party in general, and President Saddam Hussein in particular, sought self-aggrandizement of the state through extravagant military expenditures. Nationally, the Hussein regime achieved virtually total control, first of the Ba'th Party apparatus, then of Iraqi society, through a combination of ruthless coercion, financial co-optation, and a complex web of security agencies spying on the population and on each other (Makiya 1989). Regionally, the Hussein regime sought leadership of the Arab world through championing Arab causes, especially regarding the Arab-Israeli question and the plight of the Palestinian people. Internationally, by invading Iran, Saddam Hussein's regime sought to fill the geopolitical vacuum created by the collapse of the shah's regime and the emergence of an Islamic republic in Iran. This ignited an eight-year war that exhausted the state financially, bankrupted it ideologically, and took the lives of a million soldiers in total. 'The war consumed our fathers, brothers, sons, uncles,' lamented one woman. A male interviewee noted, 'My two oldest brothers were conscripted into the military when I was 14. Within two years, one was killed and the other missing. Fearing my eventual conscription, my family sacrificed everything to get me out of Iraq.' Another member of the sample explained, 'My husband is from a wealthy Najaf family. Despite the fact that some of the family members were active in the Ba'th Party, they were accused of being a fifth column for Iran and summarily deported. It was a terrifying time and we feared we would be next.'

The Iraq-Iran war ended in 1988, but the respite this brought to the Iraqi population was short-lived. In August 1990 Iraq invaded Kuwait. In response, the United Nations Security Council (UNSC) imposed on Iraq the severest international sanctions ever imposed on any country. The stated intent of the sanctions regime was to force a withdrawal by Iraq from Kuwait. UN Security Council Resolution (UNSCR) 687 called for ending the sanctions when Iraqi compliance was established by the council. However, President George H.W. Bush rejected the primary purport of Resolution 687, and opposed any relaxation of the sanctions as long as Saddam Hussein was in power. President Clinton later concurred, and Secretary of State Warren Christopher announced in 1994 that Iraqi compliance was not enough to lift the embargo, in effect changing the substance of the Security Council ruling unilaterally (Chomsky 2003: 30). Thus, the severe sanctions regime – a regime that deprived the Iraqi population of virtually all basic necessities – were not removed until 2003, after the US invaded and occupied Iraq.

Also in response to the Iraqi invasion of Kuwait, the US issued a unilateral declaration in August 1990 demanding Iraq's withdrawal; in January 1991 launched a full-scale air assault, dubbed 'Operation Desert Storm,' on Iraq, followed in February by an invasion with ground forces. A ceasefire was declared on 28 February. While the US-led military attack completely destroyed Iraq's civil infrastructure, it left Saddam Hussein's regime intact. In the immediate aftermath of the war, both of these outcomes appeared as unintended consequences. However, the resolute maintenance of the rigid sanctions regime over the next 13 years supports the contention widely accepted in the Arab world that these were covert objectives, and not unintended consequences (Ismael and Ismael 1999: 70–78). Denis Halliday and Hans-C. von Sponeck, both senior international civil servants in charge of the UN's humanitarian program under the Security Council's Iraq sanctions regime, argued that if the sanctions had been directed against preventing a weapons of mass destruction (WMD) program instead of targeting the Iraqi population – the direction they assumed under US and UK administration – the Iraqi people might have been able to send Hussein to the fate of other tyrants, such as Suharto, Marcos, Ceausescu, Mubuto, Duvalier, and others (Chomsky 2003: 249).

After the war in 1991, Iraqi per capita income fell from US \$2,279 in 1984 to US \$627 in 1991, and decreased to as low as US \$450 in 1995. Numerous surveys and reports conducted by the Government of Iraq and UN agencies over the decade following the 1991 Gulf War detailed the deepening of the complex humanitarian crisis precipitated by the war's destruction of Iraq's civil infrastructure (especially electricity and water sanitation) and exacerbated by the continuing sanctions regime (Ismael and Ismael 2004: 126–65). The 1999–2000 Report of UN Development Programme's Iraq Country Office summarized the situation as follows:

> Iraq's economy has been in crisis since the imposition of economic sanctions in 1990. Despite the Oil-for-Food program, the country continued its decline into poverty, particularly in the south. Food supplies continue to be inadequate in the centre and south of the country; the prevalence of general malnutrition in the centre and south has hardly changed. Although the rates have stabilised, this happened at 'an unacceptably high level.' In the area of child and maternal health, in August 1999, UNICEF and the Government of Iraq released the results of the first survey on child mortality in Iraq since 1991. The survey showed that under-five child mortality had more than doubled from 56 deaths per 1000 live births in 1984 to 131 deaths in the period 1994–1999. At least 50% of the labour force is unemployed or underemployed; a shortage of basic goods, compounded by a drought, has resulted in high prices and an estimated inflation rate of 135% and 120% in 1999 and 2000 respectively… Most of the country's civil infrastructure remains in serious disrepair. GDP per capita dropped to an estimated US \$715 [from US \$3508 before the Gulf War], which is a figure comparable with such countries as Madagascar and Rwanda (UNDP 2000).

Food production and availability were major factors exacerbating the problem of increasing morbidity and mortality in Iraq under the sanctions regime. Fuelled by lavish oil income, in the 1970s and 80s the Ba'th government had substituted importation of foodstuffs from the international market for domestic development. As a result, agricultural and domestic industrial sectors were not only undeveloped but languished as the market was deluged with imported goods. Under the embargo imposed by the sanctions regime, oil revenue precipitously declined and food importation was seriously curtailed. In addition there were embargoes on replacement parts for repairs to civil infrastructure destroyed by the aerial bombardment and components essential to increase agricultural production in Iraq.

As a result, dietary energy supply fell from 3,120 to 1,093 kilocalories per capita per day by 1994–1995, with women and children forming the most vulnerable sector of Iraqi society. Against a UN target of 2,463 kilocalories and 63.6 grams of protein per person per day, the nutritional value of the distributed food basket did not exceed 1,993 kilocalories and 43 grams of protein. Reflecting the economic impact of war and sanctions on Iraq's economy, the rate of inflation after the imposition of the sanctions regime increased from 18 per cent in 1975 to 2,000 per cent in 1992, and the exchange rate of the Iraqi dinar to the US dollar dropped from 1:3 in 1972 to 180:1 in 1993; in other words, the dinar was equivalent to less than one cent US (Jabar 1995: 168–69).

Prior to the start of the United Nations' humanitarian relief program in 1996, the Oil-For-Food program (a program that allowed limited sales of crude oil for food), the Government of Iraq had been distributing 1,300 kilocalories per day (Office of the Iraq Programme 2002). The prevalence of malnutrition in Iraqi children under five almost doubled from 1991 to 1996 (from 12 per cent to 23 per cent). Acute malnutrition in the centre and south regions rose from 3 per cent to 11 per cent for the same age bracket. Indeed, the World Food Program (WFP) indicated that by July 1995, average shop prices of essential commodities stood at 850 times the July 1990 level. While the humanitarian program in Iraq, initiated in 1996 with the Oil-for-Food program, successfully staved off mass starvation, the level of malnutrition within Iraq remained high and directly contributed to the morbidity and mortality rates (UNOIP 2002). In 1999, a UNICEF report estimated that sanctions had caused the death of a half million Iraqi children (UNICEF 1999). The 2003 Report on the State of the World's Children, which UNICEF issued, stated, 'Iraq's regression over the past decade is by far the most severe of the 193 countries surveyed' (Chomsky 2003: 126). The impact of the sanctions regime on Iraq was overwhelming and multifarious. While it pauperized the Iraqi people, it also strengthened the grip of the Hussein regime by creating a highly dependent and beleaguered population.

Under the suzerainty of the UNSC, the Iraqi state lost control of its airspace in the north and south; nonetheless, it maintained territorial jurisdiction in the central and southern parts of the country, and nominal power in the north where the Kurds enjoyed de facto autonomy under American protection. In this aberrant context, the Iraqi people, excluding the Kurds, suffered a cynical game of brinksmanship played by the US-UK-led Security Council. Bombed back to a pre-industrial stage of development by Operation Desert Storm, the Iraqi population was pushed to the brink of humanitarian disaster by the unrelenting sanctions regime, as detailed in numerous international reports (see UNICEF 1993; UNFAO and UNWFP 1997; UNICEF 1999; WHO 2003). With the infrastructure of public health, education and social welfare destroyed, the national institutions of the state were in effect compromised and the structural foundations of society marginalized.

A plight-and-flight theme was common in the narratives represented in our interviews of émigrés from this period. As one person explained, 'The Iraq-Iran war killed our sons and brothers, and sanctions killed our spirit... We escaped through the north and made our way to Jordan.' Another stated, 'Sanctions punished us for Saddam, and he thrived while we languished. We had to get out or die. That's what you do when your house collapses around you.' The collapsing house metaphor was symbolic of the implosion of Iraq's socio-economic infrastructure under the weight of sanctions. Another common theme for this cohort was related to the dependence of families on remittances from relatives living abroad. 'I am a doctor,' said one interviewee, 'but the only way I could feed my family was to leave Iraq and work outside.'

Based on this examination, we suggest that the population-displacement tsunami referred to earlier to describe the mass movement of the Iraqi population following the 2003 invasion actually began decades before the US-UK invasion in 2003. Throughout the post-World War II era, Iraq's political context was framed by the juggernaut of global geopolitics. In other words, its political development was subordinated to Cold War politics. Initially, it was the young, educated activists of the urban centres whose lives were dislocated; displacement was one of the outcomes of their dissatisfaction. Though just a ripple initially, by the 1980s the reverberations of political shock had set off large-scale waves of displacement (Al-Jazeera 2009). This would suggest that the mass displacement of Iraq's population following the 2003 invasion was the culmination of a long sequence of political shocks induced by global geopolitics.

Home is Where the Heart is

There were both objective and subjective dimensions of bonds with Iraq amongst our interviewees. In the objective dimension, ties with kin in Iraq provided the most overt example common across the interviews. The indicator of strong ties was regular communication (e.g. phone, email), referred to incidentally in the course of the original interviews and weeded out in the secondary analysis. Such references were explicit in 39 of the interviews. Given the original purpose of the interviews, it can be inferred that family ties remained a significant bond with the homeland for émigrés.

While family ties may form a strong physical bond to place, it is the subjective symbols of home that tie identity to location. In the subjective dimension, the dominant theme was one of connectivity. The concept of connectivity is used here to relate to the connection between identity and location. One interviewee explained, 'My roots are in Iraq – not only my history but my connection with human history.' Another stated that 'I am an Iraqi. That's who I am. That's not only where I come from. It's my address when I feel lost in this world.' And yet another recited a famous Iraqi poem by Ma'ruf al-Rusafi (1875–1945): 'My country, even though it abused me, is still the dearest. And my people, even when they are selfish, are still the most generous.'

Symbols of this intersubjective connectivity were manifest in items brought from Iraq and displayed in the homes we visited for many of the interviews. Art, books and music were on prominent display, and when any of the items caught the interviewer's attention, this elicited stories of home. One interviewee boasted, 'I have the best collection of Iraqi *maqam* [classical Iraqi music]. Since the libraries were burned and the radio stations ransacked [after the invasion], my collection is an important repository for old Iraqi *maqam*.' Old books bound in leather were another common item brought from Iraq. One woman told us, 'I brought this [book] from my grandfather's house. When I was a child, I used to spend hours in his library. This book reminds me of that time.'

One respondent declared: 'See all these lovely things. I brought them from Iraq. Each one has a story, and each story has a family connection. They are the repositories for my memories, and are my children's heritage.' Though her children were born outside Iraq, they seemed to represent for her a strong, continuing connection with her homeland. The declaration was an incidental comment in a long interview about the Iraqi household. In effect, the interviewee was arguing that the Iraqi household exists in the stories and memories passed on from generation to generation. Because this was part of a secondary analysis of existing interviews, we did not have a chance to explore her comments further. Although it was the only interview in which offspring were referred to directly, the possibility of children as a bond seemed significant. As Leilah Nadir notes in her memoir, 'I feel Iraq in my bones, though I have never been there. I have never lazed in the shade of the date palm… or underneath the grape leaves hanging on the vine… My father Ibrahim has…' (2007: 15–16).

Symbols are significant, for they reflect emotional bonds. The artifacts from Iraq represented connections with home for our interviewees, and home symbolized belongingness. Sentiments of home are deeply ingrained in most folk cultures; home represents both place and social bonds. One member of our sample recited lines from a popular song by the Iraqi pop-star Sadun Jabir to describe the sense of loss among displaced Iraqis: 'He who loses gold can replace it from the gold market. But he who loses his country, where can he replace it from?'

Diaspora: A Hard Place

Throughout most of the twentieth century, Iraq's political identity evolved from backwater outpost of the British Empire in the pre-World War I era to modern nation state in the post-World War II period (Ireland 1937: 160–370; Tripp 2007:

57–169). During the interwar period, ideological politics became a primary mode for the process of value determination and articulation in the political culture of Iraq. A plethora of nationalist, socialist and communist groups emerged, all of them espousing the construction of social equity as a principal tool of nation-building (Salih 1955: 69–123; Batatu 1978: 709–21). On this trajectory of political development, Iraq developed an unambiguous secular political culture and egalitarian social ethos (al-Wardî 1965: 379–83). However, beginning with the Ba'thist coups in the 1960s, this trajectory of political development was subjected to successive political shocks culminating in the 2003 invasion and occupation of Iraq. Under the control of occupying powers, the last vestiges of a secular-egalitarian state infrastructure were dismantled, and in their place a sectarian model of government constructed (Ismael and Fuller 2008: 443–55).

In this framework of occupation and sectarian government, Iraq disintegrated into sectarian violence, unleashing mass population displacement in its wake. Ethno-sectarian divisions emerged between Arab and Kurd, Sunni and Shi'a, Muslim and non-Muslim (Christian, Mandaen, Shabak, Yezidi), and ethnic cleansing of minorities ensued neighbourhood by neighbourhood in Baghdad and other population centres (see Lamani 2010: 239–53). The issue of social identity comes into question under this circumstance. One of the concerns addressed in our re-examination of the interviews was the question of the nature of the primary lens through which Iraqi expatriates explain their experiences of leaving Iraq. Table 14.3 provides a breakdown of this in the sample.

As the table reveals, Assyrians and Kurds explained their experiences in terms of their status as a distinct cultural minority. There was an overt sense of being an oppressed community under the Iraqi state. Among the Arabs, for the 16 whose religious identity was primary, seven were Christian and nine were Shi'a. For the 36 Arabs who saw their flight from Iraq as political, one was a Christian, four were Mandaean, 10 Shi'a, and 21 Sunni. Among the 64 individuals in the sample, religion was a stronger identifier among the Christians than among the Muslims, and stronger among the Shi'a than the Sunni.

The concept of social identity is used here to describe the correlation for individuals between social context and social group. As indicated above, 44 per cent of the sample described their departure from Iraq in ethno-sectarian terms, and 56 per cent described it in political terms. What social groups did they identify with in the context of foreign lands? The common theme that emerged in this dimension may be

Table 14.3   Social Identity

	Religious	Ethnic	Political
Arabs	16	0	36
Kurds	0	6	0
Assyrians	0	6	0

represented by the observation of one respondent who noted, 'We [Iraqi expatriates] live between our memories of the oppression we escaped and the home we lost. We are connected with each other by these memories.' Another noted that 'I came here as an immigrant and aspired to assimilate. But the US invasion of Iraq changed that. It transformed me into a displaced Iraqi patriot.' Similar sentiments of a shared social identity among displaced Iraqis were echoed in many of the interviews, and several used the term diaspora to describe their experiences.

Conclusion

The secondary analysis of interviews with Iraqi expatriates yielded a rich array of information relevant to an examination of Iraqis in diaspora. Originally conducted in the framework of an exploratory study, a secondary analysis of these interviews may be expected at best to yield interesting observations that may warrant further study. This is what we offer by way of conclusion.

As it relates to Butler's three basic features of diaspora, regarding the first attribute, scattering, we observed a relationship between political shocks and waves of population displacement over several decades. In Iraq's case, we maintained that the mass population displacement following the country's invasion and occupation in 2003 was preceded by decades of what might be called brain-drain displacement – that is, the displacement of political activists, intellectuals and conscious citizens. Mass displacement, in other words, was not an isolated event. Rather, it was the culmination of a process of displacement that had its origins in the dynamics of global politics, and not local events, as demonstrated in the series of political shocks that were initiated in Iraq in the early 1960s.

Like most tsunamis, mass population displacements have their origin in underlying tectonic forces, in this case, geopolitical fault lines. While these forces occur in local space, they emanate from plate tectonics that are global in dimension. The case of Iraq suggests that mass population displacements, like tsunamis, may also have their origin in transnational fault lines; that is, they are a local manifestation of a global dynamic. With more than fifty million displaced people in refugee camps by the new millennium, and mass population displacements occurring at an increasing rate, it seems imperative that we try to understand their nature and causes.

With regard to relationship with the homeland, Butler's second feature of a diaspora, we examined both the objective and subjective bonds that connected the émigré respondents to Iraq as a homeland. The objective dimension was manifest in ties with family in Iraq, and the subjective dimension in terms of artifacts that represented sentimental attachments with the country. The significance of these bonds may be manifest in their role in transmitting the relationship across time in the absence of space. In other words, while displaced Iraqis had lived in Iraq at one time, the children and grandchildren of these émigrés could inherit the bonds but have no real relationship with the place. From this perspective, Butler's reference to 'an actual or imagined homeland' has tangible meaning in terms of both the Iraqis who experience displacement and the offspring who inherit bonds but have no direct experience of Iraq as a homeland.

Self-identification as a member of a diasporic group, Butler's third attribute, was examined in the context of Iraq's political development over the course of the twentieth century. Dimensions of this history were palpable throughout the interviews, and manifest in the way the respondents explained their experiences of fleeing Iraq. Three types of explanatory lenses were identified – religious, ethnic and political – that were commensurate with the political contexts discussed earlier. Irrespective of these differences, however, the interviews suggested a sense of shared identity among displaced Iraqis, a sensibility triggered by the 2003 invasion of Iraq. Even though all of the respondents had emigrated from Iraq years, if not decades, before that momentous event, the invasion catalyzed a sense of collective loss, echoed in a *maqam* refrain cited by one respondent: 'On what basis were we dispossessed and separated [from our home]? After that, joy was replaced by misery. The old days will never return.'

References

Batatu, H. (1987), *The Old Social Classes and the Revolutionary Movements in Iraq.* (Princeton: Princeton University Press).

Butler, K.D. (2001), 'Defining diaspora, refining a discourse', *Diaspora: A Journal of Transnational Studies* 10(2): 189–219.

Chomsky, N. (2003), *Hegemony or Survival: America's Quest for Global Dominance.* (New York: Henry Holt and Company).

Cohen, R. (1997), *Global Diasporas: An Introduction.* (Seattle: University of Washington Press).

Ireland, P.W. (1937), *Iraq: A Study in Political Development.* (London: Jonathan Cape).

Ismael, J.S. (2008), 'Living under War, Sanctions and Occupation: The Voices of Iraqi Women', *International Journal of Contemporary Iraqi Studies* 2: 3.

Ismael, J.S. and Ismael, T.Y. (1999), 'Cowboy Warfare, Biological Diplomacy: Disarming Metaphors as Weapons of Mass Destruction', *Politics and the Life Sciences* 18(1): 70–78.

——— (2004), *The Iraqi Predicament: People in the Quagmire of Power Politics.* (London: Pluto Press).

Ismael, T.Y. and Fuller, M. (2008), 'The Disintegration of Iraq: The Manufacturing and Politicization of Sectarianism', *International Journal of Contemporary Iraqi Studies*, 2(3): 443–55.

Jabar, F.A. (1995), *Al-Dawla, al-Mugtam'a al-Madani wa al-Tahawul al-Demokrati fi al Iraq.* (Cairo: Markaz Ibn Khaldoun li al-Dirasat al-Inma'iyya).

Al-Jazeera (2009) 'The Iraqi Diaspora', *Al-Jazeera Net*, 16 October, http://english. aljazeera.net/programmes/insideiraq/2009/10/2009108132427530259.html (accessed 1 February 2010).

Klein, N. (2007), *The Shock Doctrine: The Rise of Disaster Capitalism*. (Toronto: Alfred A. Knopf Books).

Lamani, M. (2010), 'Minorities in Iraq: The Other Victims,' in R. Baker, S.T. Ismael and T.Y. Ismael (eds) *Cultural Cleansing in Iraq: Why Museums Were Looted, Libraries Burned and Academics Murdered.* (London: Pluto Press).

Makiya, K. (1989), *The Republic of Fear.* (Berkeley: University of California Press).

Moghissi, H. et al. (2008), *Diaspora by Design: Muslims in Canada and in Britain, Iran and Palestine.* (Toronto: University of Toronto Press).

Nadir, L. (2007), *The Orange Trees of Baghdad: In Search of My Lost Family.* (Toronto: Key Porter Books).

Salih, Z. (1955), *Muqaddimah fî Târîkh al-'Irâq al-Mu'âsir.* (Baghdad: Matba'at al-Râbitah).

Tripp, C. (2007), *A History of Iraq*, 3rd Edition. (Cambridge: Cambridge University Press).

United Nations Children's Fund (UNICEF) (1999), *Iraq Child and Maternal Morbidity Surveys*, August.

—— (1993), *Iraq: Children, War and Sanctions,* April.

United Nations Development Program (UNDP) (2000), '1999–2000 Report,' Iraq Country Office.

United Nations Food and Agricultural Organization (UNFAO) and United Nations World Food Program (UNWFP) (1997), *Special Report: FAO/WFP Food Supply and Nutrition Assessment Mission to Iraq*, 3 October, http://www.fao. org/docrep/004/w6519e/w6519e00.htm (accessed 1 February 2010).

United Nations High Commissioner for Refugees (UNHCR) (2009), 'Statistical Snapshot', 2010 UNHCR Country Operations Profile – Iraq, January, http://www.unhcr.org/cgi-bin/texis/vtx/page?page=49e486426# (accessed 1 February 2010).

United Nations Office of the Iraq Program (UNOIP) (2002), 'Oil-for-Food: Basic Figures', 18 May, http://www.un.org/Depts/oip/background (accessed 1 February 2010).

al-Wardî, A. (1965), *Dirâsah fî Tabî'at al-Mujtama' al-'Irâqi*, 2nd edition. (London: Al-Warrak Publishing Ltd).

World Health Organization (WHO) (2003), *Potential Impact of Conflict on Health in Iraq*, briefing note, March, http://www.who.int/features/2003/iraq/briefings/ iraq_briefing_note/en/index.html (accessed 1 February 2010).

Zaher, U. (ed.) (1986), 'Political Developments in Iraq, 1963–1980', Committee Against Repression and for Democratic Rights in Iraq.

Chapter 15

Conclusion:
A Plea for a Positive and Inclusive Rhetoric

Halleh Ghorashi

From the end of 1990s to the beginning of the new century we witnessed the growing marginalization of ideals such as equality, public engagement and tolerance. World leaders with messages of destruction and war replaced leaders with messages of peace and tolerance. Cultural, ethnic, and national tensions rose. The dominance of conflict, pessimism, and insecurity came to usurp the belief in ideals such as solidarity and the struggle against inequality. In part, this can be understood as a result of our era, which many scholars describe as late modernity, comprising fluidity (Bauman 2001), greater reflexivity (Giddens 1991), and increased concern with perceived risks (Beck 1992). The events at the beginning of the century have provided us with unforgettable justifications for this growing sense of insecurity and sense that we live in an unsafe world.

New Realism and the Islamization of the Discourse

Although we need to be wary of overemphasizing the impact of historical occurrences, I believe that the events of September 11th, 2001 accelerated already growing negativity in diverse societies. In many European countries, the most visible aspect of this negativity has been aimed at migrants from Islamic countries. Since 2001, many in the West have come to view the cultures and the religion of these migrants as a source of discomfort and fear. The fact that much of the European media overemphasizes news of various forms of violence (domestic and public) related to migrants from Islamic countries has overwhelmingly contributed to this impression. This negativity increased because of the number of attacks that followed September 11th around the world, including in Madrid, London, and Mumbai. In Europe, the growing fear of migrants from Islamic countries has led to demands for the assimilation of their culture into that of the dominant host societies. This, in turn, has resulted in an increasing gap between migrants and the rest of the society. The main message emerging (for example in the Dutch public space) is that we need to distance ourselves from a 'naïve' and idealistic approach towards cultural difference and become realistic about its threats. Baukje Prins (2002) calls this new era in the Netherlands the era of 'new realism.' The new realist is someone with guts; someone who dares to call a spade a spade;

someone who sets himself up as the mouthpiece of the common people and then puts up a vigorous fight against the so-called leftist – read idealistic – 'politically correct' views of cultural relativism. An increase of negative feelings combined with growing public and political space for expressing those feelings has given rise to a disapproving and cynical tone within the dominant discourse of most European countries. In the following sections of this conclusion I will sum up a number of the common components of this new negative rhetoric.

Essentialism versus Differentiation

The first component of the new exclusionary rhetoric in the West is essentialism. The culture of Muslim migrants is considered to deviate from Western norms. This notion is based on a static and essentialist approach to culture, in which cultural content is considered the determining factor governing the actions of individuals. In this discourse, we observe construction of us-them dichotomies. We, Westerners, are secular, rational and modern, while the Muslim migrant 'other' is represented as religious, irrational and traditional. In various chapters throughout this book we see a range of possible objections to this dichotomous representation of cultures. They show that the assumed categories of secular West and religious others do not hold up. Not only is Islamic positioning much more differentiated than often presented, the presumed secularism of dominant societies, such as Sweden and the Netherlands, is also much more layered than assumed. The importance of religion in Western societies and its relation to the state has changed over the past decades, yet this relationship is anything but simple and clear-cut as it is often presented within the constructed dichotomies of 'the secular self' and 'the religious other.' While some of the chapters differentiate the notion of 'the secular self' (e.g., the chapters written by de Koning and Roald), there are other chapters that differentiate the notion of 'the religious other' (e.g., the chapters written by Moghissi, Sunier, Farahani, Farkhondeh and Balchin).

Many chapters in this book show that an essentialist approach of the Islamic other leaves little space for individual interpretations and creativity with regard to cultural and/or religious background. Although individuals embody various discourses from their past, they are quite different in the ways in which they bring these past discourses to bear on the present discourses they have entered. It is in this constant negotiation between the past and the present discourses that individuals shape and reshape their positioning. Although the contexts and discourses available to individuals are not endlessly open, the whole process of negotiation makes what precedes any kind of positioning dynamic. These chapters show how dynamic and situational this layered process of negotiation and positioning are. These data show a clear gap between a static and closed representation of migrants from Islamic as opposed to the dynamic reality of the everyday life of these migrants. Buitelaar and Stock, for example, show in their chapter how the sense of belonging is not naturally linked to the country of origin, as the dominant discourse often portrays.

They show how this sense transcends either/or categories and that one can be at home in more than one locality or community.

In addition to exploring the multi-layeredness of positioning and belonging, many authors emphasize the impact of the gaze of others on how people position themselves. They show that the layers of positioning and belonging are very much defined by the power of the dominant discourse on Islam in the countries of residence for migrants. This aspect was convincingly presented in the chapter of Thurfjell. He shows how the essentialized image of Islam and Islamic migrants contributes to the extreme forms of positioning among migrant youths who either choose extreme secularism or extreme Islamism. In this chapter we see how the power of the dominant discourse affects the positioning of all citizens (migrants or not). It also shows that although the positions of migrants can by layered, the framework in which they negotiate their position is influential and, in many ways, limits their choices. The dominance of an exclusionary framework does not leave much room for nuanced positions in relation to Islam. In the chapters written by Ahmed and other authors, in which gender issues are central, we see that another kind of dichotomy is presented: the binarism of 'oppressed and passive Muslim (Third World) women' vs. 'liberated and independent Western women.' Balchin shows effectively in her chapter that in most policy manners women are invisible. Policy-makers often focus on the most traditional and conservative male migrants, who lack the dynamic positioning of migrant women both inside and between nation-states. In these chapters it is shown how migrant and/or Muslim women try to deal creatively with the dilemmas of emancipation, sexuality and leadership in contexts where exclusionary discourse defines their position so deterministically. We read about the variety of choices made and positions taken in relation to dominant discourses in a number of societies. Some positions are reactions to the dominant discourse and, as such, reproduce the discourse in one manner or another; others are searching for space for reflection and self-definition. These chapters present the multiplicity of the ways individuals engage with the dominant discussions in the societies studied.

The chapters of this book give us a broad range of reality, allowing us to rethink the present harshness of the dominant discourse towards migrants with an Islamic background. They also help us to reconsider the assumptions underlying this negative, hard-line approach. Since in the dominant discourse Muslim migrants are seen as a major source of the present tensions in societies (see also Parekh 2006), a key assumption is that a hard-line approach can solve societal problems. In most hard-line, short term, and instrumental approaches, the justification of the costs of programs is related to the immediate satisfaction of individual voters, defining the terms of action because of their visibility within the opinion polls. The public attention given to certain issues – such as honour-related violence, radicalization of Islamic youth, increasing reports of crime – is very much related to the feelings of loss of safety and security based on individual incidents. In this way these incidents and feelings dominate the election polls and give rise to populist politics. Populist leaders, with their one-liners addressing the existing fear and discomfort, have come to dominate the present-day politics in many Western countries. As a result, addressing long-term public issues is disregarded as being too idealistic or too unaccountable. I will show below how this short-term attitude towards satisfaction of the immediate needs of individual citizens endangers the culture of democracy in the long run.

Extreme Individualism and the Culture of Democracy

In the present condition, which Zygmunt Bauman (2000) refers to as the condition of late modernity, we see individuals becoming the worst enemies of the citizen. Within this framework, the citizen is understood to be one whose well-being is connected to the 'city', while the individual seeks only self-satisfaction. The impact of negative discourse and feelings of loss and distrust push individuals into a defensive position: a position in which the connection to the long-term considerations of the well-being of society are reduced to incidental, short term, individual satisfactions. Inspired by Bauman's line of thinking I believe that extreme individualization could lead to a slow disintegration of citizenship, with the consequence that 'public' becomes colonized by the 'private.' The greatest challenge of this second modernity is to learn collectively to tackle public issues without reducing them solely to private needs. To be able to do that, we need to bring hope and trust, which are the cornerstones of democratic culture, back into the public discourse.

In a democratic, legal state, democratic society concerns the field of tension between two components, namely state-run institutions and those of 'civil society' (citizens' initiatives). Theorists from the 1970s and 1980s emphasized what Rawls called 'the basic structure' of society, meaning, constitutional rights, political decision-making processes, and social institutions that enable democracy. By now it has become widely accepted that in addition to this basic structure, attention should be given to the qualities and attitudes of citizens operating within these structures (Kymlicka and Norman 2000: 6). This 'basic attitude' – what de Tocqueville calls lifestyle – is mandatory for maintaining and protecting a culture of democracy. Protecting a democratic culture that is inclusive of diversity is one of the features of communality. One of the basic preconditions for this democratic culture is tolerance. Yet, tolerance in terms of *allowing space* for otherness, has, in the Netherlands for example, proven over the past decades to promote indifference. Collective issues are not tackled through indifference. This is also what de Tocqueville warned us about: 'Setting people free makes them indifferent' (in Bauman 2000: 36). What is lacking is the growing sense of a collective notion of citizenship. In order to create a collective notion of citizenship, it is necessary to make room for interaction through difference and address the tensions involved in the process. What individuals need to do to become citizens is to take an additional step: not only *to allow* space but *to make space* as well. Making space involves the will to meet the other and requires the ability to step to the side in order to create a common, shared space between cultures, in which we can admit, meet, and connect with the other. The next step in a democratic outlook would then be one towards *guarded space*. In other words, a democratic citizen needs to be prepared to make an effort to guard and, if necessary, defend another person's liberty and space.

Yet it seems that in the light of negative tendencies in our time there is not much space for some of the virtues of democratic culture such as respect and tolerance. Democracy goes beyond the liberty to go to the polls. In contrast to what is often maintained, democracy is not simply about the will of the majority; it requires creating space for the minority as well. This is exactly what constitutes the difference between a constitutional democracy and a populist democracy: in the latter, the voice of the majority is given relatively free reign but the voice of the minority is not secured. Democracy without opposition is not democracy (see Janssens and Steyaert 2001; Ghorashi 2006). Through the dominance of the negative Islamized discourse, the emphasis on the frightening and endangering elements of cultural difference have been so overemphasized that there is little space for accepting the presumed 'cultural others' or for commonality instead of difference. Instead of solving problems, this focus on culture has contributed to a growing gap in many European societies between the European self and the migrant other. The main explanation for this is the notion that culture is presumed to be a problem, predicated on the idea of cultural contrasts, that may increasingly cause migrants to regroup within their ethnic boundaries to defend their culture. Feelings of social insecurity and lack of recognition tend to encourage radicalization both for majorities and minorities. When people feel threatened, they will go to extremes to defend their boundaries. The growing threat of extreme Islamic and extreme right-wing groups is a case in point here.

Connecting the Individual back to the Public

The growing sense of distrust and strong negativity of the discourse is damaging for any society, but it is especially so for a democratic one. The core notion of any democratic society is that the citizens believe in their ability to change and to trust the representatives they have chosen. For individuals to become citizens it is essential to create societal interspaces in order so they can co-produce long-term actions. In order to be innovative within the political system representing them, engaged citizens need to have a productive and sceptical attitude, and not a cynical one. In keeping with this argument, negative rhetoric that breeds extreme cynicism and extreme individualism is the most damaging force for any democratic society. Thus, to start with, we need a more positive rhetoric in order to tackle the dominant negativity of our time, such as growing insecurity and distrust in general and specifically towards individuals and groups within societies. Such positive rhetoric can inspire citizens to believe in their ability to take action within their societies.

In spite of the growing criticism of President Obama of the United States, based on his first year's performance as a president, I think that his role during the presidential campaign can be seen as one of the most inspiring examples of our time. The hopeful and empowering rhetoric of Obama during the campaign period helped the United States believe in its potential after years of cynicism and destruction. What Obama did was simply to remind citizens of their value to the society and their essential role in democracy. As a result, civic activities during the campaign and participation in the election were very high. He reminded citizens of their role in society by simply asking for their help. His campaign clearly demonstrated that positive rhetoric is a key step towards a more engaged society. Public participation and diverse forms of connections between citizens across culture, gender and age are essential ingredients of the culture of democracy. For this kind of public engagement people need to feel safe enough to interact and to connect across boundaries of culture, ethnicity, religion and otherness. To create this sense of safety, it is necessary to have leaders who do not base their approach on the results of opinion polls, but are able to inspire and motivate citizens to stay engaged publicly, especially in difficult times. This needs to go beyond the protection of one's own boundaries and include the protection and well-being of society as a whole. In this time of the rise of extreme realism and extreme individualism, citizens need to defend the space for ideals such as solidarity and societal engagement. There is a need to put long-term public issues on the agenda and not be forced or rushed by the individual incidents dominating public and political agendas. We need to bring the individual back to citizenship: that is the only way that communities can be more than the sum of their parts. To realize that we need to create interspaces of communality that can become the foundation for collective actions that are inclusive.

Creating Interspaces

The essential contribution of positive rhetoric can be to provide an alternative to the sense of powerlessness towards the local, national and global problems of our time. It creates a space for people to trust one another as citizens within the public arena in spite of their individual prejudices. A positive rhetoric can provide the necessary safety that is essential for any social encounter, but most importantly for encounters that are often considered difficult. The major conditions for social encounters with individuals from diverse backgrounds are openness and curiosity (Tennekes 1994). These two conditions can only be met when feelings of safety and trust return to the public space. For a more profound encounter with the other, however, yet another step must be taken. This is the step that philosopher Theo de Boer (1993) considers a prerequisite for intercultural dialogue. This step is called *epochè*, which is a temporary suspension of the truth of one's own judgment. We cannot listen to another person without temporarily putting a question mark over our own convictions. Janssens and Steyaert (2001) write about a similar condition that they define as setting a step to the side. This does not involve casting doubt on our own ideas but rather creating a common space in which we can listen to the other and get closer to him or her. What is salient in De Boer's view is that, without suspension, discussion is pointless; without conviction, there is nothing at stake.

For a social encounter to take place we should be able to approach, look at, and listen to, the other. For this to happen, it is important to create an interspace by temporarily stepping to the side to make space for the other, before we judge, or even condemn, him or her. Importantly, making space is the only way to counter the dominant discourse. By encountering each other in as open an atmosphere as possible, and by virtue of the courage to step to the side, we can create temporary interspaces that can lead to diverse forms of connection. These connections will enable us to initiate social activities across boundaries of difference. Thus it becomes possible to overcome, to a certain extent, the self-evident power of the dominant discourse. It is exactly these interspaces that give us the opportunity to adopt new ideas and creations and to forge new connections.

To sum up, the Islamization and culturalization of the dominant discourse in Western democratic countries has reached a point where it is beginning to erode the most valuable foundations of democracy, such as openness and tolerance of the other. In a proper balance between being similar and being different, dialogue, encounter and innovation can arise. In the awareness that culture is only one aspect of our lives together, working together, and living together, ethnicity-transcending connections can be made. Thus, the greatest challenge of our time is to bring some idealism back to the public: solidarity instead of instant satisfaction, a sense of collective gains rather than immediate individual profits, resistance to short-term, quick-fix solutions in favour of long-term solutions. The chapters of this book provide us with food for thought to reflect upon the process of inclusion and exclusion in our societies. This reflection could be on the level of discourse, organizing difference, policy-making or gender issues. It is necessary to create the sensitivity and reflexivity to transcend the obvious and that which we take for granted because of the dominance of certain discourses in our societies. In this conclusion I have tried to show the importance of a positive and inclusive rhetoric for creating societal interactions that go beyond fear and enable civic engagement beyond populism.

References

Bauman, Z. (2000), *Liquid Modernity.* (Cambridge: Polity Press).

Beck, U. (1992), *Risk Society: Towards a New Modernity.* (London: Sage Publications).

Boer, T. de (1993), *Tamara A., Awater en andere verhalen over subjectiviteit.* (Amsterdam: Boom).

Ghorashi, H. (2006), *Paradoxen van culturele erkenning: Management van diversiteit in nieuw Nederland.* (Inaugural lecture at VU University Amsterdam).

Giddens, A. (1991), *Modernity and Self-Identity: Self and Society in the Late Modern Age.* (Cambridge: Polity Press).

Janssens, M. and Steyaert, C. (2001), *Meerstemmigheid: Organiseren met verschil.* (Leuven: Universitaire Pers Leuven).

Kymlicka, W. and Norman, W. (2000), 'Citizenship in Culturally Diverse Societies: Issues, Contexts, Concepts', in W. Kymlicka and W. Norman (eds) *Citizenship in Diverse Societies.* (Oxford: Oxford University Press), 1–45.

Parekh, B. (2006), 'Europe, liberalism and the "Muslim question"', in Modood, T., Triadafyllidou, A. and Zapata-Barrero, R. (eds) *Multiculturalism, Muslims and Citizenship: A European Approach.* (London: Routledge), 179–204.

Prins, B. (2002), 'The Nerve to Break Taboos. New Realism in the Dutch Discourse on Multiculturalism', *Journal of International Migration and Integration* 3(3–4): 363–79.

Tennekes, J. (1994), 'Communicatie en cultuurverschil', *M&O, Tijdschrift voor organisatiekunde en sociaal beleid* 48(2): 130–44.

Index

RESEARCH IN MIGRATION AND ETHNIC RELATIONS SERIES

Full series list

Turks in European Cities
Housing and Urban Segregation
*Edited by Sule Özüekren and
Ronald Van Kempen*

Multicultural Policies and the State
A Comparison of Two European Societies
Edited by Marco Martiniello

Long-Distance Nationalism
Diasporas, Homelands and Identities
Zlatko Skrbiš

Education and Racism
A Cross National Inventory of Positive
Effects of Education on Ethnic Tolerance
*Edited by Louk Hagendoorn and
Shervin Nekuee*

New Chinese Migrants in Europe
The Case of the Chinese Community
in Hungary
Pál Nyíri

European Nations and Nationalism
Theoretical and Historical Perspectives
*Edited by Louk Hagendoorn,
György Csepeli, Henk Dekker and
Russell Farnen*

Transitions
Russians, Ethiopians, and Bedouins
in Israel's Negev Desert
*Edited by Richard Isralowitz and
Jonathan Friedlander*

Comparative Perspectives on Racism
*Edited by Jessika ter Wal and
Maykel Verkuyten*

Arguing and Justifying
Assessing the Convention Refugees'
Choice of Moment, Motive and
Host Country
Robert F. Barsky

Patriarchal Structures and Ethnicity in the
Italian Community in Britain
Azadeh Medaglia

South Africa's Racial Past
The History and Historiography of Racism,
Segregation, and Apartheid
Paul Maylam

Poland's Post-War Dynamic of Migration
Krystyna Iglicka

Ethnicity and Nationalism in
Italian Politics
Inventing the *Padania*: Lega Nord
and the Northern Question
Margarita Gómez-Reino Cachafeiro

Integration and Resistance
The Relation of Social Organisations,
Global Capital, Governments and
International Immigration in Spain
and Portugal
Ricard Morén-Alegret

New European Identity and Citizenship
*Edited by Rémy Leveau, Khadija Mohsen-
Finan and Catherine Wihtol de Wenden*

Globalizing Chinese Migration
Trends in Europe and Asia
Edited by Pál Nyíri and Igor Saveliev

Illegal Immigrants and Developments
in Employment in the Labour Markets
of the EU
Jan Hjarnø

European Encounters
Migrants, Migration and
European Societies Since 1945
*Edited by Rainer Ohliger, Karen
Schönwälder and Triadafilos
Triadafilopoulos*